THE
CIVIL WAR
on the
WEB

THE
CIVIL WAR
on the
WEB

A GUIDE TO THE VERY BEST SITES

Completely Revised and Updated

ALICE E. CARTER & RICHARD JENSEN

Foreword by Gary W. Gallagher

New Introduction by John C. Waugh

A Scholarly Resources Inc. Imprint
Wilmington, Delaware

Scholarly Resources Inc.

104 Greenhill Avenue

Wilmington, DE 19805–1897

www.scholarly.com

Library of Congress Cataloging-in-Publication Data
Carter, Alice E., 1964–
   The Civil War on the Web : a guide to the very best sites / Alice E.
Carter & Richard Jensen ; foreword by Gary W. Gallagher and
new introduction by John C. Waugh. — Rev. & updated.
        p. cm.
   Rev. and updated ed. of: The Civil War on the Web / William G. Thomas,
Alice E. Carter.
   Includes bibliographical references.
   ISBN 0-8420-5134-1 (alk. paper) — ISBN 0-8420-5135-X (pbk. : alk.
paper)
   1. United States—History—Civil War, 1861–1865—Computer network
resources—Directories. 2. Web sites—Directories. I. Jensen, Richard J.
II. Thomas, William G., 1964– Civil War on the Web. III. Title.
E468.9 .C35 2003
025.06'9737—dc21

                                                                2003009604

♾The paper used in this publication meets the minimum requirements of the
American National Standard for permanence of paper for printed library materials, Z39.48, 1984.

Acknowledgments

The authors would like to thank Will Thomas, who co-authored the first edition and who developed the book's organization and focus. Will's scholarship, leadership, and innovation in putting history on the web have made the Internet a better place.

ABOUT THE AUTHORS

ALICE E. CARTER is the director of project management at Interactive Media Associates, an Internet consulting firm in New Jersey. She holds an M.A. in U.S. history from the University of Virginia, Charlottesville, and is a former project manager for the *New York Times on the Web* and the former associate director of the Virginia Center for Digital History at the University of Virginia, Charlottesville.

RICHARD JENSEN is professor emeritus of history at the University of Illinois, Chicago, and research associate at the National Center for Supercomputer Applications. In 1992 he founded H-Net, the groundbreaking and highly successful web-based book review, information, and scholarly discussion source for the academic community. He has written extensively on using the web for historical research and has conducted computer research training programs all over the world. In addition, he has written a number of articles on World War II. Jensen is a recognized authority on reviewing military history web sites.

CONTENTS

PART I

THE VERY BEST CIVIL WAR WEB SITES— REVIEWS AND RATINGS

PART II

SITES WORTH A VISIT—A TOPICAL INDEX

Political and Military Leaders

General History, Historic Documents, Links, and Online Bookstore Sites   **233**

FOREWORD

Gary W. Gallagher

Future generations might know the official statements of generals and the outlines of major battles, observed Walt Whitman, but they would "never know the seething hell and black infernal background of countless minor scenes and interiors ... of the Secession War." Contemporary Civil War scholarship promises to deliver all that Whitman envisioned and much that he did not. Long considered primarily the province of military historians, the field embraces an increasingly spacious definition of the conflict, extending from superlative work on campaigns and generals to treatments of subjects well beyond the battlefield. The daily lives and concerns of common soldiers stand out in sharper relief than before. Studies relating to emancipation, civilian morale, and gender complement books on military and political history. Authors increasingly attempt to show the reciprocal influence of home front and battlefield, a sign that long-standing barriers between scholars of military and nonmilitary bents may be eroding. In short, it is a very productive time for anyone interested in the nation's greatest crisis, and all signs point to continued expansion of the field.

Some of the most striking evidence of that expansion lies in the profusion of Civil War–related sites on the World Wide Web. The online offerings appeal to scholars who write about the war as well as to lay readers who seek to understand it better. A number of sites include documents and images of potential benefit to serious researchers, and literally thousands of others beckon nonprofessional readers who already confront a surfeit of published materials. Many sites are amateurish, clearly reflecting the zealous interests of single individuals. Others contain a mass of information but are so poorly constructed as to defy easy use. Any online search for "Civil War" reveals the intimidating scale and chaotic nature of the offerings— and highlights the need for assistance in separating the grain from the chaff.

As one who cannot devote a great deal of time to trying to differentiate among the many web sites, I was delighted when I learned about *The Civil War on the Web: A Guide to the Very Best Sites*. My enthusiasm grew on reading an advance version of the manuscript. The authors had saved me countless hours of frustrating work by examining thousands of sites, then selecting those they considered particularly valuable and placing them in nine broad categories. They also adopted a sensible and effective format. As well as analyzing contents, the entry for each site rates aesthetics and ease of navigation. Excellent introductory essays open each chapter, and brief bibliographies point toward some of the best published material. In terms of organization, clarity, and utility, the *Guide* stands as a model. It is limited in the sense that the web does not include sites relating to all facets of the war. But its entries address enormously important dimensions of the war and should afford welcome guidance to most people, whether they are interested in generals and military campaigns or events behind the lines.

Beyond its value as a superior reference tool, the *Guide* provides an excellent overview of the current state of Civil War scholarship. The opening sections of the chapters lay out basic issues in the field, address some of the tensions between popular and academic approaches to the conflict, and offer insights into why web sites do not engage the full spectrum of current work on the Civil War era. In this way, the *Guide* highlights the rich and often contentious nature of the field.

The World Wide Web will occupy an increasingly important place in the field of Civil War studies. The Lincoln and Soldiers Institute at Gettysburg College a few years ago announced a new "eLincoln Prize" that will award $50,000 annually to the best web site, CD-ROM, or other scholarly high-technology contribution to exploring the Civil War era. This inducement should promote the creation of more impressive sites that will yield benefits to scholars and lay students alike. For now, anyone hoping to gain some mastery over current sites should consult the *Guide*. It deserves a place on any short shelf of basic reference books on the Civil War.

I NTRODUCTION

John C. Waugh

The Internet is moving Civil War research—indeed, all historical research—into an entirely new dimension. That has not always been the case. In its early years the World Wide Web offered very little that working Civil War historians could reliably use to penetrate the past. That situation is dramatically changing. Today, a decade since its beginning, the web is becoming a bona fide research tool. It reaches out not just to Civil War buffs, lay browsers, and web junkies but also to serious historians. Its emergence as a viable research venue is potentially the single most important development in historical research since Johannes Gutenberg invented moveable type in the fifteenth century.

More and more the web can be used with confidence. Primary documents, the heart and soul of all serious research, are coming online in gratifying numbers. Only a small fraction of the important primary documents have yet made their way to the web, but their volume increases daily. And with each increase the web becomes a happier, more fruitful source for historians. The quickening torrent of information, however, presents a major problem: how to navigate through this sea of plenty and push aside the overabundance of flotsam in the hundreds of thousands of web sites on the Civil War.

This new revised edition of *The Civil War on the Web*, now carefully updated from its excellent first edition, emphatically solves that problem. It penetrates the bewildering flood of sites with laser-like clarity to sift through, lift out, and leave only what are the most important, comprehensive, and accessible. Its descriptions of what it considers the 100 premier sites on the web and its listing of 300 others definitely worth visiting do the browsing for us and save us endless hours of frustrated sifting on our own.

The web is a constantly shifting world. In the three years since the first edition of this book was published, much has changed in that fast-moving universe. However, the great majority of the sites highlighted in the original edition are still online and improving. Only a handful from the original premier list have disappeared or fall-en below the standard set by this guide. Twenty-three new sites have been added to replace the very few dropped. In the wider list of sites worth visiting, seventy-five were dropped, but 100 new ones were added.

The added sites are in part what make this revised edition so necessary and so increasingly desirable and useful. Two political entries—a site on presidential elections from 1860 to 1884 and the Library of Congress's Abraham Lincoln Papers—are important additions. Alluring sites on the Great Locomotive Chase, feeding Union soldiers, and the Confederate commerce raider CSS *Alabama* have made the premier list. Four sites on blacks and slavery—the Dred Scott Case, *Harper's Weekly* reports on Black America, *Uncle Tom's Cabin* and American Culture, and advertisements for Virginia runaways—constitute the biggest new bloc. They are impressive.

There is also an entirely new chapter, not in the first edition, that describes sites in general history, collections of important historic documents, key links to other sites, and leading online bookstores. This addition is a splendid one. As a working Civil War historian, I particularly relish the full text of any primary source. And here in this revised edition we are led to new sites of great primary wealth—secession-era editorials, the entire *New York Times* and *Congressional Globe* for the war years, archival material on the Southern homefront, and the full texts of important public speeches from John Winthrop's 1625 "On Liberty" to President George W. Bush's address nine days after September 11.

All that and much more are found in this indispensable guide to *The Civil War on the Web*. In the 400 sites, whether described in depth or simply listed, are represented virtually the full repertoire of the most important elements of the war—specific sites on all the major campaigns and battles, maps, photographs, biographies of key fig-ures, key states and cities, and an ever-building archive of official reports and per-sonal letters and diaries. Here also is our entry to the prose, poetry, music, emotion, and passion of the war.

The web is without question becoming a superhighway into history. Alice E. Carter, one of the authors of this guide, believes that "this open, democratic forum for sharing research and ideas can help us become more enlightened and informed." Indeed, it can—for searchers at all levels of interest and expertise. But it is a very busy and crowded highway, and we cannot find our way without a roadmap. Fortunately, the roadmap is laid out for us in this wonderful guide.

USER'S GUIDE

Alice E. Carter

The World Wide Web contains many sites rich with content about the Civil War. Researchers can go online to read soldiers' letters and diaries, examine diagrams of cannons and gunboats, and study official reports of major battles and minor skirmishes. But this valuable material can be difficult to find. Entering "Civil War" into a typical search engine will produce a list of hundreds of thousands of sites, most of which are of little value to serious researchers. Many are nothing more than pages of links. Others provide only the hours of operation of a historic site or museum in a distant state. Researchers relying on search engines can find themselves sifting through site after site looking for high-quality material. Searching for sites about certain aspects of the Civil War, such as emancipation, soldiers' lives, or a particular battle, can be even more frustrating. The designers of the best Civil War web sites tend to be educators, government employees, and lay researchers. They generally are inexperienced with "metatags" and costly promotion schemes designed to ensure that the sites will be found by commercial search engines.

Sites such as The United States Civil War Center (http://www.cwc.lsu.edu) and The American Civil War Homepage (http://sunsite.utk.edu/civil-war/) begin to meet the needs of serious researchers, but they too are of limited usefulness. The hundreds of thematically categorized links on these sites take visitors to material that varies widely in quality. Some of the linked sites consist only of short excerpts of out-of-print books. Others contain a few paragraphs of poorly researched secondary material. The true gems linked from most links pages are outnumbered by sites that are quite mediocre.

Unlike search engines and links pages, this book identifies only those sites that are of value to serious researchers. A guide rather than a series of lists, this book provides over one hundred in-depth reviews of the best Civil War sites on the World Wide Web. Each review in Part I gives a detailed description of the site's subject matter. For example, the book's discussion of Civil War Women, part of Duke

University's Digital Scriptorium, explains that the site features the personal papers (http://scriptorium.lib.duke.edu/collections/civil-war-wmen.html) of three women: Rose O'Neal Greenhow, a famous Confederate spy and diplomat; Alice Williamson, a young Tennessee woman coping with life under Union occupation; and Sarah Thompson, a pro-Unionist who aided federal efforts against Confederate guerrilla activity around her Tennessee home. The reviews also describe the type of content on the site. Civil War material on the web ranges from excerpts of previously published but important historical accounts, to collections of documents with explanatory introductions, to original hypertext essays. Digital library sites that consist exclusively of searchable, exquisitely digitized rare primary texts represent another extreme.

The detailed reviews found here are designed to help students, educators, genealogists, academic scholars, and lay historians find web sites that match their interests and needs. In reviewing only a selection of sites, this book emphasizes quality over quantity. Taken together, however, these sites offer endless opportunities for exploration and research.

Some of the sites reviewed were created and maintained by enthusiastic individuals on their own time, with the navigation and page design that one would expect from amateur designers. Others represent years of work by professional historians and archivists, graphic designers, and programmers. The common element in all the sites reviewed is high-quality content. To be selected for a review, a site needed to meet several criteria. First, it had to have material that would help researchers learn about the American Civil War. The content had to be extensive, accurate, and well documented. Second, the site had to make effective use of the medium of the World Wide Web. The information superhighway has the potential to give anyone with a computer and a phone or cable line access to otherwise unavailable material. A site with content that could be found in most bookstores or public libraries did not qualify for a review. The best sites reviewed here feature innovative navigation and searching techniques possible only on the Internet. A selection was never made solely on the basis of aesthetics and technical sophistication, but sites hampered by poor appearance or navigational problems were generally disqualified.

The reviews are divided into eight topical chapters and one catchall chapter titled General History, Historic Documents, Links, and Online Bookstore Sites. The topical chapters are titled Battles and Campaigns, Political and Military Leaders, Life of the Soldier, Naval Operations, The Experience of the U.S. Colored Troops, Slavery and Emancipation, Women in the Civil War, and Civil War Regiments. These subjects are certainly not the only important areas of Civil War study, but they reflect the current focus of Civil War resources on the web. With the exception of Secession Era Editorials Project (http://history.furman.edu/~benson/docs/) and Part I of The Valley of the Shadow (http://valley.vcdh.virginia.edu), there are no significant sites on the coming of the Civil War. The home front experience has also been largely neglected by web site designers.

Each of the eight topical chapters opens with an introduction that provides a historic overview of the subject and that serves as a jumping-off point to the reviews themselves. The reviews describe the contents and structure of the site and provide some navigational hints. They close with ratings on the site's content, aesthetics, and navigation with five stars indicating "excellent," four stars indicating "good," and three stars indicating "average." A list of books at the end of each chapter invites the reader to explore the topic in greater detail. The ninth chapter, new to this edition, features reviews of excellent sites that do not fall neatly into any of the topical chapter categories.

The sites given a rating of five stars for content generally feature extensive collections of primary documents placed in an explanatory context. Although almost all of the reviewed sites receive four or five stars in the content category, the ratings for aesthetics and navigation are not as consistently high. The bulk of the sites reviewed here were not made by professional web designers but by librarians and archivists, reenactors and preservationists, students and educators—people more interested in the Civil War than in slick appearance or sophisticated menus. The few sites that earned ratings of "excellent" in the navigation category are those that cleanly separate historic content from other information, give visitors a clear sense of what lies behind each link, allow easy movement from section to section, and invite visitors to chart their own paths through the material. Of the three categories, aesthetics generally show the lowest ratings, with quite a few sites earning only three stars. The pages in these sites are generally well laid out but make clumsy use of background images, colors, headings, or icons. Sites earning four stars in aesthetics have clean design and effective graphics, and the few sites with five stars for this category are of extraordinary quality, constructed with a level of professionalism that warranted special mention.

Part II, the topical index at the end of the book, provides the names, addresses, and short descriptions of more than 400 Civil War web sites. Most of them were not deemed Best of the Web and so are not reviewed in the main chapters. Although the sites in this category provide valuable historic content, they generally do not have the level of scholarly engagement, depth of analysis, or breadth of coverage exhibited by the reviewed sites. Many of the sites listed in the topical index but not deemed Best of the Web have less effective page layout and navigation.

These sites are still worth a visit. Some are extremely interesting but not sufficiently engaged with central issues of the Civil War study to warrant a full review. For example, The Trial of Captain Henry Wirz (http://www.law.umkc.edu/faculty/projects/ftrials/wirz/wirz.htm), a site made by a team of law students at the University of Missouri–Kansas City, offers a fascinating look into the trial and execution of the commander of the notorious Andersonville Prison. Another example is Civil War Richmond (http://www.mdgorman.com), which contains an impressive collection of documents about businesses, hospitals, and prisons in the Confederate capital city. This site would be of use to people interested in Richmond during the war, although researchers seeking an in-depth study of issues such as the home front, medical care, and prisons will not be satisfied here.

Creating print guides to web sites is always a risky undertaking. Most web sites, including many of the ones reviewed and listed here, are works in progress, and the layout, navigation, and content can be altered fundamentally without notice. Readers of this book may find that some of the sites reviewed here have been transformed considerably since the time the review was written. In revisiting the sites while writing the second edition, we found that the changes were almost always for the better, with new material, better appearance, and improved overall design. Sadly, some sites may still simply disappear or fall into disrepair. Many of the sites reviewed and listed here are constructed and financed by private individuals or non-profit organizations. Changes in interests, priorities, and resources may result in the site's decay or ultimate demise. With luck, this problem will not occur with more than a few of the sites reviewed or listed here. Fortunately, it is often possible to partially recreate sites that have disappeared or radically changed. The Internet Archive's "Way Back Machine" (www.archive.org) allows users to type in a URL, select a date, and then view an archived version of the site.

Even more now than when the first edition of this book was published, the World Wide Web is dominated by e-commerce and other for-profit enterprises. So it is important to recognize the sites that provide a genuine public service. For the most part, the men and women who made these web sites—those reviewed and those not reviewed—did so with little or no remuneration. They were motivated not by profit but by a desire to share their knowledge, their family papers, or their library's or archive's resources with the general public. Thanks to the builders of these fine sites, history still has a secure place in this medium.

The Internet hype has largely evaporated in the past few years. But interestingly, only three of the ninety or so sites picked as Best of the Web in the first edition disappeared over this time period. The rest are still being maintained, and many have been significantly improved. The endurance of these free, public service, research and educational web sites suggests that perhaps the Web is returning to its original vision. The information superhighway will not make us all multimillion-aires after all. But this open, democratic forum for sharing research and ideas can help us become more enlightened and informed.

THE VERY BEST
CIVIL WAR
WEB SITES

REVIEWS

AND

RATINGS

CHAPTER 1

BATTLES AND CAMPAIGNS

Anyone who has browsed the U.S. history sections of bookstores can attest to the enduring fascination that Civil War battles and campaigns hold for scholars and readers. The vast quantity of published works about the Battle of Gettysburg alone could easily fill a small library. The attention is not misplaced. Generals and armies determined the outcome of the conflict.

Military histories of battles and campaigns in the Civil War abound. During the past decade these books have become progressively more detailed and microscopic in their approach. A 600-page volume published in 1987, for example, is devoted to a single day of the battle of Gettysburg. Every year, publishers release new books on major battles and even on secondary engagements, such as Port Republic and Kernstown. These books tend to concentrate on the movements of troops and the orders and counterorders at the regimental level.

Despite the excruciating detail of current battle histories, their coverage confirms the widely held notion that battles and campaigns determined the political outcome of the war. While some historians have looked to the home front to explain Confederate defeat and Northern victory—focusing on such aspects as loss of popular will, uneasiness about slavery, and dissent within the civilian population—battles and campaigns played an obvious role in the outcome, so obvious that they are often overlooked or taken for granted.

The public and the politicians in both North and South measured victories and defeats in the calculus of political, economic, and diplomatic outcomes. Early conquests in the Mississippi Valley provided the North with control over important western transportation networks, and the Union's success at Antietam and Gettysburg halted large-scale Confederate incursions into Northern territory. These and other timely victories on the battlefield bolstered Northern public support for the war effort and headed off British assistance to the Confederacy. The Northern victory at Atlanta in September 1864 virtually ensured reelection for President Abraham Lincoln and the continuation of the war.

The South shared in the experience of timely victory and costly defeat. The Confederacy's Army of Northern Virginia handed defeat after defeat to the Union's Army of the Potomac in 1862–63, or so it seemed to many observers. As the conflict dragged on through these years and casualties mounted, Northern public support for the war diminished while Southern hopes for independence brightened. Even a battle such as Antietam, widely viewed as a marginal Northern victory, gave the Northern public serious cause for concern, as the losses there amounted to the single bloodiest battle in American history. The number of American casualties on this hot day in September in Maryland was four times the number of Americans killed or wounded on D-Day in World War II. In the shadow of Antietam, many Northerners in 1862 wondered about the human costs of fighting the war. Congressional elections in the North in 1862 showed weakening support for the war, as Republicans lost ground to Democrats and Lincoln's ability to prosecute the war without opposition eroded. For the South, though, the loss at Atlanta in 1864 ended any hope of altering the Northern political landscape.

Victory and defeat on the battlefield helped reshape the war's goals in unforeseen ways. Union failures, by lengthening the war far beyond what most Americans had expected, served to alter the war's aims. After the battle of Antietam, President Lincoln drafted the Emancipation Proclamation. When the proclamation was enacted on January 1, 1863, the war became a war to end slavery, not just a war to save the Union. In the South also the war's aims shifted with the armies' fortunes on the battlefields. Offensive campaigns into Northern states followed military success for the Confederacy in 1862 and 1863, and the influence of these campaigns on Northern and foreign public opinion was never far from the minds of Confederate strategists.

Civil War campaigns and battles are popular for reasons other than their strategic significance alone. The development and use of technology over the course of the war is still of interest to scholars of the military, and strategies and tactics employed by generals on both sides of the war are hotly debated by Civil War roundtables, online discussion groups, and academic historians. Perhaps the factor most responsible for the enduring fascination with the war is the role of the common soldier in the conflict. In no other war did so many American men fight. The Confederacy mobilized between 750,000 and 850,000 men in all, almost 75 to 85 percent of its draft-age white male population. The North mustered in 2.2 million soldiers, about 50 percent of its draft-age population. By the end of the war, more than 600,000 men had died of wounds or disease, and hundreds of thousands more were permanently disabled. The number of casualties in the Civil War surpasses American casualties in World War I, World War II, the Korean War, and the Vietnam War combined.

Every year, millions of Americans make pilgrimages to archives and battlefields in search of a connection with these figures from the past. Americans are still struggling with the meaning of the Civil War. Many are seeking answers by studying battles and campaigns, and by building web sites to share their knowledge with the public. Civil War battle and campaign web sites have also been made by custodians of the battlefields, such as the National Park Service and other government organizations. As a result, the online researcher will be rewarded with a wealth of excellent material.

 EB SITE REVIEWS

GENERAL SITES

The Civil War Artillery Page
http://www.cwartillery.org

As the authors of the Civil War Artillery Page point out, artillery played a crucial role in many battles, even though only 6 percent of Civil War soldiers served in artillery units. This site contains practically everything a person would want to know about this important component of the war. Informative essays and excellent illustrations make the Civil War Artillery Page one of the best Civil War sites on the World Wide Web.

Sections include Organization and Drill, which explains how artillery (both heavy and light) fit into the general organization of the Union and Confederate armies and displays the flags and insignia of different units and ranks. The Weapons section explains in simple terms how different types of artillery guns worked and how the design of cannons changed over the course of the war. Black and white drawings are used to illustrate the text. The Ammunition section explains the difference between shells, case shot, grape shot, solid shot, and canisters. The section also contains excellent photographs and diagrams of ten types of projectiles, from the Schenkl shell used by the Union army to the Confederate army's Read bolt. A page titled The Effects of Artillery Fire contains first-hand accounts of the horrible carnage inflicted by these weapons.

The section Famous Weapons describes the history and current condition of important Civil War artillery pieces, such as the Widow Blakely, which fired on federal boats attacking Vicksburg, and the 17,000-pound gun called the Dictator that pounded Confederate forces during the Siege of Petersburg. Quoting Napoleon's belief that the best generals have served in the artillery, a page titled Famous Artillerists summarizes the contributions made by men such as John Pelham, a captain in Stuart's Horse Artillery, and Robert Parker Parrott, whose innovations in cannon production proved essential to the Union's war effort.

The Civil War Artillery Page is exhaustive but never tedious. All of the information is presented in a lively fashion, and visitors will find themselves fascinated as they explore this excellent site.

CONTENT   ★ ★ ★ ★ ★
AESTHETICS   ★ ★ ★ ★
NAVIGATION   ★ ★ ★ ★

Civil War Sites Advisory Commission Battle Summaries

http://www2.cr.nps.gov/abpp/battles/tvii.htm

Created by the American Battlefield Protection Program of the National Park Service, this site contains brief summaries of both major and minor Civil War battles. The descriptions can be accessed from two menus: one listing the battles by theater and campaign, and the other by state. The site provides the following information for each battle: all names that the battle has been known by, location (county and state), campaign, date(s), principal commanders, forces engaged, estimated casualties, description, and result(s).

The descriptions are minimal, with none of the details necessary to create a sense of the battle experience or of its larger significance, and the site contains no maps. With information on more battles than any other single Civil War web site, however, this site is an excellent source for basic information.

CONTENT   ★ ★ ★ ★
AESTHETICS   ★ ★ ★
NAVIGATION   ★ ★ ★ ★

Selected Civil War Photographs in the American Memory Collection

http://memory.loc.gov/ammem/cwphtml/cwphome.html

Shortly after the beginning of the Civil War, Washington, DC, portrait photographer Matthew Brady dispatched a corps of photographers to battlefields and encampments. These men created some of the most powerful records of the conflict, providing Brady with over 1,000 negatives. The Library of Congress bought these negatives from collectors in 1943, and now excellent digital versions can be seen as part of the Library of Congress American Memory Collection.

You will not find dramatic combat scenes among the Brady photographs. The tradition of the heroic combat photographer risking his life to capture the excitement of the heat of the battle still lay far in the future. Photographic technology at the time did not permit moving objects to be captured on film, and photographers preferred to remain safely behind battle lines until the fighting was over.

Rather, the photographs tend to be of battlefield landscapes and structures (taken hours or days after the battle) and camp scenes. Visitors to the site can find the photographs they are looking for in three ways. First, they can search by the name of a battle (or other term). The second option, browsing by subject, takes the visitor to a table of terms arranged alphabetically, which visitors would click to get actual subject headings. (Browsing by subject would be very difficult for anyone not highly familiar with Library of Congress subject terms.) The third and most useful gateway to the photographs is the site's timeline. Each year of the war has its own page containing brief summaries of that year's major battles and campaigns as well as links that automatically execute searches for relevant images.

Any search, whether launched from the search page, a subject term, or the timeline, generates a new page with a list of items that match the search criteria. The items on the list can be clicked to access a thumbnail version of the image and corresponding catalog information. Clicking on the thumbnail accesses a large version of the same image as well as a link to download a high-quality tiff file.

By far the most extensive collection of Civil War photographs available on the web, this Library of Congress site should not be missed.

CONTENT   ★ ★ ★ ★ ★
AESTHETICS ★ ★ ★ ★
NAVIGATION ★ ★ ★ ★

Shotgun's Home of the American Civil War: Battles

http://www.civilwarhome.com/records.htm

The work of one extremely enthusiastic individual, Shotgun's Home of the American Civil War shares many of the characteristics of privately made sites: incomplete citations, grammatical and spelling errors, and an admitted pro-South bias.

But it is the most comprehensive single source on the web for orders of battle, *Official Records*, and other firsthand accounts of practically every major Civil War engagement. As with the Civil War Sites Advisory Commission Battle Summaries site (reviewed above), Shotgun's Home of the American Civil War does not provide enough details or the context necessary to gain a good understanding of Civil War battles and campaigns. But with primary sources on more battles than any other single site on the web, this is a valuable source for researchers.

CONTENT   ★ ★ ★ ★
AESTHETICS   ★ ★ ★
NAVIGATION   ★ ★ ★

The Valley of the Shadow: Two Communities in the American Civil War—The War Years

http://jefferson.village.virginia.edu/cwhome.html

By focusing on two communities, Franklin County, Pennsylvania, and Augusta County, Virginia, the Valley of the Shadow site creates a sense of the Civil War as it was experienced by the people who lived it.

Interesting material on battles can be found in the site's Images, Newspapers, and Letters and Diaries sections, but the best material for the study of battles and campaigns is found in its collection of interactive theater maps. These maps, which require a free plug-in to view, show troop movements of three Augusta County and three Franklin County regiments as they participated in the major battles and campaigns of the Eastern theater.

The base map shows topography and rivers, and additional details (such as modern and historic roads, major cities and towns, and railroads) can be clicked on and off. Clicking the play button starts a movie, and clicking on a battle location opens a summary page with basic facts on that unit's experience there, such as the weather and the number of casualties. The summary page also contains links to soldiers' letters, official reports, and individual dossiers for the men of that unit who were killed and wounded in the battle. These maps can take up to five minutes to load over a modem connection during heavy Internet traffic, but they are worth the wait.

CONTENT ★ ★ ★ ★
AESTHETICS ★ ★ ★ ★
NAVIGATION ★ ★ ★ ★

ANTIETAM/SHARPSBURG

Antietam National Battlefield

http://www.nps.gov/anti/home.htm

Entrusted with the care of dozens of Civil War battlefields and with educating the public about these places, the National Park Service has become the most prolific producer of online material on the Civil War. A visitor to the Antietam National Battlefield web site will find excellent content on this crucial battle.

The Battlefield Information section provides a detailed description of the battle with links to eyewitness accounts, casualty figures, biographical sketches, and photographs. Separate sections include portraits of six generals killed in the battle, photographs of the battlefield by Alexander Gardner, and several paintings made after the battle by eyewitnesses. A page dedicated to the use of artillery shows Union superiority in firepower at Antietam. Other highlights include an explanation of events leading to the battle titled Why Lee Invaded Maryland, an analysis of the role that the battle played in Lincoln's Emancipation Proclamation, and a description of the Dunker church, which stood at the center of the battlefield.

This site also contains information for visitors interested in more general aspects of the Civil War. The frequently asked questions answered in the Special Subjects section include, "What were the tactics of battle in those days?" and "Who exactly were the Zouaves?"

The only primary documents consist of six eyewitness accounts (for which no citations are provided) and the Gardner photographs. This Park Service web site provides visitors with a basic understanding of the Battle of Antietam, but those seeking a more in-depth analysis of the battle will probably be better served at other sites.

CONTENT ★ ★ ★ ★
AESTHETICS ★ ★ ★
NAVIGATION ★ ★ ★

Brian Downey's Antietam on the Web

http://www2.ari.net/brdowney/index.html

Brian Downey's Antietam on the Web is one of the best privately made Civil War
battlefield web sites. A visitor can read a brief overview of the entire battle as
well as a more detailed description of its three major stages. Some of these
descriptions are accompanied by excellent maps made by the author. The site
also contains biographical sketches of Union and Confederate generals who
fought at Antietam. The Exhibits section features dozens of memoirs, letters,
and official reports from battle participants, with helpful explanatory text
accompanying every document. Included among these are Robert E. Lee's letter to Confederate president Jefferson Davis in which he makes the case for taking Southern troops into Maryland, and official reports filed by key individuals
after the battle. Throughout the site, Downey carefully documents and credits
his sources.

This is a well-designed site. Downey makes good use of navigational frames and
attractive menu icons, and he does not clutter his pages with extraneous images
and links. Brian Downey's Antietam on the Web should be a required stop for
anyone interested in the Battle of Antietam as well as for anyone looking for
a good model of a privately made history web site.

CONTENT   ★ ★ ★ ★
AESTHETICS ★ ★ ★
NAVIGATION ★ ★ ★

APPOMATTOX

See Richmond

CHANCELLORSVILLE

See Fredericksburg

CHATTANOOGA

Chattanooga: A Road Trip Through Time

http://www.mediaalchemy.com/civilwar/

This gorgeous site chronicles the journey of its two designers to the major landmarks
of the Battle of Chattanooga. As they go from place to place, they tell the story
of the battle that put an end to the Confederate siege of Union-held Chattanooga
and that set the stage for Sherman's March to the Sea. The history, while not

terribly detailed or analytical, is beautifully written. The authors describe the balance of troops at the start of the battle, the successful Union attacks on Lookout Mountain and Orchard Knob, the foiled attack on Tunnel Hill, and the final victorious advance up Missionary Ridge. On the spot where General Philip Sheridan supposedly raised a glass of whiskey to Confederate officers atop the ridge, the authors paused to toast and drink in Sheridan's honor.

One of the few Civil War sites created by a professional design firm, this site features many artistic photographs taken on their trip as well as a series of maps depicting the military balance before the battle and the events on Lookout Mountain, Tunnel Hill, and Missionary Ridge. A final map of the authors' journey contains links to discussions of various locations important during the battle.

CONTENT   ★ ★ ★ ★
AESTHETICS   ★ ★ ★ ★ ★
NAVIGATION   ★ ★ ★ ★ ★

COLD HARBOR

See Richmond

CORINTH

See Western Theater

FLORIDA

Battle of Olustee

http://extlab1.entnem.ufl.edu/olustee

The Battle of Olustee, Florida's largest Civil War battle, took place in February 1864, when federal troops ventured from Jacksonville into central Florida seeking to cut off supply routes and recruit black soldiers. Confederate forces under Brigadier General Joseph Finegan stopped the Union advance near the town of Olustee. Northern troops suffered heavy casualties and retreated back to Jacksonville, never to attempt another large-scale movement into the Florida interior.

A labor of love on the part of one passionate individual, this site contains photographs of battle reenactments, a large collection of public domain primary documents, invitations to join a battlefield preservation group, and a poem penned in 1989 ("The mist hung low o'er Ocean Pond / That frosty winter's morn; / Many hopeful hearts at dawning's light, / By night would be forlorn").

The site provides an informative account of a little-studied Civil War battle, with a capsule history of the battle as well as a more detailed account titled Ambush at St. Mary's River. Primary documents include official reports filed after the battle and numerous letters and newspaper articles written by participants. A section on the U.S. Colored Troops in the battle includes a detailed description and many additional primary documents.

CONTENT   ★ ★ ★ ★ ★
AESTHETICS   ★ ★ ★
NAVIGATION   ★ ★ ★ ★

FREDERICKSBURG

Battle of Fredericksburg

http://members.aol.com/lmjarl/civwar/frdrksburg.html

This site, created by a private individual, features a detailed account of the battle and excellent maps. Full-scale treatment of topics such as Burnside Takes Over, Day of Battle, Union Order of Battle, and Casualties makes for an extremely informative visit. The illustrated narratives portray the squabbles that took place between Union commanders during the battle and convey a sense of the courage and suffering of the Union soldiers who made the doomed assaults on Confederate positions. The site also contains a lengthy bibliography and credits page.

CONTENT   ★ ★ ★ ★
AESTHETICS   ★ ★ ★
NAVIGATION   ★ ★ ★ ★

Fredericksburg and Spotsylvania National Military Park Visitor Center

http://www.nps.gov/frsp/vc.htm

The Fredericksburg and Spotsylvania National Military Park Visitor Center web site is a useful starting point for studying the battles of Fredericksburg, Chancellorsville, the Wilderness, and Spotsylvania. It contains detailed descriptions of the battles, an explanation of why the area was the scene of so much fighting (titled "Why War Came This Way"), and an excerpt of a Fredericksburg woman's diary kept just before and after the battle there.

The description of the Battle of Fredericksburg opens with General George B. McClellan handing over his command to Ambrose Burnside and concludes with Burnside's withdrawal of his men from Fredericksburg after suffering more than

12,500 casualties. The description is not overly detailed, but it provides enough texture to create a sense of drama. The site now features a link to an animated map of the battle with blue bars depicting units of federal forces and red bars representing Confederate forces. The map shows blue bar after blue bar crossing the Rappahannock, advancing through the streets of the town to join the disastrous Union attack on Marye's Heights. Visitors would be well served by spending a long session with this map, perhaps first looking only at the action in and just above the town, and then focusing on action elsewhere.

The essay on Chancellorsville credits the Confederate victory to bold leadership, particularly that of Stonewall Jackson, who led more than 30,000 troops on a 12-mile trek to launch a surprise attack on Union forces. The essay concludes that the Confederate victory there was a hollow one: Jackson's death cost the South one of its most important heroes, and overconfidence inspired by his success at Chancellorsville caused Lee to launch his ill-fated invasion of Pennsylvania.

The site features two essays on the battles of the Wilderness and Spotsylvania Courthouse. One describes the battles in straight chronological order and concludes with a discussion of the heavy cost that the South paid for its tactical victory there. The second essay covers the events at Todd's Tavern, where Confederate soldiers harassed the Union army as it marched toward Spotsylvania Courthouse.

A sense of the experience of civilians during the fighting is provided in an excerpt of the diary kept by Jane Howison Beale, a Fredericksburg woman. Her diary gives an interesting account of the effect of the proximity of Federal soldiers on the town's slaves and slaveholders.

The enemy has interfered with our labor by inducing our servants to leave us and many families are left without the help they have been accustomed to in their domestic arrangements. . . . I love my servants, they are part of my family and their happiness has been my care as well as that of my own children. I can but hope that no evil influences will be brought to bear upon their minds inducing them to place themselves and me in a more unhappy position than that which we now occupy.

Reflecting the Park Service's initiative to include the experience of civilians, particularly those of women and African Americans, documents such as these show how events on the battlefield affected not only the outcome of campaigns but also the economics and ideologies of the home front.

CONTENT   ★ ★ ★ ★
AESTHETICS ★ ★ ★
NAVIGATION ★ ★ ★

GEORGIA

 The Great Locomotive Chase: The Definitive Story of the Andrews Raid, April 12, 1862

http://www.andrewsraid.com

On April 12, 1862, federal spy James J. Andrews and nineteen Union soldiers in civilian clothes boarded the northbound General in Marietta, Georgia. As the General's crew and passengers were eating breakfast in an inn near the train's first scheduled stop, the Union men took control of the engine, decoupled all but three boxcars, and sped toward Chattanooga. The General's original crew pursued the stolen engine by foot, platform car, and a series of trains they commandeered along the way. After a dramatic chase, the General was overtaken by its pursuers in the town of Ringgold, about fifteen miles south of Chattanooga. The Union men had failed to significantly damage the tracks, and the covered bridge they tried to burn was saved when the pursuing engine simply pushed the smoldering boxcar out of the structure. Andrews and his crew were soon captured and charged with seizing the train and severing the Western & Atlantic Railroad's Atlanta-to-Chattanooga rail link. Andrews was hanged as a spy the following June.

This Great Locomotive Chase web site provides a dramatic, illustrated account of this little-known event along with an interesting analysis of the raid's memorialization in print and film. Railroad enthusiasts will appreciate the site's detailed histories of the General and of the engine that ultimately caught up with the stolen train, the Texas. Both engines were made in Paterson, New Jersey, within one year of each other. After the war, the General became a traveling exhibit, while the Texas remained in use by the Western & Atlantic Railroad for the remainder of the century.

CONTENT   ★ ★ ★ ★
AESTHETICS   ★ ★ ★ ★
NAVIGATION   ★ ★ ★

GETTYSBURG

Carl Reed's Gettysburg Revisited

http://home.sprynet.com/~carlreed/

Novices and experts alike will find Carl Reed's Gettysburg Revisited well worth their time. The Analysis section contains essays by Reed about issues that have long preoccupied Civil War scholars, such as whether General James Longstreet should have attacked earlier on the second day and whether J. E. B. Stuart was truly AWOL at the beginning of the battle. Although rather inelegantly written, Reed's essays are well documented and balanced. Simple but effective computer-generated maps accompany many of the site's essays. The section titled Resources contains the standard fare of official reports and orders of battle as well as excerpts of previously published firsthand accounts such as Robert Johnson and Clarence Buel's edited 4-volume series titled *Battles and Leaders of the Civil War* and William F. Fox's *New York at Gettysburg*. Not a professional historian, Reed does not provide full citations for these materials, but he clearly took pains to document his work.

Each page of Gettysburg Revisited is clean and attractive. Reed makes skillful use of background images and arranges his text carefully. His menu items are intuitive, and, just in case one needs a little help, a site map lists all the contents on one page.

CONTENT	★ ★ ★ ★
AESTHETICS	★ ★ ★ ★ ★
NAVIGATION	★ ★ ★ ★ ★

Gettysburg Discussion Group

http://www.gdg.org

The stated mission of the Gettysburg Discussion Group is to digitize and preserve documents related to the battle. Their effort in this area has been focused on the papers of Union brigadier general Henry Hunt, a Library of Congress collection that has been partially transcribed by group members and made available on the site. The papers include Hunt's postwar correspondence with other Union officers about their units' actions during the battle and letters to Hunt from William Tecumseh Sherman about the proper organization of the peacetime army. Since the site provides no information about Hunt or his role in the Battle of Gettysburg, the nonexpert may find this section's contents confusing.

The bulk of the material on the Gettysburg Discussion Group site consists of secondary accounts of different aspects of the battle, most of which were written and submitted by group members. Topics in this category include Devil's Den: A History and a Guide, and Who Saved Little Round Top? A small collection of essays by National Park Service senior historian Kathleen Georg Harrison covers the formation and early planning of the Gettysburg National Cemetery and Park. The third source of secondary accounts is *Gettysburg Magazine*, which allows the site to post one article from every issue.

The volume of content on this site is overwhelming. Attempting to impose some order on this abundance of material, site designers have created several entry points. One of these is titled The Research Page, which organizes the contents into thematic categories ranging from "Index of Generals" to "The Gettysburg Park Commission Reports, 1893–1921." For the most part, the site is of value primarily to members of the organization and other knowledgeable Gettysburg scholars. In general, nonexperts will find it difficult to judge the quality of the pieces submitted by members of the group and would be better served by other sites.

CONTENT   ★ ★ ★ ★
AESTHETICS   ★ ★ ★
NAVIGATION   ★ ★ ★

Gettysburg National Military Park

http://www.nps.gov/gett/home.htm

This web site contains a vast amount of material for people interested in the Battle of Gettysburg as well as in the Civil War in general.

The virtual tour takes the visitor through each day of the battle, with lengthy explanations of the main events. Links to pages covering locations of interest, such as McPherson's Farm and Oak Hill, contain photographs and detailed accounts of what took place there. Several animated maps that show the general movements of troops for each day and an extensive collection of firsthand accounts round out the tour. Taken in its entirety, this is probably the single most informative web site about the Battle of Gettysburg.

The Gettysburg National Military Park web site also contains exhibits on topics not strictly about Gettysburg but about the Civil War in general. Informative essays in Soldier Life list the contents of a typical soldier's pack, explain how soldiers passed the time in camp, and describe their tents, food, and arms. Separate discussions of cavalry and artillery describe how these divisions were organized and the role that they played in the war. A beautiful exhibit of objects from the Gettysburg Museum, including prayer books, letters, and musical instruments carried by soldiers, can be accessed in Camp Life.

Most of the material on the site is well suited for secondary school students, and several sections are designed strictly with children in mind. Be a Junior Historian presents in simple terms topics such as causes of the war ("What were they fightin' about?"), food and medical care for soldiers, and backgrounds of the war's major leaders. The Teacher's Features section in the Teacher's Guide offers a comprehensive lesson plan, essay topics about the battle, and bulletin board ideas.

CONTENT   ★ ★ ★ ★
AESTHETICS   ★ ★ ★
NAVIGATION   ★ ★ ★

Military History Online—Battle of Gettysburg

http://www.militaryhistoryonline.com/gettysburg

Military History Online is a high-quality commercial site with valuable Civil War material. Its section on the Battle of Gettysburg contains analysis, documents, and highly detailed descriptions of the battle. The descriptions vary from overviews of the events of each day to more focused pieces such as The Peach Orchard and Pickett's Charge. The Articles section contains pieces contributed by various writers, including "First Night, First Mistake: Lee and Ewell" and "A Matter of Numbers and Good Timing." The articles vary in quality of analysis and writing, and all suffer from a lack of citations. The primary documents (accessed by clicking the Reference link in the menu) consist of orders of battle. The site also features a large collection of beautiful photographs of the present-day battlefield.

Every inch of practically every page is filled with text and images, but restrained use of colors and tables prevents the site from seeming cluttered, and it has a very professional overall appearance.

CONTENT ★ ★ ★ ★
AESTHETICS ★ ★ ★ ★
NAVIGATION ★ ★ ★ ★ ★

MANASSAS/BULL RUN

Manassas National Battlefield Park

http://www.nps.gov/mana/home.htm

This National Park Service site is designed primarily for secondary school students, but it will be of value to anyone interested in Civil War battles and campaigns.

The site's brief history of the First Battle of Manassas provides an account of the early Federal success on Henry Hill and of the Confederate reinforcements that forced Northern troops to retreat toward Washington. Thumbnail portraits of key figures such as General Irvin McDowell and General Joseph E. Johnston are linked to larger images and biographical information. The battle account describes the overconfidence felt by both North and South as they headed toward this first significant encounter with the enemy.

The narrative on the Second Battle of Manassas describes how General John Pope, commanding the Union Army of Virginia, ordered an attack on General Stonewall Jackson's units, unaware that Jackson would soon be reinforced by men under General James Longstreet. After suffering heavy losses, the Union army retreated, just as it had a year earlier in the same place. The one primary document about the Second Battle of Manassas is the report filed by Lieutenant Colonel C. B. Brockaway of the First Pennsylvania Artillery. Finding his men without infantry support, he surrendered to Confederate soldiers and was marched to Libby Prison in Richmond.

Material designed specifically for teachers rounds out the offerings on the Manassas Park web site. Educational material includes classroom activities designed to prepare students for a class trip to the park as well as a vocabulary lesson plan in which students learn terms such as *recruitment, bounty jumper,* and *regimental colors.*

The most comprehensive single source of online material on the First and Second Battles of Manassas, the Manassas National Battlefield Park Online Visitor Center provides online researchers with an excellent overview of these two battles.

CONTENT ★ ★ ★
AESTHETICS ★ ★ ★ ★
NAVIGATION ★ ★ ★

MISSOURI

See Western Theater

NEW MARKET

The Battle of New Market, Virginia, May 15, 1864

http://www.vmi.edu/archives/Civil_War/cwnm.html

The Virginia Military Institute (VMI) is closely intertwined with the history of the Civil War. According to historian James M. McPherson, in 1861, 1,781 of the 1,902 current and former students of VMI joined the Confederate armed services, and its alumni led one-third of Virginia's regiments. In 1864, as Union forces were advancing up the Shenandoah Valley, VMI's superintendent sent students from their classrooms to join Confederate forces in a successful attempt to halt the Union advance. These young men had their first combat experience at the Battle of New Market. Ten cadets died on the battlefield or afterward from wounds inflicted there, and forty-five others were wounded.

The VMI New Market exhibit consists of a brief background essay, the names and portraits (if available) of the entire corps that fought, and biographical sketches of the men who were killed during, or from wounds sustained in, the battle. Transcriptions of the superintendent's records are also available, including two letters to the families of young men who died. The superintendent assured the brother of Henry Jenner Jones that "Providence has so ordained it that these young men should be sent off in early youth—they fell nobly fighting in a just cause, in which all Southern youths are willing to pour out [their] heart's blood."

In addition to the material on New Market, VMI's archives contain an extensive collection of online Civil War manuscripts. Clicking Civil War Resources at the bottom of the main New Market page takes the visitor to the home page of the archives' Civil War Resources section. Clicking the Unit and Battle Resources Guide, about halfway down the opening page, and then clicking Civil War Battles take the visitor to a list of manuscripts organized by battle. All combined, there are twelve online collections of letters and diaries that cover sixteen Eastern theater battles and campaigns.

Few sources can match the power of letters and diaries to convey the experience of the Civil War battle. Clayton G. Coleman, a lieutenant colonel in the 23rd Virginia Infantry, wrote to a friend after the Battle of Antietam, "Our brigade lost eight out of ten in the last fight, and my company lost 22 out of 23 men. . . . Every one of your acquaintances in the 4th Alabama and 11th Mississippi were either killed or wounded and indeed I reckon it is almost the case in every Regiment." A member of the 33rd Virginia Infantry, Derastus E. W. Myers, wrote about Chancellorsville, "I was in a thicket and there was not a twig as thick as a man's finger that was not struck with a ball."

This site also contains a letter from Sidney Marlin, who served in one of the Pennsylvania regiments that burned VMI buildings to the ground in June 1864. Marlin wrote his wife, "This is a nice place. There is about 6 thousand inhabitants and the buildings are good. There was a military school here but we have burnt all the buildings. It was a pitty to do it but I suppose it could not be helpt."

VMI's close connection with the Civil War and its extensive archival material have allowed it to make a significant contribution to the World Wide Web.

CONTENT   ★ ★ ★ ★ ★
AESTHETICS ★ ★ ★
NAVIGATION ★ ★ ★ ★

NORTH CAROLINA

Bentonville Battleground
http://www.ah.dcr.state.nc.us/sections/hs/bentonvi/bentonvi.htm

Created by the North Carolina Division of Archives and History, this site provides a highly informative account of the last major Confederate offensive. As the Battle Synopsis section explains, the battle occurred after Confederate general

Joseph E. Johnston quickly assembled scattered units from various Confederate armies in an attempt to halt the advance of General Sherman's Union army through North Carolina. After several minor engagements, the mass of the Confederate and Union troops met near the town of Bentonville on March 19, 1865. Rebel troops retreated after three days of fighting, and Johnston accepted Sherman's surrender terms less than four weeks later. The site's excellent account of this little-studied battle is accompanied by maps, orders of battle, and lists of units engaged on both sides.

The navigation and appearance of this site are generally strong. The links found under The Battle in the left frame provide the best way to move about. Although most of the illustrations are good, the maps have not been scanned at a resolution high enough to make them entirely readable.

CONTENT   ★ ★ ★ ★ ★
AESTHETICS   ★ ★ ★ ★
NAVIGATION   ★ ★ ★ ★

PENINSULA CAMPAIGN

See Richmond

PETERSBURG

Petersburg National Battlefield

http://www.nps.gov/pete/mahan/PNBhome.html

This National Park Service site rewards patient visitors with a wealth of material about the crucial events that took place around Petersburg, Virginia, during the Civil War. Designed primarily with the needs of teachers and students in mind, the site is also extremely valuable to lifelong learners of all ages.

Most of the valuable content lies behind the "Education" link on the site's home page. Visitors can read biographical sketches of dozens of historic figures including Ambrose Burnside, Clara Barton, and Richard Eppes, a civilian living near Petersburg. A physician and planter who owned over one hundred slaves at the outset of the war, Eppes saw all but twelve of them leave for Union lines in 1862. Two years later, his City Point home was turned into General Ulysses S. Grant's headquarters.

Clicking "History" from the main education page invites the visitor to explore subjects ranging from African Americans to Battles to the U.S. Military Railroad. The discussion of African Americans contains a lengthy description of the role played by U.S. Colored Troops regiments in the siege and discusses how members of Petersburg's free black community worked as laborers for the Confederate army. The Battles section takes the visitor through a chronological sketch of the deadly events of 1864 and 1865. The narrative is illustrated by excellent computer-generated maps.

Entire sections devoted to teachers and students support the Park Service's educational mission. Teachers can choose from pre- and post-visit lessons about slavery, prisoners of war, and military strategy. The Kids' Pages include an illustrated dictionary of terms such as *carbine*, *hardtack*, and *primer*. This section also invites students to complete a series of activities that will allow them to qualify as a "junior ranger." In one, students are instructed to outfit a soldier for service using the items described in the illustrated dictionary.

Civil War enthusiasts of all ages will enjoy the Siege Challenge. Visitors are encouraged to test their "Siege IQ" by taking a series of tests. The "Cavalry" level questions, such as "How many patients could the Depot Field Hospital hold?" can be answered using material found on the Petersburg National Battlefield web site. Answering the "Artillery" questions requires exploring additional National Park Service web sites. Finally, the "Infantry" level involves writing a 1- to 2-page essay on topics such as "Did the Siege of Petersburg insure the demise of Gen. Lee's army or did it keep the army alive longer than it could have hoped for otherwise? Or both?"

Although the site suffers somewhat in its navigation and appearance, the sheer wealth of excellent content and its integration of social and military history make it an outstanding example of a battlefield site and serve as a testament to the creativity, hard work, and enthusiasm of Park Service historians and interpreters.

CONTENT   ★ ★ ★ ★ ★
AESTHETICS   ★ ★ ★
NAVIGATION   ★ ★ ★

The Siege of Petersburg

http://members.aol.com/siege1864/

This site, produced by Jim Epperson, the organizer of Civil War newsgroups and web rings, will be appreciated by users seeking a greater level of detail about the Siege of Petersburg than that provided on the Park Service site.

One of the most valuable sections can be accessed by clicking Chronology of the Siege on the opening page. It presents day-by-day details of the entire ten-month campaign, beginning with the arrival of 10,000 Union men under General W. F. "Baldy" Smith to the Petersburg fortifications on June 15, 1864, and ending on April 2, 1865, the day that Union forces penetrated three separate Confederate lines guarding the city, forcing General Lee to order the evacuation of both

Petersburg and Richmond. Another section, Brief Accounts of Each Action in the Siege, contains illustrated descriptions of specific events, such as the fighting around the Crater, First and Second Hatcher's Run, and the Beefsteak Raid. The site includes maps of the Petersburg and the Deep Bottom areas, which Epperson has traced from various authoritative sources.

The design of this site is very simple, and the navigation is straightforward, with menu items clearly indicating the nature of the linked material. The Siege of Petersburg is a valuable site for researchers seeking details about the military aspects of these crucial events in the Civil War.

CONTENT   ★ ★ ★ ★
AESTHETICS   ★ ★ ★
NAVIGATION   ★ ★ ★ ★ ★

RICHMOND

Appomattox Courthouse National Historic Park
http://www.nps.gov/apco/

This National Park Service site provides basic information on Lee's surrender to Grant and the events leading up to it. The Appomattox Campaign section contains a description of the Confederate army's retreat from Petersburg and Richmond in search of rations, supplies, and reinforcements. Northern forces confounded the Confederate troops' escape, first by cutting off their initial route at the Battle of Sailor's Creek and then by beating them to the town of Appomattox. On April 9, 1865, Lee accepted Grant's surrender terms, disbanding the Army of Northern Virginia. The site provides a description of Lee and Grant's meeting in the McLean house as well as an interesting explanation of how the more than 28,000 parole forms were printed, signed, and distributed to the defeated Confederate army. For the most part, the historic material on this site consists of secondary accounts, with few documents. This site provides a good introduction to the important events that took place at Appomattox.

CONTENT   ★ ★ ★ ★
AESTHETICS   ★ ★ ★
NAVIGATION   ★ ★ ★

NEW The 1862 Peninsula Campaign
http://www.peninsulacampaign.org/

This attractive site provides a brief outline of Major General George B. McClellan's attempt to capture the Confederate capital in 1862 and bring an early and swift end to the war. The page titled The Campaign provides a concise summary of the Union general's plan to land Federal troops near the eastern tip of the peninsula formed by the York and James Rivers, take control of the rivers and railroads, and advance on what was sure to be a helpless Richmond. As the summary explains, things did not go as planned. Repeatedly (and mistakenly) convinced that he was badly outnumbered and deprived of the troop reinforcements he believed were necessary, McClellan failed to move decisively at several key points and the campaign failed after four frustrating months.

The site offers additional details about seven important events of the campaign, which can be found by clicking The Battles link on the home page. This section consists of brief descriptions of the clash of the ironclads as well as the battles of Dam No. 1, Williamsburg, Eltham's Landing, Drewry's Bluff, and Seven Pines (Fair Oaks). Several of the descriptions are accompanied by helpful battle maps. The site also features a brief discussion on the use of earthworks and fortifications during the campaign as well as an essay titled "Technology and War," which discusses the pioneering use of ironclad ships, hot-air balloons, antipersonnel land mines, and the rapid-fire gun during the campaign.

The remainder of the site seems designed to encourage tourism to the area. There is an out-of-date calendar of events and a description of places to stop along a 70-mile, 2-day tour. (No map of this tour is provided, and several of the links yield "file not found.")

Researchers already familiar with the Peninsula Campaign will not learn much new here. The narratives merely scratch the surface, and there are no primary sources or other opportunities for further exploration. Nonetheless, it serves as a good starting point for study.

CONTENT   ★ ★ ★
AESTHETICS   ★ ★ ★ ★
NAVIGATION   ★ ★ ★

Richmond National Battlefield Park Homepage

http://www.nps.gov/rich/home.htm

Only sixty miles from Washington, Richmond seemed an easily attainable goal for the Union army, but successive campaigns against it failed. In the spring of 1862, General George B. McClellan launched the ill-fated Peninsula Campaign to take Richmond, only to be stopped seven miles outside of the city. It took more than two years of bloody fighting for Union troops to make significant advances toward the city, which was only evacuated in 1865 after a 10-month siege of Petersburg left Richmond defenseless.

Two sections of the Richmond National Battlefield Park discuss the Peninsula Campaign. Embattled Capital provides an overview of Richmond during the entire Civil War and briefly sketches the main facts of the campaign. A separate page on Drewry's Bluff explains how Confederate gunfire stopped the Union naval advance up the James River just miles from Richmond.

Most of the material on the site covers battles around Richmond that took place in 1864 and 1865. A day-by-day account of the Battle of Cold Harbor includes a description of the fourth day of fighting, when Union forces, pinned down by Confederate gunfire, desperately dug protective trenches with bayonets, cups, and plates. As the site explains, the costly Union defeat at Cold Harbor led Grant to abandon attempts to attack Richmond directly and to opt for taking Petersburg instead. The site also discusses the Battle of Chaffin's Farm, or New Market Heights, and has a large, separate section on the role of the U.S. Colored Troops there. This section has a completely different design from the rest of the Richmond National Battlefield site and is the only part that contains any primary documents.

The site was not designed with the needs of researchers in mind. Rather, its purpose is to inform visitors about historically significant locations in the Richmond area. As a result, the historic content is not highlighted and can be difficult to find. Researchers seeking a basic understanding of some of the events around Richmond during the Civil War will nevertheless be rewarded by the good material here.

CONTENT   ★ ★ ★ ★
AESTHETICS   ★ ★ ★
NAVIGATION   ★ ★ ★

SPOTSYLVANIA

See Fredericksburg

VICKSBURG

See Western Theater

WESTERN THEATER

The Battle of Perryville
http://www.battleofperryville.com/

The Battle of Perryville ended Confederate general Braxton Bragg's Kentucky offensive and kept this critical border state in Union hands for the duration of the war. This web site, the work of enthusiastic lay historians and preservationists, gives an informative account of the battle and its significance and assembles a large collection of primary documents for those interested in more detailed study.

The site provides details of Bragg's invasion of Kentucky, the battle itself, and the post-battle Confederate retreat into Tennessee. The Confederate offensive started as a great success, bringing Frankfort and Lexington under Southern control and threatening the important cities of Louisville and Cincinnati. But Federal reinforcements forced Bragg's army to retreat southward to the crossroads town of Perryville. After failing to repulse Federal forces converging on his men there, Bragg was forced to withdraw even farther. His men returned to Tennessee, and Bragg was soon summoned to Richmond to account for the failure of his campaign.

Readers may find two additional parts of the web site to be helpful companions to the narratives. The chronology provides an exhaustive (almost minute-by-minute) color-coded summary of the events of the main day of the battle. The maps section features two modern maps that clearly identify the locations of the roads, creeks, and towns mentioned in the narratives.

Primary sources on the Battle of Perryville site consist of the standard fare of orders of battle, *Official Records*, and excerpts from *Battles and Leaders of the Civil War* as well as several interesting eyewitness accounts published in newspapers shortly after the battle.

CONTENT   ★ ★ ★ ★
AESTHETICS   ★ ★ ★
NAVIGATION   ★ ★ ★

Corinth: Crossroads of the Confederacy

http://www.corinth.org/

The Siege and Battle of Corinth Commission developed this site to educate the public and to encourage tourism in the Corinth, Mississippi, area. The best content can be found in the section titled Background, which consists of a series of pages that summarize the events leading up to the Union occupation of Corinth in April 1862 and describe the battle that took place when Rebel forces attacked that fall. The narration includes an explanation of the strategic importance of Corinth and of Union general Henry Halleck's leadership. It also does a nice job of placing the battle in the context of events taking place in other theaters of the war. The walking and driving tours described on the site contain photographs of locations that were significant in the siege and battle. The Letters section is actually a collection of various primary sources, ranging from official reports filed by military leaders to the diaries of various soldiers.

Unfortunately, compiling all of these sources into one page makes for extremely difficult navigation.

Navigation within the Background section takes place through a series of forward buttons at the top and bottom of each page. Although there is a site map, it is generated by a Java applet that can take up to thirty seconds to be executed on a home computer. The slide show has been improved since the first edition of this book; it is easier to view on a home computer. It shows historic structures—some still standing and some not—and photographs of troops and encampments.

The Corinth web site makes an important contribution to the online study of the Civil War. There are few sites devoted to the Western theater, and the material found here helps the researcher begin to gain an understanding of events in this important region.

CONTENT   ★ ★ ★ ★
AESTHETICS   ★ ★ ★
NAVIGATION   ★ ★ ★

Vicksburg National Military Park

http://www.nps.gov/vick/home.htm

This is among the best of the National Park Service Civil War web sites. Clicking the Battle for Vicksburg hypertext link on the home page accesses a timeline of the entire Vicksburg campaign with links to informative, illustrated descriptions of the events and their significance. Links at the bottom of many of the descriptions reveal large color maps showing the location of the events described.

Genealogists and other researchers will particularly appreciate the database of thousands of parole records given by the Union army to captured Confederate soldiers after the Vicksburg surrender. To search for a particular individual, a visitor can click the first letter of the soldier's last name to be taken to a page containing all the records for that letter in alphabetical order. Each record gives the full name, rank, and unit of the individual. (Visitors should avoid searching the database using the Park Service search engine because doing so will search not only the Vicksburg parole records but also every web page on the entire National Park Service server.)

The site also includes an interesting presentation about the USS *Cairo*, an ironclad warship sunk by a Confederate mine during the siege and restored one hundred years later. The presentation includes a full listing of the crew of the *Cairo*, giving not only the enlistees' name but also their place of enlistment, date of birth, occupation before the war, and physical appearance. Finally, tailor-made educational packets on the siege are provided for different school subjects and subject levels.

The extensive content on this site compensates for its design, which is marred by intrusive background images on most pages.

CONTENT ★ ★ ★ ★ ★
AESTHETICS ★ ★ ★
NAVIGATION ★ ★ ★ ★

Wilson's Creek National Battlefield

http://www.nps.gov/wicr

This National Park Service site provides a description of the Battle of Wilson's Creek as well as an interesting account of Missouri during the Civil War. After Missouri's governor and state legislators expressed their secessionist leanings in the spring of 1861, Captain Nathaniel Lyon, the commander of the U.S. arsenal in St. Louis, secretly moved the weapons stored there to a secret location, raised a pro-Union regiment, and took control of the state capital. The Battle of Wilson's Creek, fought on August 1, 1861, was a clash between Lyon's regiment and units raised by Missouri's exiled pro-Confederate governor. Lyon was killed while leading a charge during this 5-hour battle, and Federal forces eventually retreated. Although the battle was a Southern victory, Missouri remained in the Union and largely under Federal control, despite the fierce guerrilla warfare waged by groups on both sides.

The Wilson's Creek National Battlefield web site contains only one page with historic content, with the rest of the site providing information for people planning physical trips to the battlefield. Despite its limitations, this site provides a good starting point for researchers unfamiliar with this battle or with Missouri during the Civil War.

CONTENT ★ ★ ★
AESTHETICS ★ ★ ★
NAVIGATION ★ ★ ★

WILDERNESS

See also Fredericksburg

The Battle of the Wilderness: A Virtual Tour

http://home.att.net/~hallowed-ground/wilderness_tour.html

Site designers and Civil War enthusiasts Jim Schmidt and Curtis Fears tell the story of the Battle of the Wilderness by way of a virtual tour. The tour begins with photographs of modern-day Germanna and Ely's Fords. Accompanying text explains how units under Generals Ulysses S. Grant and Winfield Hancock crossed the Rapidan River at these places in May 4, 1864. The tour continues with Saunders' Field, Widow Tapp Farm, the Brock Road–Orange Plank Road Intersection, Ellwood/Grant's Knoll, and the Massaponax Church. Each stop on the tour contains at least several paragraphs of explanatory text and a small collection of photographs.

This site is recommended for researchers seeking a sense of the landscape in which the Battle of the Wilderness was fought and would aid in preparation for a physical visit to the area. For an explanation of the main events of the battle, the best place would be the Fredericksburg and Spotsylvania National Military Park Visitor Center site reviewed above.

CONTENT　★ ★ ★
AESTHETICS　★ ★ ★
NAVIGATION　★ ★ ★ ★

SUGGESTED READINGS

Catton, Bruce. *The Centennial History of the Civil War.* 3 vols. Garden City, NY, 1961–65.

———. *The Army of the Potomac.* 3 vols. New York, 1951–53.

Coddington, Edwin B. *The Gettysburg Campaign: A Study in Command.* New York, 1984.

Cozzens, Peter. *The Shipwreck of Their Hopes: The Battles for Chattanooga.* Urbana, IL, 1994.

Davis, William C. *The Imperiled Union, 1861–1865.* 2 vols. Garden City, NY, 1982–83.

Foote, Shelby. *The Civil War: A Narrative.* 3 vols. New York, 1958–74.

Gallagher, Gary. *The Fredericksburg Campaign: Decision on the Rappahannock.* Chapel Hill, NC, 1995.

———. *The Confederate War: How Popular Will, Nationalism, and Military Strategy Could Not Stave Off Defeat.* Cambridge, MA, 1997.

———. *The Wilderness Campaign.* Chapel Hill, NC, 1997.

Gallagher, Gary, ed. *The Third Day at Gettysburg and Beyond.* Chapel Hill, NC, 1994.

———. *Chancellorsville: The Battle and Its Aftermath.* Chapel Hill, NC, 1996.

———. *The Spotsylvania Campaign.* Chapel Hill, NC, 1998.

———. *The Antietam Campaign.* Chapel Hill, NC, 1999.

Hennessy, John. *Return to Bull Run: The Campaign and Battle of Second Manassas.* New York, 1993.

Josephy, Alvin M., Jr. *The Civil War in the American West.* New York, 1991.

McPherson, James M. *Battle Cry of Freedom: The Civil War Era.* New York, 1988.

Rhea, Gordon C. *The Battle of the Wilderness, May 5–6, 1864.* Baton Rouge, LA, 1994.

CHAPTER 2

POLITICAL AND MILITARY LEADERS

It might surprise even Civil War readers to know that generals suffered the highest combat casualties. They were 50 percent more likely to be killed in action than privates were. The list of fallen generals in the Civil War is long: Garnett, Armistead, Stuart, Jackson, Reynolds, and Kearny, to name a few. Historians, artists, and writers have glorified these leaders, casting images of their deeds across generations. Among the engravings of Civil War action in *Frank Leslie's Illustrated* is that of Lewis A. Armistead leading the assault on the stone wall at Gettysburg with his hat held high on his sword. One of the most recognizable and reprinted paintings concerning the Civil War is E. B. D. Julio's *The Last Meeting of Lee and Jackson*. Both generals are on horseback at the edge of a wood, and Lee is gesturing to his right, presumably indicating his approval of Jackson's plan to attack the far right flank of the Union army at Chancellorsville. More recently, artists such as Mort Kunstler have continued to make the heroics of generals a main part of their work. Civil War history enthusiasts today can buy chess sets with Lee and Jackson as the Confederate king and bishop, respectively.

Historians agree that leadership—both political and military—played a decisive role in the outcome of the war. Many note the advantage that the Confederacy seemed to maintain in officer-level leadership, especially in the beginning of the war. The presence in the South of seven of the eight military colleges in the United States helps to explain the initial disparity. Just as important, the regular U.S. Army officers and their units were kept intact rather than interspersed with the new volunteers; Union forces, therefore, failed to benefit from their highly trained leaders.

Both North and South witnessed the appointment of "political generals." In the North the term became synonymous with incompetence and failure. Governors of the states, as well as Lincoln and Davis, were under considerable pressure to satisfy political debts and obligations. Seeking to placate Democrats and present a united front to the South and to foreign nations, Lincoln assigned generalships to Benjamin F. Butler, Daniel E. Sickles, and John A. Logan, prominent Democrats all. He also appointed ethnic leaders such as Carl Schurz, Franz Sigel, and Thomas Meagher. Davis also named "political generals" to gain the support of various state leaders.

Despite the appointment of political generals, graduates of West Point held the vast majority of high-level appointments, so much so that one historian has labeled the war "preeminently a West Pointers' fight." In perhaps one of the most widely read essays on Civil War leaders, historian T. Harry Williams argues in *Why the North Won the Civil War* that "it is the general who is the decisive factor in battle." He pointed out that in the sixty biggest battles in the war West Pointers commanded the armies of both sides in fifty-five of them. He also argued that the dominance of the Jominian strategy of warfare, which is divorced from political considerations, hindered the growth of both Union and Confederate generals. In another essay in that slim but important book, historian David Potter suggests that "there is a great deal of evidence to justify placing a considerable share of the responsibility for the Confederacy's misfortunes directly at the door of Jefferson Davis."

Leadership questions litter Civil War histories. They are at the center of many interpretations of strategic battles and turning points. Was Union general George McClellan afraid to commit his troops to battle and too slow to move, hence losing an opportunity in the Seven Days battles to win the war by capturing Richmond? Did Confederate corps commander James Longstreet delay on the second day of Gettysburg and thereby lose the battle for the Confederates? What explains General Thomas J. "Stonewall" Jackson's slowness at the Seven Days battles? Was Union general Joseph Hooker drunk at Chancellorsville or hit in the head with a shell? Did Union general Gouverneur K. Warren act in an unprofessional manner at Five Forks?

Many military leaders of the Civil War would probably find the cutthroat criticisms of their decisions by today's scholars and enthusiasts disturbingly familiar. Even at the time, they were at the center of political recriminations, courts-martial, and public scrutiny from the newspapers. McClellan's officer corps, for example, was entrenched in political considerations, so much so that when General Ambrose Burnside succeeded McClellan a half-dozen generals schemed to limit his influence in command. Internal dissension over the leadership of Confederate general Braxton Bragg nearly led to a formal duel between him and another general in the Confederate Army of Tennessee after the battle of Stones River. Bragg court-martialed one of his generals for insubordination and threatened to do the same to the others.

Courts-martial brought down more than a few Civil War generals. Defendants' peers reviewed their decisions and conduct in battle, either absolving or condemning them. Stonewall Jackson had one of his division commanders, General A. P. Hill, arrested for failing to follow orders that gave the start time for his division to march on the morning of September 4, 1862. Hill fought the Maryland campaign at the head of his division under a cloud of potential court-martial and formally under arrest. Lee patiently resolved the conflict between the two generals. Union general Gouverneur K. Warren was not so fortunate. A hero at Gettysburg, he was court-martialed by General Philip Sheridan for failure to move on orders at the battle of Five Forks. Warren maintained that he had followed orders, that his maps were wrong, and that his corps behaved honorably. He was found guilty as charged and his reputation ruined. Finally, in 1885, Warren succeeded in having the verdict overturned by a court of inquiry.

Congressional committees and newspaper editors also took shots at military leaders, evaluating their performance not on the basis of military justice but instead on the basis of public opinion. The Joint Committee on the Conduct of the War investigated Union generals' losses and inefficiency and corruption in the army. Although no counterpart for the Joint Committee developed in the Confederate Congress, various members of the Confederate Congress led an opposition effort against Jefferson Davis, often conducting their investigations through the newspapers. Newspaper editors lambasted generals for any perceived incompetence. Few generals received such bad press as did Robert E. Lee when he took command of the Army of Northern Virginia. The *Richmond Examiner* derided him as "Evacuating Lee" for his poor performance in western Virginia in 1861.

The intense partisanship, courts-martial, infighting, and recriminations all reveal the complexities of an internecine war. It is no wonder, then, that business leaders today seek lessons from the leadership of Civil War generals and politicians, buying books about Lincoln and Lee with subtitles such as "Executive Strategies for Tough Times" and "From Battlefield to Boardroom."

The World Wide Web offers sites on Civil War leaders that will please both business leaders looking for clues to successful strategies of management and serious scholars searching for the sequence of key decisions by Civil War generals. Some of the most comprehensive come from university libraries that hold the papers of these leaders, but others are freewheeling forums on the command decisions of the war.

GENERAL SITES

NEW **HarpWeek: Presidential Elections from 1860 to 1884**
http://elections.harpweek.com/

A privately funded venture, HarpWeek offers institutional subscribers full access to
the digitized, complete *Harper's Weekly* from 1857 to 1912. As a public service
and to help promote their main product, its creators have also produced a number of excellent exhibits that are free and open to the public. One of these
exhibits, Presidential Elections from 1860 to 1884, features impeccably digitized campaign broadsides and political cartoons from the seven U.S. presidential
elections. Scanned at three levels of resolution and accompanied by excellent
explanatory narratives, the prints provide a wonderful window onto the politics of the Civil War years.

The exhibit is organized by election. Clicking "1860" on the home page will
take users to a list of twenty-five cartoons. The first is a traditional party broad-
side with the portraits of Abraham Lincoln and running mate Hannibal Ham-
lin enclosed in rustic twig frames with the messages "The Union must and
shall be preserved," "Free Speech, Free Homes, Free Territory," and "Protection to American Industry." Less complimentary is Nathaniel Currier's "The
Republican Party Going to the Right House," which shows Lincoln carried on
a rail into a lunatic asylum by *New York Tribune* editor Horace Greeley. A Mor-
mon, a suffragette, a free black, a socialist, and two common criminals follow
closely behind. As the accompanying narrative explains, Horace Greeley had
backed Lincoln throughout the nomination race, and critics of Republicans
depicted the party as an association of radicals, eccentrics, and thugs.

Nineteenth-century political cartoons drew on images from the popular culture of the time that would be lost on most twenty-first-century researchers.
So it is helpful that HarpWeek not only explains the political events or con-
troversies being illustrated but also the cultural references. The *Vanity Fair* cartoon, "A Modern Pyramus and Thisbe," shows Stephen Douglas and John C.
Breckinridge being held apart by President James Buchanan. The explanation
summarizes the Babylonian folk tale of two lovers separated by a wall and
reminds those of us who need to brush up on our Shakespeare that this story

appears in a subplot of *A Midsummer Night's Dream*. According to the text, the cartoonist holds President Buchanan responsible for the 1860 division of the Democratic Party.

In addition to the cartoons and descriptions, HarpWeek provides explanatory material on each election. The 1860 election material includes biographies of eighteen political figures. "Overview" gives a one-page account of the splitting of the Democratic Party, the appeal to sectional harmony made by the Constitutional Union Party, and the Republican nomination of Lincoln over early frontrunner William Seward. The thirty-two cartoons from the 1864 election include "That reminds me of a little joke," a *Harper's Weekly* cartoon showing Lincoln holding a doll-sized George B. McClellan in his hand. As the accompanying narrative tells us, the cartoonist was referring both to Lincoln's tendency to pepper important meetings and conversations with jokes and anecdotes and to McClellan's short stature.

This site is enormously valuable to researchers at a variety of levels. For those seeking a basic introduction into the electoral politics of the Civil War era, the symbolism of the cartoons and the explanatory narratives are an excellent starting point. More advanced researchers will spend hours enjoying the large collection of beautifully reproduced historic prints.

CONTENT ★ ★ ★ ★ ★
AESTHETICS ★ ★ ★ ★ ★
NAVIGATION ★ ★ ★

Shotgun's Home of the American Civil War: Biographies
http://www.civilwarhome.com/biograph.htm

Evidently the work of one energetic individual, Shotgun's Home of the American Civil War is the largest single source of Civil War biographical material on the web. The Civil War Biographies section contains biographical sketches of more than seventy military and political leaders, from U.S. Major Robert Anderson to CSA Brigadier General Felix Kirk Zollicoffer. Most of the biographies consist of summaries of secondary accounts, and some contain portraits and full-text excerpts of public domain sources. The site features little historical analysis, few images, and almost no primary source documents. But its sheer breadth makes it an excellent starting point for the study of Civil War leaders.

CONTENT ★ ★ ★ ★
AESTHETICS ★ ★ ★
NAVIGATION ★ ★ ★ ★

The *War Times Journal* Civil War Series: Grant, Longstreet, Sherman, Hood, and Gordon

http://www.wtj.com/wars/civilwar/

The *War Times Journal* is a professionally made, commercial site devoted to military history and science. Its section on the Civil War contains lengthy excerpts from the public domain memoirs of five important Civil War generals: U. S. Grant, James Longstreet, William Tecumseh Sherman, John B. Hood, and John B. Gordon.

The selections from Confederate general James Longstreet's 1912 memoirs *From Manassas to Appomattox* cover his Civil War and post–Civil War career. In the three chapters devoted to the Battle of Gettysburg, Longstreet presents a highly detailed defense of his actions in an attempt to silence postwar critics who blamed him for the Confederate defeat there. The final chapter chronicles Longstreet's postwar career as the Republican-appointed surveyor of customs in New Orleans and describes the opprobrium brought down on him for suggesting that white Southerners cooperate with the federal government during Reconstruction.

The excerpts from General William Tecumseh Sherman's *Memoirs* cover the Battle of Shiloh and the Union capture of Memphis. The site also contains two chapters from Confederate lieutenant general John B. Hood's *Advance and Retreat*, published in 1880. The excerpts discuss Hood's experience at Gainesville, Antietam, Fredericksburg, Gettysburg, and Chickamauga. Included in the selections from Confederate general John B. Gordon's *Reminiscences of the Civil War: From Manassas to Gettysburg* is Gordon's version of the Battle of Gettysburg, which, not surprisingly, differs sharply from Longstreet's.

Excerpts from Grant's memoirs have been added since the first edition of this book. At the time this volume went to press, the excerpts begin with his account of his operations in Mississippi and end with the march to Cold Harbor in 1864.

The memoirs will prove daunting to a researcher unfamiliar with the battles discussed and with the careers of the five generals. But they are essential for anyone seeking a full understanding of the careers of Grant, Longstreet, Sherman, Hood, or Gordon. This is a simple site in that the transcripts cannot be searched and there are few images, but the layout is clean and the navigation intuitive.

CONTENT   ★ ★ ★ ★
AESTHETICS   ★ ★ ★ ★ ★
NAVIGATION   ★ ★ ★ ★

DAVIS, JEFFERSON

The Papers of Jefferson Davis
http://jeffersondavis.rice.edu/

This site offers selections from the multivolume series of Jefferson Davis's collected papers edited at Rice University. The documents cover the period from 1834 to 1864 and include his speeches and letters as well as letters to Davis from the Civil War home front and battlefield.

The documents provide a vivid sense of the many pressures facing Davis as president of the Confederacy. In 1862 a woman wrote to him and demanded that her husband be released from military service. The forty slaves on the plantation she was left to manage alone could not be controlled with her husband gone: "Your Excellency is doubtless in constant attention to the ponderous business of the Government ... yet I hope your Excellency will find time enough amidst all this, to give me a hearing and grant me the relief sought for." Davis was powerless to protect even his own family's plantations as Union forces took command of the Mississippi River. He advised his brother to flee with his slaves and cotton before Federal forces descended on the area. The papers also include Davis's addresses to the Confederate Congress, letters to his wife Varina, and a dispatch to Davis from General Robert E. Lee. The documents have been transcribed in full, and, although they cannot be searched, they are accompanied by helpful explanatory notes and listed in chronological order.

Other sections on the site discuss Davis's life before, during, and after the Civil War. The Jefferson Davis Chronology page gives a detailed timeline of his life, with important names and terms linked to other web pages. Because some of the linked pages are from outside sites of inconsistent quality and relevance, this feature is ultimately confusing. The Frequently Asked Questions page discusses the confusion over Davis's year of birth, his middle name, and the charges of treason brought against him after the war. The pages are illustrated by portraits of Davis in various stages in his life.

CONTENT   ★ ★ ★ ★ ★
AESTHETICS   ★ ★ ★ ★
NAVIGATION   ★ ★ ★ ★

GRANT, ULYSSES S.

The Ulysses S. Grant Association
http://www.lib.siu.edu/projects/usgrant

The Ulysses S. Grant Association has assembled Grant's correspondence, military papers, and government documents and published them in the multivolume series titled *The Papers of Ulysses S. Grant*. The association's web site contains a small selection of these documents as well as additional historic material about Grant's life.

The section titled Historical Information on U. S. Grant features a link to Grant's memoirs. The memoirs are not searchable, but a helpful table of contents sends visitors where they need to go. They open with a discussion of Grant's ancestry and conclude with a description of the grand review of the victorious Union armies in Washington in May 1865. Written in Grant's distinctive, unadorned prose, the memoirs are a compelling summary of many of the important events of the Civil War. The Historical Information section also contains the reminiscences of James Crane, a military chaplain who became close to the general during the war. Crane depicted his friend as intensely religious and took pains to refute charges that Grant was a heavy drinker.

Other material includes a lengthy chronology of the general's life, a short essay on Grant by Civil War historian Bruce Catton (accessed by clicking the "Ulysses S. Grant Chronology" link), and a variety of documents and secondary accounts published in back issues of the Ulysses S. Grant Association's newsletter, which include reminiscences from Grant's sister-in-law, "When Grant Went A-Courtin," as well as a poem by Walt Whitman.

CONTENT   ★ ★ ★ ★
AESTHETICS   ★ ★ ★
NAVIGATION   ★ ★ ★

JACKSON, THOMAS J. "STONEWALL"

Stonewall Jackson Resources at the Virginia Military Institute Archives
http://www.vmi.edu/archives/Jackson/Jackson.html

With extensive selections of documents about the life of Thomas "Stonewall" Jackson from the Virginia Military Institute (VMI) Archives, this site is an excellent resource for researchers at all levels.

Web visitors unfamiliar with Jackson's life may want to start by clicking Biographical Information. This link accesses a detailed timeline that starts with his birth in Clarksburg, West Virginia, and ends with his death from wounds sustained at the Battle of Chancellorsville. Certain events and individuals in the timeline are linked to pertinent document transcriptions. The Frequently Asked Questions page provides information as varied as how he got his nickname and where his amputated arm is buried. As with the timeline, certain names and events on this page are hyperlinked to relevant documents elsewhere in the archives. The page titled Major Jackson, Professor at VMI, chronicles Jackson's troubled teaching career at the military institute. (In 1856, Jackson proved so unpopular that the Alumni Council petitioned for his dismissal.)

The section called Stonewall Jackson Papers consists of transcriptions of several dozen letters that Jackson wrote before and during the Civil War. Many were written to his sister while he was attending the U.S. Military Academy, fighting in the Mexican-American War, and beginning his teaching career at VMI. The Civil War-era letters attest to Jackson's strong Christian faith. He wrote to a friend who had earlier congratulated him on a recent victory, "Without God's blessing I look for no success, and for every success my prayer is that all the glory may be given unto Him to whom it is properly due."

This is an extremely rich site that merits lengthy exploration. The pages are simply designed, and the navigation is intuitive without being flashy.

CONTENT   ★ ★ ★ ★ ★
AESTHETICS   ★ ★ ★ ★
NAVIGATION   ★ ★ ★ ★ ★

LEE, ROBERT E.

The Robert E. Lee Papers at Washington and Lee University
http://miley.wlu.edu/LeePapers/

This site contains images of forty-six letters written by Robert E. Lee before, during, and after the Civil War. The documents include letters written to Jefferson Davis, George B. McClellan, Jubal Early, Ulysses S. Grant, and the Washington College Board of Trustees as well as General Orders No. 9, in which Lee said goodbye to his army at Appomattox: "After four years of arduous service marked by unsurpassed courage and fortitude, the Army of Northern Virginia has been compelled to yield to overwhelming numbers and resources."

Since the publication of the first edition of this book, some of the documents have been transcribed. But otherwise, this site recreates the experience of true archival research: there are no summaries of the letters' contents and there is no information to provide background or context. As a result, the site is not particularly easy to use. But as the largest online source of material penned by Lee, it will prove valuable to serious researchers.

CONTENT   ★ ★ ★ ★
AESTHETICS   ★ ★ ★ ★
NAVIGATION   ★ ★ ★

LINCOLN, ABRAHAM

Abraham Lincoln Online

http://www.netins.net/showcase/creative/lincoln.html

This site contains a variety of material on the man who was president of the United States during the Civil War. The section called Lincoln This Week lists three or four events that occurred during particular weeks from various periods in Lincoln's life. Of most value to researchers is the section titled Speeches/Writings. Each of the several dozen documents in this section opens with an introduction that provides useful background information. The documents are generally well known, such as the Gettysburg Address, Lincoln's First and Second Inaugural Addresses, and his letter to *New York Tribune* editor Horace Greeley about emancipation, wherein he wrote, "if I could save the Union without freeing any slave I would do it, and if I could save it by freeing all the slaves I would do it; and if I could save it by freeing some and leaving others alone I would also do that." Within months of this letter, Lincoln issued the preliminary Emancipation Proclamation and fundamentally transformed the nature of the war.

A volunteer effort of a group of Lincoln enthusiasts, the site also contains an exhaustive bibliography, links to other sites, and the Lincoln Mailbag, to which visitors contribute their thoughts about Lincoln.

CONTENT   ★ ★ ★
AESTHETICS   ★ ★ ★
NAVIGATION   ★ ★ ★ ★

NEW Abraham Lincoln Papers at the Library of Congress

http://lcweb2.loc.gov/ammem/alhtml/malhome.html

With the exceptions of the small exhibits on the Emancipation Proclamation and Lincoln's Assassination, this site is not designed for the novice researcher. Its overwhelming volume and its general lack of explanatory or narrative material may intimidate those not already fairly familiar with Lincoln's life. But lay researchers would still benefit from a visit here.

Selecting April 2–April 8, 1861, when browsing by date, shows that in the midst of the Fort Sumter crisis, Lincoln was besieged by officeseekers and their supporters. The majority of the 120 documents from this week regard appointments to patronage posts. However, quite a few were letters to Lincoln advising him on Fort Sumter. Some of the advice was solicited, but some was not, such as this note from an Illinois Republican:

Bellefontaine Ohio

April 3. 1861—

Sir—

The reinforcement of Fort Sumpter under existing circumstances, would secure to you an immortality of fame, which Washington might envy— The Surrender of Fort Pickens under any circumstances, will consign your name, and fame, to an ignominy, in comparison with which that of your immediate predecessor, will be tolerable, and Arnolds illustrious.

I but reflect the universal sentiment when I say, the loyal people of the North West would tolerate any stretch of power on your part, & prefer to see you, "wade through Slaughter to a throne" rather than have our country humiliated, and its glorious flag dishonored by a voluntary Surrender. Pardon this obtrusion but Save us from Shame— Yours Truly—

W H WEST
A Chicago Delegate

In addition to browsing by date, users can also take advantage of the Library of Congress's excellent search function. Searching for "Grant" yields a long list of correspondence between the president and Ulysses S. Grant, including a telegram sent by the general on March 31, 1865, during his final offensive in Virginia:

From Boydtown Road 1865.

Our troops after being driven back onto Boydtown plank Road turned & drove the enemy in turn & took the White Oak Road which we now have. This gives us the ground occupied by the Enemy this morning

I will send you a rebel flag captured by Our troops in driving the Enemy back. There has been four (4) flags Captured today. The one I send you was taken from a Va Regiment of Hunters Brigade.

The documents have been digitized from microfilm rather than the original paper, so they are generally unattractive and quite difficult to read. Most of the letters written by or directly to Lincoln have been transcribed, and some have been annotated with helpful explanations. Unfortunately, it is not possible to tell which documents have been transcribed and/or annotated without calling up the document itself.

CONTENT   ★ ★ ★ ★ ★
AESTHETICS   ★ ★ ★
NAVIGATION   ★ ★ ★

Abraham Lincoln Research Site
http://members.aol.com/RVSNorton/Lincoln2.html

Created by a former teacher of U.S. history, the Abraham Lincoln Research Site is a rich source of interesting material. It is designed primarily for school children, but it is of value to adult learners as well.

The Especially for Students page provides a thorough overview of Lincoln's life, with important names and terms linked to outside web sites such as Grolier's Encyclopedia. Photographs of Lincoln in various stages of his life accompany the text. Visitors seeking a more detailed account of Lincoln's life can visit the Chronology page, which is similarly illustrated and hyperlinked. The site also contains separate sections on Mary Todd Lincoln and Lincoln's assassination, both of which are complete enough to stand alone as their own sites. The section called The Lincoln Special provides a fascinating account of the journey of Lincoln's funeral train from Washington to Springfield, Illinois. On its 14-day route, the train stopped at ten cities where Lincoln's open coffin was placed for public viewing. Thousands of people lined the railroad tracks to watch the train pass while it traveled between cities.

The bulk of the material concerns Lincoln's personal life. The site features a page about Ann Rutledge, who is billed as his first romance; a page about each of his sons; and a page about his wedding day. The site contains little about Lincoln's presidency or the Civil War.

CONTENT   ★ ★ ★
AESTHETICS   ★ ★ ★
NAVIGATION   ★ ★ ★ ★

Lincoln/Net: The Abraham Lincoln Digitization Project
http://lincoln.lib.niu.edu/

Based at the University of Northern Illinois, the Abraham Lincoln Digitization Project focuses on Lincoln's life and career in Illinois. Since the first edition of this book went to press, Lincoln/Net has evolved into one of the best sources of online archival material about this essential figure.

The site features a collection of sixty-nine campaign songs from Lincoln's 1860 and 1864 presidential campaigns. The collection can be searched by variables such as title, lyricist, composer, arranger, or a word or phrase in the lyrics. Searching for "rail splitter" in the lyrics yielded three matches, including one titled "Western Star": "Mechanics and farmers / Hail the glad day, / When Free Labor gives them / Good price and pay. / Brightly the Western Star / O'er us appears— / LINCOLN, the 'Rail-Splitter!' / Give him three cheers." The songs can also be accessed through a browsable list. A transcription of the lyrics and a scan of the page from the original sheet music are available for each song. Seven of the songs can be heard with a free plug-in.

The site also contains a collection of material on topics such as Frontier Settlement, Law and Society, and the Lincoln-Douglas debates. Each collection consists of a brief scholarly essay and digitized primary sources that can be searched or browsed. Novices may feel daunted by the primary sources, which are unaccompanied by any explanatory material or reading aids, although specialists will find the extensive collection of otherwise inaccessible primary source material extremely valuable. More about frontier Illinois society than about Lincoln himself, Lincoln/Net provides visitors with an excellent sense of the president's background as well as the political culture of the midnineteenth century.

CONTENT   ★ ★ ★ ★
AESTHETICS   ★ ★ ★
NAVIGATION   ★ ★ ★ ★

LONGSTREET, JAMES

The Longstreet Chronicles
http://tennessee-scv.org/longstreet/

General James Longstreet, who fought beside Robert E. Lee throughout the Civil War, fell out of favor with many of his fellow officers in the decades that followed Appomattox. His detractors, whose accounts formed the basis of early interpretations of the war, blamed Longstreet for a series of missteps, most notably at Gettysburg.

The Longstreet Chronicles site represents an attempt to rehabilitate Longstreet's reputation. The section titled The Controversy contains essays by Brian Hampton, the site's author, which attribute the accusations against Longstreet to the need for a scapegoat to blame for the South's defeat. Longstreet, who became a Republican after the war and urged his fellow Southerners to accept negro suffrage, was an easy target. His public criticism of Lee's tactics at certain battles further fanned the flames of the anti-Longstreet clique. Hampton's essay also describes the formation and influence of the "Lee cult," which elevated Robert E. Lee to godlike status and cast Longstreet as the villain.

The Life and Career section contains a mixture of more than one hundred public domain primary and secondary accounts of various aspects of Longstreet's military record. Taken together, these accounts provide a rigorous defense of his career. The site also features an annotated bibliography of eleven books that address Longstreet's record.

CONTENT   ★ ★ ★ ★
AESTHETICS   ★ ★ ★
NAVIGATION   ★ ★ ★ ★

MEADE, GEORGE GORDON

The Meade Archive

http://adams.patriot.net/~jcampi/welcome.htm

The reputation of Union general George Gordon Meade suffered permanent damage as a result of his actions (or lack thereof) after the Union victory at Gettysburg. The Meade Society created this archive of essays and primary documents to defend him against these charges.

The site presents the accusations against Meade in the His Critics section, which includes anonymous critical letters published in the *New York Herald* and *New York Times* and the testimony of Major General Daniel Sickles to Congress's Joint Committee on the Conduct of the War:

QUESTION. In your opinion, as a military man, what do you think of the propriety of again encountering the enemy at the river before he recrossed [after the Battle of Gettysburg]?
ANSWER. He should have been followed up closely, and vigorously attacked before he had an opportunity to recross the river.
QUESTION. Under the circumstances, as you understand them, could there have been any great hazard to our army in venturing an engagement there?
ANSWER. No, sir. If we could whip them at Gettysburg, as we did, we could much more easily whip a running and demoralized army, seeking a retreat which was cut off by a swollen river; and if they could march after being whipped, we certainly could march after winning a battle.

The defense of Meade is set forth in excerpts from a complimentary previously published biography, numerous contemporary and firsthand accounts of Meade's career, and his own letters and addresses. In his testimony to the Joint Committee on the Conduct of the War, Meade maintained that the Confederate army was not as weakened as Sickles had claimed:

QUESTION. Did you discover, after the battle of Gettysburg, any symptoms of demoralization in Lee's army, such as excessive straggling, or anything of the kind?

ANSWER. No, sir; I saw nothing of that kind. . . .

The site is illustrated with portraits of Meade and his critics as well as photographs of the Gettysburg battlefield.

CONTENT   ★ ★ ★ ★
AESTHETICS   ★ ★ ★ ★
NAVIGATION   ★ ★ ★

SUGGESTED READINGS

Catton, Bruce. *Grant Moves South*. Boston, 1960.

———. *Grant Takes Command*. Boston, 1969.

Connelly, Thomas L. *The Marble Man: Robert E. Lee and His Image in American Society*. New York, 1977.

Connelly, Thomas L., and Archer Jones. *The Politics of Command: Factions and Ideas in Confederate Strategy*. Baton Rouge, LA, 1973.

Donald, David Herbert. *Lincoln*. London, 1995.

Freeman, Douglas Southall. *R. E. Lee: A Biography*. 4 vols. New York, 1934–35.

———. *Lee's Lieutenants: A Study in Command*. 3 vols. New York, 1942–44.

Jones, Archer. *The Politics of Command: A Military Study of the Civil War*. 5 vols. New York, 1949–59.

Marszalek, John F. *Sherman: A Soldier's Passion for Order*. New York, 1993.

Nolan, Alan T. *Lee Considered: General Robert E. Lee and Civil War History*. Chapel Hill, NC, 1991.

Pitson, William G. *Lee's Tarnished Lieutenant: James Longstreet and His Place in Southern History*. Athens, GA, 1987.

Simpson, Brooks D. *Let Us Have Peace: Ulysses S. Grant and the Politics of War and Reconstruction*. Chapel Hill, NC, 1991.

Warner, Ezra J. *Generals in Gray*. Baton Rouge, LA, 1959.

Williams, Kenneth P. *Lincoln Finds a General: A Military Study of the Civil War*. 5 vols. New York, 1949–59.

Williams, T. Harry. *Lincoln and His Generals*. New York, 1952.

Woodworth, Steven. *Jefferson Davis and His Generals*. Lawrence, KS, 1990.

CHAPTER 3

LIFE
OF THE
SOLDIER

In the 1940s and 1950s, Bell Irvin Wiley pioneered the history of the common soldier with his books *The Life of Johnny Reb* and *The Life of Billy Yank*. He contended that if you threw the letters of the common soldiers from both sides in the air, you would not be able to tell the difference between North and South. His books examined camp life, training, music, punishment, hospital treatment, prison life, religion, homesickness, food, weapons, and other daily experiences of the soldiers.

Historians and others interested in the Civil War continue to find the world of the common soldier fascinating. Thousands of Americans participate in Civil War reenactments, painstakingly recreating the minutiae of the soldier's daily life. Some take the living history to extremes by using only authentic materials in camp, speaking in supposedly authentic tones and dialects, and mimicking the movements of their historical counterparts in every respect. The urge among Civil War enthusiasts to live the life of the common soldier seems almost as pervasive as the urge to second-guess the leading commanders.

The average Civil War soldier was twenty-five years old and volunteered for duty. He was most likely single, although 30 percent of his fellow soldiers were married. Approximately 78 percent of the men in the army served in the infantry, with 15 percent in the cavalry and 7 percent in the artillery. About 5 percent of the Union forces fought in the navy. On the Union side, 9 percent of the soldiers were African American, and about 33 percent of the Confederate soldiers' families owned slaves. Because so many sons of slave owners fought for the Confederacy, the war can hardly be labeled "a rich man's war and a poor man's fight." That saying was nevertheless commonplace at the time in both the North and South and suggests the internal divisions within both societies.

Disease presented a graver danger to common soldiers than did enemy bullets. Nearly two Civil War soldiers died of disease—most often diarrhea or dysentery, typhoid fever, pneumonia, or even malaria—for every one killed in action. For all the deaths by disease, Civil War soldiers were better off than their counterparts in earlier wars. This was hardly comforting news to soldiers who faced time in a Civil War hospital, however. Most believed that these institutions were places of failure from which few returned. Drunken doctors, dirty conditions, and rampant disease threatened to make a soldier's hospital stay short and terminal.

Common soldiers were imprisoned if captured and had to wait a long time in desperate conditions for possible exchange. Early in the war, field commanders sometimes agreed to an informal exchange or mutual parole of prisoners. Parole simply meant that the prisoner swore not to take up fighting again until he had been formally exchanged with a counterpart on the other side. The Confederacy's resources were strained, and it could barely feed its growing prisoner of war population. In 1862 both sides agreed to an exchange cartel in which most prisoners were exchanged smoothly. The practice was halted in 1863 because Northerners objected to Confederate threats to reenslave or execute black prisoners of war and because the Confederacy began treating parolees as if they had been fully exchanged. Andersonville Prison in Georgia became the North's symbol of the mistreatment of prisoners of war in the Confederacy. The prison was severely overcrowded, and more than one hundred men died there each day in 1864. Elmira Prison in New York was generally considered the worst Union prisoner of war camp, but its conditions did not compare in severity to Andersonville.

Soldiers who managed to avoid both disease and enemy capture faced the hardships of marching and battle. Casualties in the war were extremely high, especially for the Confederacy. In his book *The Confederate War*, historian Gary Gallagher shows that the Confederacy sustained a casualty rate of 37 to 38 percent of its men under arms, whereas the North's casualties amounted to 17 percent. Gallagher compares this rate with other American wars, such as World War II, where American forces experienced a lower casualty rate of 5.8 percent.

Many soldiers wrote letters or kept diaries. Their stories tell the full range of human emotion in war. One Union soldier's August 1862 letter from his post in Port Royal, South Carolina, to his relatives in Pennsylvania suggests the complexity of these documents:

> We have only about six thousand men here, but I wish they would bring forty thousand and try to lick us. . . . You may do as you think proper with the money, put

in the bank or keep it yourself, change is getting scarce here too. At first you could see nothing but gold, now you get all one dollar bills. We get paid in United States Bank Notes. That was a fine turtle you was writing about, but it was not as large as the one the boys brought in about two weeks ago. It came out on land to lay— they were out on picket and five of them run their bayonets in to it and could hardly master it. It weighed two hundred and thirty five pounds. . . . Leave me know how recruiting takes in York. If they would know what I know, it would be a hard time to raise a company in York. I'm afraid the nigger question will raise a rum- pus in the army yet. If I ever get back I'll shoot all the niggers I come across. Give my respects to all of my enquiring friends. No more at present. The boys are catch- ing plenty of fish about here. We are making a large seine to drag. Write Soon.

This document and many others from the period raise difficult questions that can apply to both sides in the war. What were soldiers fighting for? How did soldiers view African Americans and Emancipation? What did soldiers think of these distant places they visited and how did they report these impressions to their family and friends at home? What effect did their letters have on recruiting and the morale of the home front? How did soldiers spend their time? How did national issues, such as fiscal and currency policies, filter down to the common soldier? Did these nation- al policies affect the morale of the troops and the home front?

Web sites about the common soldier address many of these questions through the use of effective primary sources such as letters, diaries, and items of material cul- ture. Researchers can find a wealth of firsthand accounts from the Civil War on the World Wide Web. Both universities and government agencies have led the way in the digital publication of soldiers' letters and diaries, but individuals and nonprofit organizations have contributed sites examining camps, hospitals, prisons, and other aspects of daily life in the army.

WEB SITE REVIEWS

CAMP LIFE

Camp Life: Civil War Collections from Gettysburg National Military Park
http://www.cr.nps.gov/museum/exhibits/gettex/

As the authors of this National Park Service site point out, a typical soldier's day was passed neither in battle nor on the march but in camp, where troops lived for months at a time. Using artifacts on display at the Gettysburg National Bat-tlefield Park, this site conveys a vivid sense of soldiers' day-to-day life in these temporary homes.

The exhibit shows how men tried to make themselves as comfortable as possi-ble under difficult conditions. Although officers had trunks in which to carry their possessions, enlisted men were limited to what they could carry on their backs. Their tents consisted of little more than tarps draped over poles. Men mended their own clothes using sewing kits known as "housewives" and attacked head lice with special combs.

The exhibit also features cards, dice, and dominoes that soldiers used to battle boredom. Wood and bone carvings, musical instruments, and sheet music pro-vide examples of more creative means of passing the time. Soldiers also spent hours reading and writing letters, several of which are on display here. Prayer books and Bibles indicate that troops attended to their spiritual needs as well.

Although the site is beautifully designed, it is cumbersome to view on an 800 x 600-pixel or smaller monitor. Nonetheless, the beautiful digital images of sol-diers' common possessions and the helpful explanatory text create a powerful sense of life in a Civil War camp.

CONTENT   ★ ★ ★ ★
AESTHETICS   ★ ★ ★ ★ ★
NAVIGATION   ★ ★ ★

ETHNIC GROUPS

Jews in the Civil War
http://www.jewish-history.com/civilwar.htm

This section of a large Jewish history and genealogy site contains interesting docu-ments about the experience of Jewish soldiers in the Civil War. Many of them are transcriptions of postwar articles contributed by Union veterans to *The Jewish Messenger*. In the 1867 article "Passover—A Reminiscence of the War," a former member of the 23rd Ohio Regiment recalled celebrating Passover while stationed in West Virginia. The Jewish sutler of his unit purchased matzo and prayer books from stores in Cincinnati. Cider, lamb, chickens, and eggs were obtained from the countryside, and in lieu of horseradish the men ate a bitter-tasting weed found in the woods. As the author recalled, the weed proved to be troublesome: "The herb was very bitter and very fiery like Cayenne pepper, and excited our thirst to such a degree, that we forgot the law authorizing us to drink only four cups, and the consequence was we drank up all the cider. Those that drank the more freely became excited, and one thought he was

Moses, another Aaron, and one had the audacity to call himself Pharaoh." Despite the disruption, the ceremony proceeded according to custom. "There, in the wild woods of West Virginia, away from home and friends, we consecrated and offered up to the ever-loving G-d of Israel our prayers and sacrifice."

The site also contains an interesting collection of correspondence from official records on the campaign to allow rabbis to serve as Union military chaplains as well as material related to General Grant's order to expel all Jews from the Department of the Tennessee. Grant's order stated that "Jews, as a class violating every regulation of trade established by the Treasury Department and also department orders, are hereby expelled from the department within twenty-four hours from the receipt of this order." Protested vehemently by Jewish soldiers and civilians, the order was revoked by General Halleck within weeks.

Documents about Jews in the Confederacy include a prayer for victory written by a Richmond rabbi and distributed to Jewish troops, biographical sketches of prominent Jewish Civil War veterans, and previously published letters, memoirs, and diaries of Jewish soldiers, such as Louis Leon, of the 53rd North Carolina Infantry, who wrote of his participation in the Battle of Gettysburg. The Confederate collection also contains General Robert E. Lee's letter denying Richmond rabbi M. J. Michelbacher's request that Jewish Confederate soldiers be granted furloughs for the holy days: "It would give me great pleasure to comply with a request so earnestly urged by you, & which I know would be so highly appreciated by that class of our soldiers. But the necessities of war admit of no relaxation of the efforts requisite for its success, nor can it be known on what day the presence of every man may be required. I feel assured that neither you or any member of the Jewish congregation would wish to jeopardize a cause you have so much at heart by the withdrawal even for a season of a portion of its defenders."

One of the most impressive features of this site is the Jewish Civil War veterans database. A search using the name "Schwartz" led to the records for fourteen men from five different states. Four of these men were wounded in battle, and one died. All but one, who enlisted in the 17th Virginia Infantry, fought for the Union.

This rich collection of documents and searchable individual-level data sheds light not only on the experience of Jews in the American Civil War but also on the life of Civil War soldiers in general. Interesting documentary content, intuitive navigation, and uncluttered (if amateur) design make this site valuable to a variety of researchers.

CONTENT   ★ ★ ★ ★
AESTHETICS   ★ ★ ★
NAVIGATION   ★ ★ ★ ★

FOOD

NEW **Feeding Billy Yank: Union Rations between 1861 and 1865**
http://www.qmfound.com/feeding_billy_yank.htm

This informative essay, part of the U.S. Army Quartermaster Museum web site, provides a lively account of how Union soldiers managed to remain comparatively well fed throughout the course of the war. Official rations, although deficient in vitamin C, prone to infestation, and hardly tasty, were still more generous than those provided to the men behind Confederate lines or to European armies at the time. Moreover, soldiers could supplement their rations with packages from home, purchases from sutlers, and occasional foraging.

The essay traces the route of army rations from source to stomach, starting with the Commissary General soliciting bids, awarding contracts, and procuring food in one of five major Union cities. Once collected, it was shipped by the Quartermaster Department to the men in the field via sailing ship, steamship, barge, or train. Food delivered to the field army's base of operations was then divided and hauled by wagon to individual brigades, where it was divided again among regimental commissaries and finally into separate allotments for each company. The challenge at that point was parceling out the rations evenly by eye, without the aid of scales. Men's names were called in random order for them to come forward and claim a pile of food as their own.

A much-appreciated, though hardly free, supplement to official rations could be obtained from army sutlers, who bought canned fruit and vegetables, meat, and dairy products on the open market and then resold them to the men in camp. Even more valued, of course, was food sent by friends and family, which came without a price tag and carried with it fond reminders of home.

The essay's author maintains that foraging was rare; but, when conducted, it was usually carried out in an orderly fashion. The well-known exception was in South Carolina, where General Sherman gave Union soldiers free rein to seize and destroy civilian food supplies. Even there, the foraged foodstuffs did not significantly improve soldiers' diets.

Filled with informative articles on the history of providing for men and women in uniform, the U.S. Army Quartermaster Museum web site will delight military historians for hours despite its difficult navigation and clumsy page design.

CONTENT   ★ ★ ★ ★
AESTHETICS   ★ ★
NAVIGATION   ★ ★

H O S P I T A L S   A N D   M E D I C I N E

Whitman's *Drum Taps* and Washington's Civil War Hospitals
http://xroads.virginia.edu/~CAP/hospital/whitman.htm

A student at the University of Virginia has created an interesting online account of Washington's Civil War hospitals in this exploration of Walt Whitman's experience in caring for wounded soldiers there. The site explains that soldiers hospitalized in the first months of the war found themselves in makeshift structures set up by their regiments that consisted of little more than tents with bare floors. These impromptu arrangements soon proved inadequate, and the military converted sections of the Patent Office, the Capitol, and other buildings into hospitals for wounded soldiers. New hospital buildings were constructed as well, under the direction of the U.S. Sanitary Commission.

Poor security, sanitation, and nutrition rendered a soldier's hospital stay harrowing. Little could be done to prevent the theft of soldiers' possessions. Surgeons, unaware of the dangers of microbes, wet suture thread with saliva and sharpened instruments on the soles of their boots. Unsafe drinking water carried even more hazards. Fresh fruit and vegetables were rarely part of a patient's diet, so scurvy and other types of malnutrition were common.

For wounded soldiers, the transport from the battlefield to the hospitals may have proved to be more terrifying than the hospital stay. Ambulance drivers, according to a surgeon quoted on the site, were "the most vulgar, ignorant, and profane men I ever came in contact with ... such as would disgrace ... any menials ever sent out to the aid of the sick and wounded."

Although centered on the effect of Civil War hospitals on Whitman's poetry, the well-researched narrative and Civil War-era photographs will be of interest to anyone seeking a basic understanding of Civil War hospitals.

CONTENT	★ ★ ★ ★
AESTHETICS	★ ★ ★ ★
NAVIGATION	★ ★ ★ ★

L E T T E R S   A N D   D I A R I E S

American Civil War Collection at the Electronic Text Center
http://etext.virginia.edu/civilwar/#Letters

This site, part of the University of Virginia's Electronic Text Center, is one of the largest online collections of letters and diaries of American Civil War soldiers. A sizeable portion of the letters and diaries were transcribed and indexed in collaboration with the Valley of the Shadow project. Since the Valley project follows the experience of Augusta County, Virginia, and Franklin County, Pennsylvania, over the course of the Civil War, most of the letters and diaries in this Electronic Text Center site are written by men and women from these two places.

The site allows researchers to examine a number of issues regarding Civil War soldiers, such as the controversial practice of hiring substitutes. James Booker wrote to his cousin in the summer of 1862: "[S]ome of our boys are getting very anxious to put in substitutes, John Milner . . . put in a substitute last week. . . . I dont blame no man to put in a substitute if he can, tho I think if it is kept up much longer it will ruin our army." James's brother John was less charitable about substitutions in a letter written a year later: "[N]early all the men say they will [desert] if they [don't] call out all the men that have put in substitute. . . . I am a posed to desertion as much as any boddy can bee but I say put every one on equal footting for this is a rich mans war an a por mans fight, I be leave thare are some of the men that have put in substitute are dooen a great deal of good but the most of them are doo en more harm than good they are just speculaten on the poor people, an soldiers."

Many of the letters provide a vivid sense of a soldier's life on the march. Samuel M. Potter, an assistant surgeon in the 16th Pennsylvania Cavalry, gave a wry account of his diet and shelter in a letter to his wife. If his son wants to play soldier, Potter wrote, he should

put his cup full of water on the fire. Let it boil. Put in a spoonful of coffee & let it burn his fingers when it boils over & he tries to take it off. Then take a piece of fat pork. Get a rod about 2 feet long. Sharpen one end & stick it in the pork. Then hold it over the fire. The grease dripping will make it blaze. Nicely roast his meat a little then put some water over it to wash off the salt which the fire draws out. Then hold it over the fire again & it is done & very good it will be to eat if he has not had anything to eat since yesterday morning. That is our style of cooking sometimes on the march. Then if he wants a bed let him go into a fence corner when it rains. Put a blanket on the ground, an over coat over him & an oil cloth over all & let it rain.

With much less humor than Potter, John Snider, of the14th Virginia Cavalry, wrote to his sister about having to buy meat at inflation prices: "[I]t was for one week that we did not get no meet only what we bought. our mess bought one side of bacon and it cost us four dollars and thirty cts apiece. it was seventy five cts a pound. we have the half of it et and the side that Jacob Anderson brought with him. we are getting plenty of beef a gain it is dried beef."

The Electronic Text Center's Civil War collection is a true digital archive, with impeccable transcriptions, detailed scans, and refined searching. As with most digital archives, only minimal background material is provided to help visitors understand the context of the letters. But visitors with even the most basic knowledge of the Civil War will enjoy exploring this site for hours.

CONTENT ★ ★ ★ ★ ★
AESTHETICS ★ ★ ★ ★
NAVIGATION ★ ★ ★

American Civil War Resources in the Special Collections Department, University Libraries, Virginia Tech
http://spec.lib.vt.edu/civwar/

The Virginia Polytechnical Institute Library has made much of its impressive Civil War manuscript collection available to researchers over the World Wide Web. The memoirs, diaries, and letters found here allow visitors to read about the experience of Civil War soldiers in their own words and in the words of their loved ones at home.

The documents capture the pain that soldiers suffered by being separated from their families. Lorenzo Dow Hylton, away from his home in Rockbridge County, Virginia, missed the birth of his daughter. One month after he enlisted in the 54th Virginia Infantry, his wife sent him the news: "I can inform you that I have another Daughter, it was born April 17th. . . . [S]end the name that you choose that it should be called. Your Father and Brothers will do all they can to get our corn in. . . . I want you to come home about harvest if you can." Far from their families, soldiers not only missed significant events such as the birth of a child, but they were also unable to help with household production. Hylton never returned to his wife. The final letter in the collection was written by a fellow soldier to inform Hylton's wife that her husband had died in a Georgia hospital.

Similar anguish was felt on the Union side. William Latham Candler, a captain on General Hooker's staff, wrote about his fear of leaving his new wife a widow: "I have but one life and could not render that in a better cause. But I cannot bear to think about Fannie, should anything happen to me."

After years of fighting, soldiers fervently hoped for an end to the war, but only on terms favorable to their side. In his third year as an assistant surgeon in three different Virginia regiments, Isaac White wrote to his wife, "The Lord [I] think is on our side. . . . I hope he will soon put a stop to the diffusion of blood; for I and all of us are tired of it and desire peace (honorable)."

Helpful introductions accompany each group of documents, and for at least one of the sets of letters, key terms are linked to explanatory information. There are, however, two drawbacks to this rich site. First, the contents page does not indicate whether the collections referred to have been transcribed, whether they have been photographed, or whether only descriptions have been provided. Users only discover whether they will be able to actually read the sources by going into the collection description itself. Second, some of the collections are hampered by confusing navigation and distracting colors. On the whole, however, this is a significant contribution that should prove invaluable to online researchers.

CONTENT   ★ ★ ★ ★
AESTHETICS   ★ ★ ★
NAVIGATION   ★ ★ ★

The Calvin Shedd Papers

http://www.library.miami.edu/archives/shedd/index.htm

No well-known Civil War battles were fought in Florida, and troops stationed there experienced all of the drudgery of war but little of the terror and excitement of battle. Although grateful for their safety, these soldiers occasionally felt deprived of the glory associated with war. The University of Miami Archives has made a web site about one such soldier—Calvin Shedd of the 7th New Hampshire Volunteers. Shedd's letters, fully transcribed and nicely indexed, capture the experience of Civil War soldiers serving in remote areas.

Shedd's correspondence with his wife was filled with news of illness, bad food, and boredom. He vented his frustration at being so far from the main action of the war, while still acknowledging his relative comfort. In one letter, he wrote, "LATER I should like to see active service somewhere I dont care much where it is for we dont seem to be doing the Country much service, but I suppose it is just as neccessary to keep this Fort well defended as any other, but I want to see a rebel before I am discharged." More serious than boredom was the threat of small-pox. In one letter, Shedd reported that a man a day was dying of the fatal disease. Almost as bad, according to Shedd's letters, were meals that typically featured worm-infested food: "We had boiled Mutton & Broth with Hard-Bread for dinner the best dinner we have had for 2 weeks notwithstanding worms an inch long that came out of the Bread were crawling on the table yesterday there was one full an inch long on my plate I poked him off, and continued my dinner; nothing is supposed to turn a Soldiers stomach." Chronic diarrhea, almost certainly due to ingestion of parasites, eventually rendered Shedd unable to work. Deemed unfit for duty, he was discharged from his unit in 1863.

The opening page of the Calvin Shedd Papers contains helpful summaries of each document, a biographical sketch of Shedd's life, and a capsule history of the 7th New Hampshire Infantry. In the transcriptions, key terms in the letters are linked to helpful definitions. The combination of interesting documents and explanatory narrative makes this site a good stop for any researcher interested in the experience of Civil War soldiers, especially those far removed from the main theaters of action.

CONTENTS   ★ ★ ★ ★ ★
AESTHETICS   ★ ★ ★
NAVIGATION   ★ ★ ★ ★ ★

Civil War Diaries

http://sparc5.augustana.edu/library/civil.html

The library at Augustana College in Rock Island, Illinois, has made two Civil War diaries available on its web site. For Gould D. Molineaux's diary, the site contains only scans of the original documents, which are difficult to read on a computer screen. Fortunately, the diary of Basil H. Messler has been painstakingly transcribed and annotated, and it provides a vivid sense of the experience of Union soldiers in the Western theater. Messler served in the Mississippi Marine Brigade, an amphibious unit that patrolled the Mississippi River and suppressed Confederate guerrilla activity in Union-held areas.

Messler's diary captures the drudgery of a soldier's daily life. Poor drinking water made Messler so ill that he was bedridden for days. When well, Messler apparently spent much of his time acquiring food from the countryside: "Saturday 28th (1864) went out again after cattle again and drove in some 20 and they were killed and divided among the 3 Boats John Raine Autocrat & Fairchilds went out Berry hunting and got all I could eat Brother John and T. D. Moran was with me after eating all we wished we picked a Gallon or more it was sprinkling all the afternoon Spent the evening in reading." Like many Civil War soldiers, Messler participated in no famous battles and rarely came under enemy fire.

A helpful opening page serves as a gateway to the Messler letters. Links found there jump to particular points in the diary, and each link is accompanied by a summary of that section's contents. The opening page also provides a brief sketch of Messler's Civil War service.

CONTENT   ★ ★ ★ ★
AESTHETICS   ★ ★ ★
NAVIGATION   ★ ★ ★ ★ ★

Letters from an Iowa Soldier in the Civil War

www.civilwarletters.com

Made by descendents of the letters' authors, this site features transcripts of more than a dozen letters written by Newton Robert Scott of the 36th Iowa Infantry to friends and family at home. Accompanied by a biographical sketch of Scott and other useful background information, the letters capture many aspects of the experience of the Civil War soldier.

Like most men who fought, Scott had never been far from his hometown before the war and was amazed by his new, unfamiliar surroundings. Traveling down the Mississippi River, Scott wrote in wonder that the "little towns on the Mo. Side of the River are Hard looking Places little Dirty cabins with nothing to Sell Hardly But whiskey & the People looks to Suit the Places." Scott traveled to strange lands as far off as Arkansas and Mississippi, where his unit participated in the Vicksburg and other campaigns.

As Scott's missives illustrate, letters provided a lifeline for soldiers far from home. In his correspondence, Scott reported on the health of hometown soldiers and was occasionally forced to give the tragic news of their deaths. In return, Scott received packages of berries and butter as well as intelligence about hometown courtship and marriage. One letter carried the sad news that Scott's "sweetheart," Mattie, had married another man. Scott replied in dismay, "Well you Stated in your letter that Many changes had taken Place up in Monroe here of late and the most heart-breaking of all is my Darling has long ago Forsaken me and Married and left me to mourn my life away or in other words Do the best I can During my future life." Unlike many men in his company, Scott survived the war. He returned to Iowa in the summer of 1865 and married Hannah Cone, his most faithful correspondent.

Good design, intuitive navigation, and compelling documentary content make Letters from an Iowa Soldier in the Civil War an excellent starting point for studying the life of a Civil War soldier.

CONTENT   ★ ★ ★ ★ ★
AESTHETICS   ★ ★ ★ ★
NAVIGATION   ★ ★ ★ ★ ★

PRISONS

Alton in the Civil War: Alton Prison

http://www.altonweb.com/history/civilwar/confed/index.html

The community web site for the city of Alton, Illinois, contains an interesting section on the prisoner of war camp that operated in the area from early 1862 until the end of the war. Confederate prisoners of war first arrived at Alton Federal Military Prison in February 1862, and, by the time it closed, 11,764 prisoners had passed through its gates. As the site explains, harsh conditions in the form of overcrowding and extreme weather took a high toll on both inmates and Union guards.

The Alton Prison site contains a brief history of the prison as well as a database of approximately 1,300 men who died while imprisoned there. The records can be searched in a variety of ways. A search using "Alabama" revealed that 126 soldiers from Alabama died at Alton Prison, including James Ashbill, a private in Company B, 4th Alabama Infantry. According to his records, Ashbill was captured on August 27, 1863, at Corinth, Mississippi. He died of smallpox on January 5, 1864, and was buried near the prison on Small Pox Island. Searching the database for the word "pneumonia" showed that 234 men died of this cause.

With interesting historical narrative as well as searchable individual-level records, the Alton Prison site is an outstanding example of a local history web initiative. By inviting visitors to comb through the fragmentary records about the men who lived and died in the prison, the site illuminates a central aspect of the Civil War soldier's experience. A small gem, this site should not be overlooked.

CONTENT   ★ ★ ★ ★
AESTHETICS   ★ ★ ★ ★
NAVIGATION   ★ ★ ★ ★ ★

Archeology at Andersonville

http://www.cr.nps.gov/seac/andearch.htm

This small National Park Service site presents a brief history of the notorious Andersonville Prison, built to house captured Union soldiers in 1864. Originally designed to hold 10,000 men, the breakdown of prisoner exchanges between North and South increased the population to as high as 32,000. Strained food supplies, lack of shelter, and deadly sanitary conditions led to almost 13,000 prisoner deaths. Inmates were forced to find shelter under scraps of wood or in holes in the ground, and they subsisted on a pound of meat plus a pound and a quarter of cornmeal per day. The lack of vegetables and clean water led to rampant deadly cases of scurvy and dysentery.

In addition to a brief history of the prison, the site contains a detailed description of three seasons of archeological work at the prison site. Excavations have allowed the Park Service to reconstruct the prison's walls exactly as they were originally built. In the course of their work, field researchers found what must have been a uncompleted escape tunnel. Wide enough for a man to squeeze through, the tunnel ends underground just a few yards past the prison walls.

Archeology at Andersonville provides a basic outline of the history of the notorious prison supplemented with photographs and diagrams. Visitors seeking a basic introduction to Civil War prisons will find this site useful.

CONTENT   ★ ★ ★
AESTHETICS   ★ ★ ★
NAVIGATION   ★ ★ ★

SUGGESTED READINGS

Gallagher, Gary. *The Confederate War: How Popular Will, Nationalism, and Military Strategy Could Not Stave Off Defeat.* Cambridge, MA, 1997.

Hess, Earl J. *The Union Soldier in Battle.* Lawrence, KS, 1997.

Linderman, Gerald F. *Embattled Courage: The Experience of Combat in the Civil War.* New York, 1987.

McPherson, James M. *For Cause and Comrades: Why Men Fought in the Civil War.* New York, 1997.

Mitchell, Reid. *Civil War Soldiers: Their Expectations and Their Experiences.* New York, 1988.

———. *The Vacant Chair: The Northern Soldier Leaves Home.* New York, 1993.

Paludan, Phillip Shaw. *A People's Contest: The Union and Civil War, 1861–1865.* Lawrence, KS, 1988.

Wiley, Bell I. *The Life of Johnny Reb.* 1943. Reprint. Baton Rouge, LA, 1978.

———. *The Life of Billy Yank.* 1952. Reprint. Garden City, NY, 1971.

CHAPTER 4

NAVAL OPERATIONS

From the first battle at Fort Sumter, naval operations played a crucial role in the American Civil War. The Union naval blockade of Confederate seaports limited the South's ability to acquire crucial war material and brought practically every Southern seaport under Union control. On the western rivers, the U.S. Army and Navy coordinated a series of successful attacks that ultimately gave the Union control of the entire Mississippi River and effectively split the South in half. The war ushered in a new era of naval technology, with the advent of the ironclad ram and combat submarine. Although the Union and Confederate navies tend to be overlooked in academic and popular accounts of the war, a number of interesting web sites are giving the Civil War navy its proper attention.

By the end of the second full month of the war, U.S. Navy Secretary Gideon Welles, assisted by the capable Gustavus V. Fox, deployed dozens of ships to the waters off Southern seaports, establishing the beginning of what would become a powerful naval blockade. The blockade represented a key component of General-in-Chief Winfield Scott's Anaconda Plan, which envisioned the slow strangulation of the South by Union forces deployed along the Atlantic and Gulf seacoasts as well as on the Mississippi River. Although the Union eventually abandoned the Anaconda Plan, the blockade, which by the final year of the war was enforced by more than five hundred ships, remained essential to the Union war effort.

The blockade was far from complete. Southern merchants and their European trading partners shipped goods via specially designed blockade runners. These fast and shallow-drafted ships could outrun pursuing Union patrollers, and their gray exteriors, adjustable smokestacks, and sleek design enabled them to slip in and out of Southern ports undetected. Even as late as 1865, one of every two ships successfully eluded the blockade. Still, the Union blockade severely hampered Southern trade and limited the Confederacy's ability to equip its army. Historian James McPherson, using prewar trade volumes as a baseline, maintains that the blockade reduced the number and size of ships that merchants were willing to put to sea, creating trade levels that were one-third of what they would have been without it.

The blockade and other naval operations extended the geographic scope of the Civil War and created diplomatic complications for the Union. Seeking to capitalize on British resentment at the disruption of their lucrative trade with the South, Confederate officials encouraged the British to take armed action against the blockade. The British did not comply, choosing instead to maintain official neutrality. Their government did, however, turn a blind eye to the decidedly un-neutral activities of certain English shipbuilders, who constructed blockade runners and carried on a lively, if dangerous, trade with the South. At the urging of Confederate agent James D. Bullogh, one English shipwright built two commerce raiders for the Confederate navy. These English-built vessels, the CSS *Florida* and the CSS *Alabama*, cruised the high seas and destroyed more than one hundred American merchant ships before they were finally sunk by U.S. warships far from the American coast.

The damage inflicted by these commerce raiders stoked anti-British sentiment in the North, but the Lincoln administration, which was determined to keep the British out of the war, had few options. The Union had already angered the British with its heavy-handed enforcement of its blockade. American warships captured British vessels carrying goods destined for the South and even went as far as to board a British steamer to arrest two Confederate foreign ministers. Resentment against this insult to British sovereignty was fanned in the popular press, and tensions between the two nations increased to a dangerous level before the crisis was defused by the U.S. release of the two ministers.

With its naval strategy, the Union was able to bring about a significant reduction in Southern trade without jeopardizing British retaliation. An additional benefit of the blockade was the Union capture of major Confederate seaports. Blockading ships needed coaling stations. At the start of the war, the only Union-held coastal positions were Hampton Roads, Virginia, and Key West, Florida. Within a year, Union gunboats had captured every major port from Norfolk to New Orleans except Charleston and Wilmington, North Carolina. These toeholds provided a base for military operations into the interior.

Even before these seacoast toeholds were secured, Federal navy forces operating in the Western theater had helped to bring about some of the Union's first significant military victories. This "Brownwater Navy," led by Flag Officer Andrew H. Foote, steamed up the Tennessee and Cumberland rivers as part of General Ulysses S. Grant's successful operations against Fort Henry and Fort Donelson. Control of these rivers provided a base for naval operations against Confederate positions on the upper Mississippi. These operations resulted in the capture of Ship Island and the important city of Memphis. Meanwhile, pressure on the lower Mississippi was applied by forces under Flag Officer David Glasgow Farragut, which captured New Orleans in April 1862 and went on to take Baton Rouge and Natchez. By June 1862, while the Army of the Potomac floundered through the Peninsula Campaign, the U.S. Navy had helped the Union gain control over most of the Mississippi River. With the capture of Vicksburg a little over a year later, control over the major western river systems was complete.

The Civil War brought about important developments in naval technology. Confederate navy secretary Stephen R. Mallory initiated the naval arms race by covering the CSS *Virginia* (formerly the USS *Merrimack*) with layers of inch-thick iron plate and mounting it with ten guns. The Union responded by commissioning engineer John Ericsson to build the first Union ironclad, christened the USS *Monitor*. In March 1862 the CSS *Virginia* embarked on its first voyage against Union ships patrolling the mouth of the James River. Shots fired by these well-armed ships practically bounced off the surface of this odd-looking boat, which proceeded to ram and fire at the USS *Cumberland* and the USS *Congress* until they both sank. When the *Virginia* went out the next day to continue on its deadly mission, it was met by the *Monitor*, which had steamed down the coast from New York. The world's first battle between ironclad ships lasted several hours before it ended in a draw. The *Monitor* sank off the coast of North Carolina before it saw action a second time, and the *Virginia* was exploded by rebel forces retreating from Norfolk.

With the construction of the world's first combat submarine, the South led naval innovations in another area as well. The *H. L. Hunley*, named after its inventor, was powered by men turning a giant crankshaft. It dove by means of fins and giant ballast tanks. "The Porpoise," as it was called, was to break the Union blockade by ramming ships with a torpedo that would be detonated by a rope connected to the submarine as it pulled away. After three trial runs that resulted in the deaths of the entire crew each time, the *Hunley* went out again and successfully destroyed a Union blockade patroller off Charleston Harbor. On its return to the harbor, the *Hunley* sank a fourth time, and its entire crew drowned.

A number of individuals, organizations, and government agencies have created excellent web sites to educate the public about the Civil War navy. Online researchers can read official records of navy operations, examine diagrams of historic ships, and follow the progress of underwater excavations of the *Monitor* and other famous vessels. With material suitable for both experts and novice researchers, these sites, taken together, provide an excellent sense of Civil War naval operations.

EB SITE REVIEWS

Confederate Navy Collection Index at the Virginia State Library

http://image.vtls.com/collections/CN.html

In 1924 veteran Confederate captain W. MacElroy gathered and transcribed information on hundreds of Virginians who had served in the Confederate navy during the Civil War and typed the information onto paper cards. These cards were used to establish proof of military service for individuals applying for state pensions. The Virginia State Library has scanned these cards and made them available here. The cards provide name, rank, and information about service for several hundred individuals.

The records are not searchable, and they can be accessed only through a cumbersome alphabetical list. Finding the record for George W. Harrison requires clicking Hage on the main menu and then going through several other individuals' cards before Harrison's is reached. The card reveals that Harrison was born in the West Indies and that he commanded various Confederate ships along the Virginia and North Carolina coasts in the first year of the war, served in naval stations in Richmond and Charlotte in 1862, and commanded the CSS *Morgan* in Mobile Harbor in 1863 and 1864. For other individuals, the cards also list the names and place of residence of their descendents.

As one of the only sites that provide detailed individual-level information on hundreds of men who served in the Confederate navy, the site is of great value to genealogists and other researchers seeking to learn about particular individuals.

CONTENT   ★ ★ ★ ★
AESTHETICS   ★ ★ ★
NAVIGATION   ★ ★ ★

NEW C.S.S. *Alabama* Digital Collection

http://www.lib.ua.edu/libraries/hoole/digital/cssala/main.shtml

True to its name, the C.S.S. *Alabama* Digital Collection is composed of transcribed historic documents pertaining to the *Alabama*'s construction and 2-year career capturing and burning Union ships on the high seas. The site contains no overview or summary, so researchers unfamiliar with the story of this ship would be well served by starting with Wars and Conflicts of the United States Navy, reviewed below, and then returning to this site for its wonderful collection of documents.

The site's Virtual Journey consists of a world map showing the destructive route of the *Alabama*. Important locations are linked to pages with documents about the events that took place there. The map shows that the *Alabama* traveled as far as the Indian Ocean, where it captured and burned the *Emma Jane* of Bath, Maine.

The captain's report on the ship's activities off the coast of South America provides a sense of the *Alabama*'s ability to disrupt American commerce:

... On my passage hither from Bahia I captured the following American ships, viz, Gildersleeve, Justina, Jabez Snow, Amazonian, Talisman, Conrad, Anna F. Schmidt, and Empress. These were all valuable prizes, except the Justina, and she being a Baltimore bark, in ballast.... The Conrad being fast and well adapted for a cruiser, I fitted her out and commissioned her as a tender to this ship.... I put on board of her two brass rifled 12's, which I had captured on board the Talisman, rifles, pistols, and ammunition.

The Images section includes nicely reproduced diagrams and plans used by the shipbuilder as well as dramatic illustrations of the sinking of the *Alabama* off the coast of France in 1863.

CONTENT ★ ★ ★ ★
AESTHETICS ★ ★ ★
NAVIGATION ★ ★ ★

CSS *Neuse* State Historic Site

http://www.ah.dcr.state.nc.us/sections/hs/neuse/neuse.htm

Created by the North Carolina Department of Cultural Resources, this web site describes the CSS *Neuse*, a Confederate ironclad built in eastern North Carolina but destroyed before it could be put to use against the enemy. The remains of the ship are on display at the CSS *Neuse* State Historic Site in Kinston, North Carolina.

Menu items under the heading The Gunboat take the visitor to a host of interesting information about the *Neuse*. Background provides a concise essay about the Confederate ironclad program, which was enthusiastically endorsed by Confederate secretary of the navy Stephen R. Mallory but hampered by insufficient rail transport for the necessary iron ore. A section called "The Ram is no Myth" tells of the many delays in the construction of the gunboat and its destruction by Federal forces before it ever left the dock. In its report on the Union invasion that destroyed the gunboat, the *New York Herald* wrote, "The ram *Neuse* was destroyed by fire and sunk. Her smokestack can still be seen when the river is shallow. She must have been a formidable craft." Clicking Historical Gallery takes the visitor to an illustrated summary of the construction of the Confederate gunboat and its ultimate fate.

The CSS *Neuse* web site, like all of the Civil War sites made by the North Carolina Department of Cultural Resources, is well designed and informative. Anyone seeking to explore the Confederate ironclad construction program would be well served by a visit.

CONTENT   ★ ★ ★ ★
AESTHETICS   ★ ★ ★ ★
NAVIGATION   ★ ★ ★ ★

The *Denbigh* Project

http://nautarch.tamu.edu/projects/denbigh/index.htm

Originally used to carry goods between ports in Britain, the *Denbigh* began running the Union blockade of Mobile, Alabama, in 1863. Admiral Farragut, charged with enforcing the Union blockade, wrote in frustration after yet another failed attempt to capture this fast ship: "We came very near catching the Denbigh . . . but he was too smart for us and doubled us all and got in and now lies under the fort." After Mobile was taken by Union forces in 1864, the *Denbigh* began running to Galveston, Texas. After five successful trips, the ship came under heavy Union fire in 1865 and sank. The wreck is occasionally visible from the coast of Galveston during low tide.

The Institute of Nautical Archaeology at Texas A&M University is conducting an ongoing investigation of the wreck and has created this interesting site. In addition to providing an excellent history of the *Denbigh*, it features a variety of primary documents such as newspaper articles and official reports. One letter from the quartermaster at Richmond gives a sense of the essential nature of the supplies brought in by blockade runners such as the *Denbigh*. Writing to a colleague who was attempting to build a shoe factory in Alabama, the quartermaster reported that the "steamer *Denbigh* has fortunately just arrived at

Mobile with a large lot of shoemakers' tools and findings, and Major Barnewall, the depot officer at that point, has been instructed to send you all you may require."

The site also includes essays on the economics of blockade running. The page titled Investors describes the French, British, and Southern owners of the *Denbigh* and gives a good sense of the high risks and even higher profits associated with running the Union blockade. According to the essay, about one in four attempts to pass through the blockade resulted in destruction or capture of the ship and, subsequently, the loss of its cargo. The Erlanger Loan concerns the notes issued by the French co-owners that served as a de facto international currency for the Confederacy. With its excellent description of the ship and of blockade running in general, this site makes an important contribution to the World Wide Web.

Since the first edition of this book went to press, several new pages have been added to the site. One, titled "How Much Coal," describes the amount burned by the *Denbigh* per hour and explains that the ship relied on coal from Cuba. Completing the round trip from Havana to Galveston required carrying 3,300 cubic feet of coal.

CONTENT   ★ ★ ★ ★ ★
AESTHETICS   ★ ★ ★ ★
NAVIGATION   ★ ★ ★ ★

Friends of the *Hunley*

http://www.hunley.org

This small, interesting site was built by an organization established to raise money for the excavation of the world's first combat submarine from the bottom of Charleston Harbor. It provides an excellent account of this historic Confederate vessel.

According to the accounts found here, New Orleans merchants built the submarine in hopes that it would break the Union blockade of key Southern ports. After it was successfully tested in Mobile Bay, military authorities moved the *H. L. Hunley* to Charleston, South Carolina. Charleston residents cheered the arrival of the strange craft and nicknamed it "The Porpoise." A young Charleston woman wrote, "It is forty feet long and can contain eight or nine men. . . . It can go twenty feet under water. . . . It certainly is a wonderful thing, and we hope for its success. It was to go out Saturday to try and blow up the 'Ironsides,' but I have heard nothing since of it." Her hopes were dashed, however, and the documents and narrative on the remainder of the site chronicle the *Hunley*'s tragic end.

In addition to the historical information on the submarine, this site provides an interesting explanation about how the *Hunley* worked. With a propeller powered by men turning a crankshaft, the submarine could dive using fins and water ballast tanks. A torpedo affixed to its bow could be rammed into the sides of ships and detonated by a wire pulled as the submarine backed away.

Finally, the site describes the recent discovery of the *Hunley*'s remains by author Clive Cussler, and it encourages visitors to buy merchandise and donate funds to help with the excavation. With excellent narratives, illustrations, and primary sources, the Friends of the *Hunley* succeeds admirably in its goal of generating interest in the Confederate submarine.

CONTENT   ★ ★ ★ ★ ★
AESTHETICS   ★ ★ ★ ★
NAVIGATION   ★ ★ ★ ★

Monitor: History and Legacy

http://www.mariner.org/monitor/

This site has been created by the Mariners' Museum in Newport News, Virginia. The National Oceanic and Atmospheric Administration, which has authority over the *Monitor* shipwreck, designated the Mariners' Museum to be the official museum of this famous craft. Drawing on its collection of photographs and documents, the museum has established an informative and interesting site.

The section titled Naval Strategy of the Civil War provides the strategic context of the building of the first Union ironclad. The section titled The Revolutionary Union Ironclad *Monitor* includes the report presented by a special committee to Secretary of the Navy Gideon Welles. In outlining the advantages and disadvantages of ironclad ships, the committee concluded that "armored ships or batteries may be employed advantageously to pass fortifications on land for ulterior objects of attack, or to run a blockade, or to reduce temporary batteries on the shores of rivers and the approaches to our harbors." The committee also evaluated the proposals that had been submitted to build the ironclads. About John Ericsson's revolutionary design, the committee wrote, "This plan of a floating battery is novel, but seems to be based upon a plan which will render the battery shot and shell proof. We are somewhat apprehensive that her properties for sea are not such as a sea-going vessel should possess." Despite the committee's reservations, Welles commissioned Ericsson. The committee's concerns proved accurate. The *Monitor* survived the Battle of Hampton Roads only to sink in high seas off the North Carolina coast. The battle is discussed in the section titled The Battle of Hampton Roads: March 8 and 9, 1862, which includes eyewitness accounts that vividly render the historic clash.

Other firsthand accounts on the site include a letter from a crew member to his wife about life on the Union ironclad. He wrote the following description of a typical Sunday morning: "At 9 oclock the word is passed to get ready for muster. . . . [T]he Captain takes a look at each one as our names are called, and woe to the one who is found dirty, as he will be given over to the Master at Armes, whose business it is to take him on deck, strip him naked, and take a scrubbing brush and give him a cleaning. We have not had but one case occur; I think I had rather do my own washing."

Rounding out the offerings on this informative site are a biography of John Ericsson, a detailed chronology that begins with Ericsson's proposal to build an ironclad for Napoleon III in 1854 and ends with the sinking of the *Monitor* in December 1862, a description of recent explorations of the shipwreck, and extensive teaching materials designed for fourth graders.

Confusing organization and vague menu items make navigating this site frustrating. No distinction is made in the menus between primary sources and secondary accounts, and moving from one section to another is difficult. Nonetheless, anyone seeking a good understanding of the historic USS *Monitor* would benefit greatly from the excellent material on this site.

CONTENT   ★ ★ ★ ★ ★
AESTHETICS   ★ ★ ★ ★ ★
NAVIGATION   ★ ★ ★

Shotgun's Home of the American Civil War: Naval War
http://www.civilwarhome.com/navalwar.htm

With a large collection of excerpts from many out-of-print books and public domain primary sources on the role of the navy in the Civil War, Shotgun's Home of the American Civil War is a valuable site. The material ranges from general overviews, such as the one taken from A. A. Hoehling's book *Damn the Torpedoes!*, to General P. G. T. Beauregard's 1863 letter proposing abandoning reliance on gunboats and purchasing "swift-going steamers" instead.

The site contains *Official Records* on several interesting incidents. One set of records covers the unsuccessful Union attempt to destroy the Norfolk Navy Yard in April 1861 to prevent its use by Confederate forces. A report sent to headquarters by General John C. Frémont in August 1861 describes the pro-Southern civilian retaliation in Kentucky against the U.S. capture of the Confederate gunboat *Terry* on the Ohio River: "Yesterday the crew of the Terry, led by the captain and a few citizens, seized the steamer Samuel Orr, from Evansville, the private property of private citizens of Indiana—a retaliation more vindictive than sensible."

With material on naval action in distant seas, coastal ports, and western rivers, the Naval War section of Shotgun's Home of the American Civil War is an excellent site for novices and experts alike.

CONTENT   ★ ★ ★ ★
AESTHETICS   ★ ★ ★
NAVIGATION   ★ ★ ★ ★

Wars and Conflicts of the United States Navy: Civil War, 1861–1865
http://www.history.navy.mil/wars/index.html#anchor4162

The U.S. Department of the Navy's history web site includes a large collection of material about the U.S. Navy in the Civil War. Featuring both primary documents and explanatory essays and outlines, the Civil War section of this site is a good starting point for the study of many aspects of the role of navies in the war.

Several pages of the site are of particular value to novice researchers. Battle Streamer gives a brief overview of the role that the U.S. Navy played in securing the Union victory. Another good page for novices is Chronology of Events, a timeline of important Civil War naval events in coastal areas and on western rivers. The timeline starts with the Confederate attack on Fort Sumter in April 1861 and ends in December 1865, when Navy Secretary Gideon Welles advocated to President Johnson that the nation maintain a large, permanent naval force.

The site also features pages devoted to three famous Civil War naval craft: the CSS *Alabama*, the USS *Tecumseh*, and the Confederate submarine *H. L. Hunley*. For each of these vessels, the site provides a brief history of its construction and use as well as a description of the current state of the craft's wreck.

Rounding out the site's offerings is a small collection of primary documents, including the 1864 U.S. Navy uniforms regulation on such matters as the sorts of caps that could be worn:

Cap, of dark blue cloth; top to be one-half inch greater diameter than the base; quarters, one and a half inch wide between the seams; back of the band to be two inches wide between the points of the visor, with a welt half an inch from the lower edge, extending from point to point of the visor; band in front, one and a half inch wide; bound, black patent leather visor, green underneath, two and a half inches wide, and rounded, as per pattern, inside of the band of heavy duck.

The documents also include *Official Records* on the Confederate capture of the USS *Wachusett* in the West Indies and the Union capture of the CSS *Albemarle* off the North Carolina coast. The varied collection of material on the U.S. Navy in the Civil War makes this site well worth the visit.

CONTENT   ★ ★ ★ ★
AESTHETICS   ★ ★ ★
NAVIGATION   ★ ★ ★

The *War Times Journal*: Civil War Navies

http://www.wtj.com/archives/acwnavies/

The *War Times Journal:* Civil War Navies web site contains full transcriptions of Union and Confederate *Official Records* on the building of the ironclads USS *Monitor* and CSS *Virginia* and their historic clash at Hampton Roads. The Union records consist of dispatches between naval officers as they nervously followed the Confederates' transforming of the captured USS *Merrimack* into the ironclad CSS *Virginia*. Flag Officer Goldsborough, stationed on a Union blockade ship at Hampton Roads, wrote:

> SIR: I have received further minute reliable information with regard to the preparation of the *Merrimack* for an attack on Newport News and these roads; she will, in all probability, prove to be exceedingly formidable. The supposition of the insurgents is that she will be impregnable, and a trial of her sufficiency to resist shot of the heaviest caliber, at a short range, is to take place before she is sent out to engage us.

The records go on to cover the assignment of men to the crew of the Union ironclad USS *Monitor* and the transport of the *Monitor* to the southern Virginia coast.

On March 8, 1862, the CSS *Virginia* ventured out to the Union blockade and sank two ships. Telegrams dispatched between Union officers reveal the fear that the Confederate ironclad created.

> To General Wool.
>
> Newport News, March 8, 1862.
>
> We want powder by the barrel. We want blankets sent up to-night for the crews of the *Cumberland* and the *Congress*. The *Merrimack* has it all her own way this side of Signal Point and will probably burn the *Congress*, now aground, with white flag flying, and our sailors swimming ashore. These must come by land tonight.
>
> MANSFIELD.

To General Wool.

Newport News, March 8, 1862.

We have no more ammunition and the *Merrimack* and *Yorktown* are off Signal Point. Send us cartridges and shells for 8-inch columbiad and howitzers by land.

MANSFIELD.

To General Wool.

Newport News, March 8, 1862.

The *Congress* is now burning. The enemy's steamers have hauled off toward Pig Point. Captain Whipple is here, and so is Max Weber, the Twentieth, and the coast guard, and cavalry. We should have another light battery to resist attack by land if they come.

MANSFIELD. BRIGADIER-GENERAL.

The USS *Monitor* arrived at Hampton Roads just in time to keep the *Virginia* from inflicting further damage. The two ironclads fired at each other for several hours and then retreated.

The Confederate records on this site cover the construction of the CSS *Virginia* and the great confidence that the South had in this powerful vessel. Confederate secretary of the navy Stephen R. Mallory even proposed that after the *Virginia* broke the Union blockade, it would steam to Brooklyn and destroy the naval works there. He wrote, "Such an event would eclipse all the glories of the combats of the sea, would place every man in it preeminently high, and would strike a blow from which the enemy could never recover. Peace would inevitably follow."

The *War Times Journal* site does not contain any explanatory narrative. Researchers unfamiliar with the topic may want to first visit the *Monitor*: History and Legacy site before engaging in more in-depth research here. By making these records available for online researchers, the *War Times Journal* has made an important contribution to the World Wide Web.

CONTENT   ★ ★ ★ ★
AESTHETICS   ★ ★ ★ ★ ★
NAVIGATION   ★ ★ ★ ★

SUGGESTED READINGS

Anderson, Bern. *By Sea and by River: The Naval History of the Civil War*. New York, 1962.

Bernath, Stuart L. *Squall across the Atlantic: American Civil War Prize Cases and Diplomacy*. Berkeley, CA, 1970.

Cooling, Benjamin Franklin. *Forts Henry and Donelson: The Key to the Confederate Heartland*. Knoxville, TN, 1987.

Cunningham, Edward. *The Port Hudson Campaign, 1862–1863*. Baton Rouge, LA, 1963.

Davis, William C. *Duel between the First Ironclads*. Garden City, NY, 1975.

Fowler, William M. *Under Two Flags: The American Navy in the Civil War*. New York, 1990.

Jones, Virgil Carrington. *The Civil War at Sea*. 3 vols. New York, 1960–62.

McPherson, James. *Battle Cry of Freedom: The Civil War Era*. New York, 1988.

Niven, John. *Gideon Welles: Lincoln's Secretary of the Navy*. New York, 1973.

Perry, Milton F. *Infernal Machines: The Story of Confederate Submarine and Mine Warfare*. Baton Rouge, LA, 1965.

Wise, Stephen R. *Lifeline of the Confederacy: Blockade Running during the Civil War*. Columbia, SC, 1988.

CHAPTER 5

THE EXPERIENCE OF THE U.S. COLORED TROOPS

Unwelcome at first, discriminated against once in uniform, and in danger of being enslaved if captured by the enemy, more than 180,000 African American men nonetheless joined the effort to save the Union and end slavery. Their contributions to the Union victory have been overlooked for generations, but a recent upsurge of interest among scholars and the public has led to the development of a number of rich web sites devoted to the experience of African American soldiers.

African Americans living in Northern states offered their services to the Union army as soon as President Abraham Lincoln called for troops in April 1861, but local recruiters turned them away. In most white Americans' opinions, the aim of the war was not to end slavery but to save the Union, and the conflict was strictly a white man's fight. Furthermore, participation in local and state militias was traditionally seen as a sacred right of citizenship reserved for white men only. Bowing to public sentiment and fearful of antagonizing the slaveholding states that remained in the Union, Lincoln and his cabinet endorsed the official exclusion of black men from Union forces until the war was almost in its third bloody year.

In all parts of the Confederate states, African Americans moved toward the Union armies, ran away from slavery, and tried to enlist to fight against the Confederacy. Several Union officers with abolitionist backgrounds welcomed them into their lines. In the spring of 1861, General Benjamin F. Butler protected a group of runaway slaves from their

Virginia masters who had come to Butler's outpost at Fortress Monroe to reclaim their property. These men, Butler declared, were contraband of war, and their owners had no right to them. Butler put them to work building fortifications and manning supply lines. Other Union generals went even further. In the spring and summer of 1862, David Hunter on the Georgia coast created armed units of fugitive slaves, but Lincoln, still wary of offending pro-Union slaveholders, declined to recognize these regiments, and they were soon disbanded. In New Orleans, John W. Phelps also organized fugitive slaves into military units. Benjamin Butler, now in command of Louisiana and careful to conform to official policy, overruled Phelps. Yet by the fall of that year, the need for manpower in remote outposts under Union control compelled the Lincoln administration to accept isolated black regiments.

Meanwhile, abolitionists such as Frederick Douglass, Massachusetts governor John A. Andrew, and former Kansas senator James H. Lane petitioned Washington for the formal acceptance of black troops into the Union army. Lane, acting on his own authority, went ahead and formed two black regiments in Kansas and simply ignored War Department orders to disband the unauthorized units. Only after the Emancipation Proclamation of January 1, 1863, did the military leadership respond affirmatively to abolitionist demands, and even then only haltingly. In February of that year, Secretary of War Edwin M. Stanton authorized the governors of Rhode Island, Massachusetts, Connecticut, and Kansas to raise regiments of African Americans, and he granted formal acceptance to the regiments of runaways and free blacks that had already been formed in areas of the South controlled by the Union. Governor Andrew dispatched black recruiters across the Northern states, and African American men soon flocked to New England to enlist. Dismayed that men were leaving their homes to fill state draft quotas elsewhere, the governors of other Northern states soon demanded the authority to form their own black regiments. Secretary Stanton obliged, and by the end of 1863 black units were being raised across the North.

The movie *Glory* immortalized the 54th Massachusetts Regiment and depicted New England as the heart of the U.S. Colored Troops (USCT) effort, but most men in the USCT did not enlist in New England. In fact, of the approximately 180,000 men in the USCT, only about 38,000 belonged to units raised in Northern free states. A greater number, some 42,000, belonged to units raised in the Union slave states of Delaware, Maryland, Missouri, and Kentucky, and the remainder consisted of men in regiments raised in Confederate territory. In short, the majority of men in the USCT came from slave states. The large numbers of men who ran away from their masters to enlist in black regiments caused such an outflow of slave labor that the institution of slavery began to erode throughout the South. Thus, well before the Federal government brought official emancipation to Confederate territory, tens of thousands of black men had already freed themselves and the slave system was in the process of disintegration.

In several ways, the day-to-day experiences of African American men in the Union armed services resembled those of white men. Most days were spent marching or in camp. Combat, while infrequent, was terrifying, and death by disease was common. Many enlisted expecting glory on the battlefield and instead found themselves engaged in manual labor.

Hardships shared with their white fellow soldiers did not result in equal treatment, however. White soldiers received $13 per month, plus an allowance for clothing, but African American soldiers were paid only $10, from which $3 was deducted for clothing. In protest against this unfair treatment, the black units from Massachusetts refused to take any pay for more than a year. The men in the 3rd South Carolina Infantry reacted much more forcefully, refusing to perform any duty until pay scales were equalized. This protest was more than Union commanders could swallow, and the protest leader was charged with mutiny and executed. Eventually, dissatisfaction over unfair wages created such unrest that Congress finally equalized compensation in June 1864. Discriminatory promotion rules also hurt black soldiers. African American men were barred from serving as commissioned officers except as doctors and chaplains. Only at the end of the war did pressure from leading Republicans succeed in persuading the War Department to accept black officers.

Compounding the discriminatory policies of their own government was the particularly terrifying possibility of summary execution for black soldiers captured by the Confederate army. Almost as soon as black troops took to the field, the Confederate army announced that it refused to grant prisoner of war status to captured African Americans. As a result, captured men of the USCT faced enslavement or execution. These men dreaded the former possibility almost as much as the latter; many had risked their lives to attain freedom.

White soldiers and officers routinely suggested that black soldiers were unfit for combat duty. They variously lampooned, belittled, and maligned black fighting men. For their part, black soldiers quickly perceived that only hard-won victories and bloody sacrifices in action would begin to erode the prejudice against them. The 1st Kansas Colored Troops helped repel a Confederate advance at Honey Springs in Indian Territory in July 1863, and in the same summer African American units participated in the battle of Milliken's Bend and the Siege of Port Hudson, helping to conclude General Grant's successful campaign for Vicksburg. Other significant engagements include the attack on Fort Wagner on the coast of South Carolina, also in the summer of 1863, and the Battle of New Market Heights, Virginia, in 1864. Five African American men were awarded the Medal of Honor for heroism at this battle.

Because African Americans served the Union and fought in battle for the cause of freedom, they could make the case for equal rights more strongly. Such claims were made most forcefully during the establishment of Reconstruction governments in the Southern states. At first it seemed that black people would be successful in their quest. The Fourteenth Amendment, which guaranteed equal protection and due process to all citizens, and the Fifteenth Amendment, which held that the right to vote could not be abridged on account of race, seemed to guarantee black political equality. In many Southern states during Reconstruction, black citizens held state and local offices and represented their districts in the U.S. Congress. But the federal government's commitment to protecting African American rights waned in the 1870s, and Southern white politicians soon succeeded in curtailing black political participation.

Despite their initial exclusion from armed service, and despite unequal pay and promotion, members of the USCT fought, suffered, and died for the Union army, and in doing so helped to ensure the Union victory. Their contributions to the war effort have long been overlooked, but now, a generation after another period of African American struggle for equality, historians have begun to examine their experiences and consider their significance. A number of sites on the World Wide Web invite the interested public to join in this endeavor.

W E B   S I T E   R E V I E W S

5th Regimental Cavalry, United States Colored Troops
http://mywebpages.comcast.net/5thuscc/

Formed in Kentucky in 1864, the 5th Regimental Cavalry was composed of "contraband" slaves and served in southwestern Virginia and eastern Kentucky during the final months of the war. For almost a year after the Confederate surrender, until it was finally mustered out, the 5th patrolled sections of Arkansas. This web site, created by a descendent of a member of the 5th USCT, focuses on the controversy surrounding the first Battle of Saltville and provides a good overall regimental history as well.

The opening page of the site features a brief outline of the experience of the 5th USCT, a list of the six major engagements in which the unit participated, and links to the regimental roster. Four of the battles are linked to detailed information from the National Park Service or historic newspapers. The roster is divided into alphabetical sections and provides each soldier's name, company, original rank, and rank held when mustered out.

The best material on the site is the discussion of the events following the first Battle of Saltville, when a collection of Union forces, including the 5th USCT, made an unsuccessful attempt to capture the southwest Virginia saltworks in October 1864. After the battle, a number of the fallen men of the 5th USCT were shot by Confederate forces. Newspapers across the country reported graphic details, dubbing the episode "The Saltville Massacre." The site designer has presented a balanced account of the controversy over the details of this massacre. As the site explains, one historian maintains that more than forty wounded African American men were shot by Confederate soldiers, whereas another argues that of the list of men missing after the battle, most were eventually accounted for. According to this historian, no more than twelve men could have been murdered. The designer of the site, having conducted his own research, which he makes available on the site, takes the position that more than forty men were killed.

The 5th Regimental Cavalry USCT site reminds researchers that African American regiments fought under uniquely terrifying conditions and shows that regimental histories are still contested well over one hundred years after the war ended.

CONTENT   ★ ★ ★ ★
AESTHETICS   ★ ★ ★
NAVIGATION   ★ ★ ★

The African American Experience in Ohio, 1850–1920
http://dbs.ohiohistory.org/africanam

This site, created by the Ohio Historical Society, contains a database of materials relevant to African American history in Ohio. Creative and patient use of the search and browse features will reward web users with some fascinating documents on the USCT and its legacy.

Among its most valuable materials related to African American soldiers are scanned articles from late nineteenth-century newspapers, such as the black-owned *Cleveland Gazette*. The *Gazette* articles allow researchers to see how African Americans preserved the memory of the USCT through memorials, meetings, and complimentary obituaries of black veterans. Harry Smith, the fiery editor of the *Gazette*, was particularly defensive in regard to white politicians who claimed credit for ending slavery and who expected black votes in return:

Over 200,000 Negroes were in the rebellion. What for? In whose behalf was their blood shed? To help preserve the Union and save the government and also to gain their freedom. The blood shed by white federal soldiers, republicans and democrats, from '61–'65 was for the preservation of the Union and not in behalf of the Negro.

Smith reminded his readers that African Americans themselves, not the white leadership of the Republican Party, deserved credit for ending slavery.

This site is based on a library model. The material is carefully cataloged, but the search and browse functions are somewhat cumbersome. Like material in a library, the documents in the site are not connected or related to each other in any formal way, and little context or other explanatory material is provided.

Although not friendly to the novice researcher, the African American Experience in Ohio site is excellent. Its documentary content is rich and unique, the materials have been scanned to the highest standards, and download time is quite reasonable, given the high quality of the images.

CONTENT   ★ ★ ★ ★
AESTHETICS   ★ ★ ★ ★ ★
NAVIGATION   ★ ★ ★ ★

The African American Odyssey: A Quest for Full Citizenship
http://lcweb2.loc.gov/ammem/aaohtml/exhibit/aointro.html

The Library of Congress drew on its extensive American Memory digital collection to build this online exhibit on African American history. Section 4: The Civil War, contains rich material on the USCT, including Frederick Douglass's orders to recruit black soldiers in the Union-held areas around Vicksburg, Mississippi, and a letter from Douglass's son Charles to his father. Charles congratulates his father for doing so much to help fugitive slaves but fearfully warns him to "keep out of the hands of the rebels." Other treasures in this site include an extensive collection of USCT regimental flags, and the portrait and diary of Christian A. Fleetwood of the 4th USCT, who received the Medal of Honor for heroism at the Battle of New Market Heights.

The African American Odyssey site resembles a small museum exhibit. Navigation is straightforward: one proceeds through the site the way a visitor to a museum would walk through the rooms of an exhibit. The documents are arranged thematically and chronologically, and each is accompanied by several paragraphs of explanatory narration. The layout is simple but attractive, and the images are clear. Although not extensive, the Civil War material in the African American Odyssey site is informative, well presented, and carefully documented.

CONTENT   ★ ★ ★ ★
AESTHETICS   ★ ★ ★ ★ ★
NAVIGATION   ★ ★ ★ ★ ★

The Battle of Olustee

http://extlab1.entnem.ufl.edu/olustee/

Typical of many battlefield web sites, the Battle of Olustee site is a labor of love on the part of one passionate individual. It contains everything from photographs of battle reenactments, transcriptions of letters and official reports, invitations to join the Olustee Battlefield Citizen's Support Organization, and a poem penned in 1989 ("The mist hung low o'er Ocean Pond / That frosty winter's morn; / Many hopeful hearts at dawning's light, / By night would be forlorn").

The site provides an informative account of a significant Civil War battle and includes a good analysis of the role of the three USCT units there. The narrative on African American soldiers includes the official report filed by Captain Romanzo C. Bailey of the 8th USCT. Despite the fact that 343 of his 544 men were casualties in this battle, Bailey was most mortified that his unit's colors were taken by the enemy, and he took great pains to ward off accusations of cowardice and misconduct. Lieutenant Oliver Norton, another white officer in the 8th USCT, wrote to his sister with relief that "a flag of truce from the enemy brought the news that prisoners, black and white, were treated alike. I hope it is so, for I have sworn never to take a prisoner if my men left there were murdered."

The site attests to the ability of energetic private individuals to make valuable contributions to the World Wide Web. Drawing on public domain sources, letters donated by private individuals, and previously published narratives of the battle, the designer has made an informative, rich site.

CONTENT ★ ★ ★ ★
AESTHETICS ★ ★ ★
NAVIGATION ★ ★ ★ ★

Fort Scott National Historic Site

http://www.nps.gov/fosc/

This is a very small site, with few documents and only minimal narration, but it is one of the few National Park Service Civil War battlefield sites with significant content on African American soldiers. The Site History section contains a page on African American units raised in the area of Fort Scott, Kansas. Noting with pride that Kansas was the first state officially to raise units of black soldiers, the site also provides quotations from the unit's leaders on the bravery of their men as well as a brief explanation of how the units were raised and later incorporated into the USCT.

CONTENT ★ ★ ★
AESTHETICS ★ ★ ★
NAVIGATION ★ ★ ★ ★

Freedmen and Southern Society Project: The Black Military Experience

http://www.inform.umd.edu/ARHU/Depts/History/Freedman/bmepg.htm

The Freedmen and Southern Society Project, based at the University of Maryland, edits the excellent multivolume series, *Freedom: A Documentary History of Emancipation, 1861–1867*. Although the primary purpose of the web site is to advertise the series, which can be purchased online, it provides visitors with selected documents from the series, seven of which are relevant to the African American Civil War military experience.

The amount of material at this site is small, but the documents are extremely powerful. A letter to President Lincoln from the mother of a member of the 54th Massachusetts Infantry expresses her outrage at the Confederate practice of killing black prisoners: "Will you see that the colored men fighting now, are fairly treated. You ought to do this, and do it at once, Not let the thing run along, meet it quickly and manfully, and stop this mean cowardly cruelty." Another document shows the outrage that black soldiers felt against slave owners together with the sense of power that came from being in uniform. A soldier whose daughter remained in slavery wrote to her master that "my Children is my own and I expect to get them and when I get ready to come after mary I will have bout a powrer and autherity to bring hear away and to exacute vengencens on them that holds my Child."

The site design is strictly utilitarian and consists only of a few paragraphs of historic background and a small collection of documents. The selection of documents, however, makes it worth the visit.

CONTENT   ★ ★ ★ ★
AESTHETICS   ★ ★ ★
NAVIGATION   ★ ★ ★ ★

Museum of the Kansas National Guard: Historic Units

http://skyways.lib.ks.us/kansas/museums/kng/kngunits.html

Two regimental histories on this site make it a valuable complement to the Fort Scott web site described earlier. Developed by the Kansas National Guard, the Kansas National Guard: Historic Units site contains the histories of every Kansas-based military regiment. Included in these histories are the 1st Kansas (Colored) Volunteer Infantry and the 2nd Kansas (Colored) Volunteer Infantry, which are considered by some to be the first "officially" raised troops of African American soldiers in the Civil War.

The histories, which are drawn from out-of-copyright books, *Official Records of the War of the Rebellion*, and contemporary newspaper accounts of battles, provide vivid accounts of the dangers faced by African American men in battle. The official report for the 1st Kansas (Colored) Infantry describes the execution of a captured black soldier by Confederate forces at Poison Springs and the killing of a Confederate prisoner in retaliation: "Determined to convince the rebel commander that that was a game at which two could play, [Captain James M. Williams] directed that one of the prisoners in his possession be shot, and within 30 minutes the order was executed." Later, Williams found the massacre site: "I visited the scene of this engagement the morning after its occurance and for the first time beheld the horrible evidences of the demoniac spirit of these rebel fiends in their treatment of our dead and wounded. Men were found with their brains beaten out with clubs, and the bloody weapons left by their sides, and their bodies most horribly mutilated."

At the Battle of Jenkins Ferry, the 2d Kansas (Colored) Infantry sought to avenge the deaths of their comrades in the 1st. This site provides a dramatic account of this engagement:

Col. S. J. Crawford, of the Second Colored ... asked Gen. Rice where he should bring his regiment into action. "What regiment do you command?" was the immediate inquiry. To which the prompt reply was, "2d Kansas Colored Infantry." "They won't fight," responded Gen. Rice. To which the Colonel, in language much more emphatic than Christian, replied that they could and would go as far as it was possible for any others to go. . . . The rebel battery was taken. . . . The men of the 2d, as they rushed for the battery, nerved each other for the deadly work before them by exclaiming, "Remember Poison Springs!"

The Kansas National Guard: Historic Units site is modest, with few images and no searchable databases, and it is limited almost entirely to public domain documents. But by providing hard-to-find historical material on a subject of great interest, it is a small gem.

CONTENTS   ★ ★ ★ ★
AESTHETICS   ★ ★ ★
NAVIGATION   ★ ★ ★ ★

National Park Service Civil War Soldiers and Sailors System: History of African Americans in the Civil War
http://www.itd.nps.gov/cwss/history/aa_history.htm

In the 1990s the National Park Service embarked on an ambitious project to make an online, searchable database of the compiled military records for all men who served in the U.S. Army and Navy during the Civil War. At the time this book went to press, the only completed set of service records available on the site were for the men who comprised the units of the USCT. Today, the Soldiers and Sailors System contains the records of over 5 million of the 5.4 million men who served in the conflict. Although the emphasis has necessarily changed from only the USCT to all Civil War soldiers and sailors, it still remains one of the best sites for studying the experience of African American soldiers in the conflict.

The web address above takes the user to a page with a brief essay on the history of the USCT. A link in the top right box titled "Medal of Honor Winners" features biographical sketches and portraits of black Congressional Medal of Honor recipients. One of these men was First Sergeant Powhatan Beaty. According to his medal citation, Beaty, of the 5th USCT, "took command of his company, all the officers having been killed or wounded, and gallantly led it" at the Battle of New Market Heights.

To search for the records of the men who served in the USCT, click "soldiers" in the top menu bar. This takes the user to a search page. If you are not interested in looking for a particular individual, put a common last name in the Last Name box and select U.S. Colored Troops in the "state (or origin)" drop-down box. Doing this for the last name "Green" generates a list of 1,422 men that showed the first and last names of the soldiers and the name of their regiments. The soldiers' names are linked to a page with basic information such as unit and company name, rank when enlisted and discharged, and the National Archives record number for other material on that soldier. The names of the men's regiments are linked to brief unit histories.

Clicking the link titled "Sailors" in the top menu bar takes the user to a brief history of the 18,000 men of African descent who served in the Union navy. The makeup of these men reflects both the African diaspora that was created by the slave trade as well as the international nature of sailing men in general. Thus, the creators of the site allow the user to navigate through a series of maps, accessed by clicking "sailor origins" on the left menu. The first is a world map with regions highlighted where these sailors were born. As the map indicates, the men came from six continents. Clicking the Asian region takes the user to a more detailed map. Clicking an actual country, such as India, generates a search of the sailor database for all men of African descent in the Union navy who were born there. Six men meet this criterion. One is John Joseph, who enlisted in Peru in 1864 and served on three different vessels.

A word of warning: The navigation of the Soldiers and Sailors System site is fairly confusing, perhaps due to the project's growth from one that contains only the records of African Americans and others of African descent to one with the records of every man who served in the Union forces. Nonetheless, the

National Park Service Soldiers and Sailors System site contains the most extensive individual-level records on the USCT found on the web, and it should prove of great value to genealogists, students, and historians alike.

CONTENT   ★ ★ ★ ★
AESTHETICS   ★ ★ ★ ★
NAVIGATION   ★ ★ ★

Teaching with Historic Documents Lesson Plan: The Fight for Equal Rights—Black Soldiers in the Civil War

http://www.archives.gov/digital_classroom/lessons/*blacks_in_civil_war/blacks_in_civil_war.html*

Although classroom teachers are the intended audience for the National Archives Teaching with Historic Documents projects, the material in the Fight for Equal Rights lesson plan is so rich that anyone interested in the experience of African American soldiers would benefit from a visit to this site.

The lesson plan begins with a concise history of the USCT. The names of key individuals such as President Lincoln, General John C. Frémont, Harriet Tubman, and Frederick Douglass are linked to their portraits, and topics such as the Emancipation Proclamation and the treatment of black prisoners of war are linked to more detailed explanations and relevant primary documents. An exchange of letters between a Confederate and a Union officer provides a vivid illustration of the dangers facing black soldiers if captured. Confederate colonel William P. Hardeman, in reporting to Union forces the capture of "a negro man named Wilson," wrote that "if [Wilson's] master lives in the Confederate lines he will be returned to him, if not he will be held to slavery by the government." Other documents include the muster sheets of Douglass's two sons, both of whom fought in the 54th Massachusetts Regiment.

The lesson plan requires students to analyze a USCT recruitment poster and answer a series of questions. Follow-up assignments call for students to read Robert Lowell's poem "For the Union Dead" and to research President Harry S. Truman's 1947 Executive Order desegregating the armed forces.

Although the site is not extensive, the excellent quality of the digital images, the intuitive navigation, and the well-written, informative narrative make it valuable for anyone seeking an understanding of the experience and importance of the USCT.

CONTENT   ★ ★ ★ ★
AESTHETICS   ★ ★ ★ ★
NAVIGATION   ★ ★ ★ ★ ★

The Valley of the Shadow: Two Communities in the American Civil War

http://valley.vcdh.virginia.edu/

The Valley of the Shadow site is an extensive multimedia archive created at the University of Virginia. It takes two communities—Augusta County, Virginia, and Franklin County, Pennsylvania—through the experience of the Civil War. The War Years section contains rich material on the USCT.

Included in Student Projects is an in-depth analysis of Franklin County men in the USCT. The project, made by a group of undergraduate students at the University of Virginia, includes a fully searchable database of the compiled military service records of 138 men. It can be searched by name, age, occupation, and type of record. Searching for all Franklin County USCT soldiers who were wounded in action, for example, yields the dossier for Thomas J. Keith. As his records show, Keith was actually wounded twice—first at Williamsburg, Virginia, in February 1864, and later that same year at Fair Oaks, Virginia.

The Newspapers section details how black soldiers were perceived by white citizens on both sides of the Mason–Dixon Line. Reporting on the recruitment of black men into the Union army in West Virginia, the Augusta County, Virginia, *Republican Vindicator* patronizingly expressed sympathy for "the poor deluded African[s]." In a similar vein, the *Valley Spirit*, a Democratic Party paper in Franklin County, Pennsylvania, saw the Union army's recruitment of African Americans as proof of the ineptness of Republican military leadership. In contrast, the Republican Party newspaper, the *Franklin Repository*, commended the bravery of black men in action and condemned their inhumane treatment at the hands of Confederate forces.

Searching the database in Images allows web visitors to examine portraits of African American soldiers as well as dozens of magazine illustrations showing them in camps, on the battlefield, and on the home front. Among the *Harper's Weekly* illustrations are also dramatic depictions of the 1863 New York City draft riots, during which mobs of white protesters attacked the homes and institutions of blacks and murdered black individuals.

Visitors to this site will benefit from lengthy and patient exploration. Consisting almost entirely of documents and containing little explanatory material, the site may be overwhelming to those entirely unfamiliar with the Civil War or with nineteenth-century American life. But no Civil War site matches the Valley of the Shadow for its depth, its scholarly focus, and its emphasis on the experiences of everyday people.

CONTENT   ★ ★ ★ ★
AESTHETICS   ★ ★ ★
NAVIGATION   ★ ★ ★

SUGGESTED READINGS

Blackerby, H. C. *Blacks in Blue and Gray: Afro-American Service in the Civil War.* Tuscaloosa, AL, 1979.

Cornish, Dudley Taylor. *The Sable Arm: Negro Troops in the Union Army, 1861–1865.* New York, 1966.

Crane, Elaine, and Jay David. *The Black Soldier from the American Revolution to Vietnam.* New York, 1971.

D'Entremont, John. *White Officers and Black Troops, 1863–1865.* Charlottesville, VA, 1974.

Glatthaar, Joseph T. *Forged in Battle: The Civil War Alliance of Black Soldiers and White Officers.* New York, 1990.

Gooding, James Henry. *On the Altar of Freedom: A Black Soldier's Civil War Letters from the Front.* Amherst, MA, 1991.

Quarles, Benjamin. *The Negro in the Civil War.* Boston, 1953.

Redkey, Edwin S. *A Grand Army of Black Men: Letters from African-American Soldiers in the Union Army, 1861–1865.* New York, 1992.

CHAPTER 6

SLAVERY AND EMANCIPATION

Historians have debated the importance of slavery as a cause of the American Civil War since the first shots were fired on Fort Sumter. Many have maintained that slavery was the central issue dividing the Union. But others have minimized slavery's role, arguing that the conflict grew out of irreconcilable economic differences, the breakdown of the second party system, or disagreements over issues such as states' rights and tariffs. Whether a direct or indirect cause, *the* issue dividing the Union, or one of many issues dividing the Union, the role of slavery has generated an intense controversy that points to its importance. In fact, it is impossible to understand the Civil War without understanding the institution of slavery.

Slaves could be found throughout the North and South during the colonial period, but by the early nineteenth century, slavery had become a distinctly Southern institution. At the same time that Northern states began outlawing the practice in the 1790s, economic developments made Southern slave labor more profitable than ever. The invention of the cotton gin and power loom meant that cotton could be produced in greater quantities and sold at higher prices than ever before. Slave labor was a crucial component of this equation. In the noncotton South, slaves were valued not only for their labor but also for the price they could command from traders purchasing them for cotton growers in the Deep South. On the eve of the Civil War, one in three Southerners was enslaved.

In the first half of the nineteenth century, Southern slaveholders passionately defended the institution against abolitionists' increasingly strident charges. Slaveholders insisted that Southern slaves lived more comfortably than Northern factory laborers and pointed to the care given to the sick and elderly. Owners often referred to slaves as members of their family and demonstrated their commitment to their human property by giving gifts, holding occasional parties and festivals, and seeing to their religious instruction.

But gestures of kindness could not mask the harsh reality that slaves were legally chattel, with no rights that owners or governments were obligated to respect. State laws prohibited slaves from learning to read and write and from traveling without a pass. They could be—and were—brutally beaten and sold against their will. Families were separated by sale and by being hired out by their owners to distant employers. Slave women had no protection against being raped by their masters and then bearing their children.

In these harsh conditions, enslaved people found for themselves whatever autonomy and comfort they could. Despite the dangers of forced and permanent separations, slaves married and had children. Family names were passed down through generations, and ties of kinship were carefully documented and maintained. Slaves also developed a sustaining spiritual Christianity with distinct African American traditions that continue today.

Some blacks fought against their enslavement. The best-known and most violent incident took place in Virginia in 1831. In what became known as Nat Turner's Rebellion, a group of more than thirty slaves killed about sixty whites before they were apprehended. The most common form of resistance, however, was not armed rebellion but escape. Southern newspapers commonly carried offers of reward for the return of missing slaves. Free blacks, sympathetic whites, and slaves formed a secret network of support for runaways known as the Underground Railroad, which provided safe havens and assistance to slaves escaping bondage.

Slaves found increased opportunities for resistance when the Civil War began. They took advantage of the absence of masters and overseers away in military service by slowing the pace of their work and by refusing to exhibit the same deference that they had shown before the war. As Union forces approached their homes, authority broke down further. Many slaves left their masters' farms and crossed into Union lines.

Congress originally designated these runaways "contraband of war." Because slave labor helped the Confederate war effort, Congress stated, escaped slaves could legitimately be withheld from their masters. In the Sea Islands of Georgia and South Carolina, thousands of additional slaves came under Federal control when their white owners fled before approaching Union forces. Government officials and missionary men and women came to the Sea Islands to raise cotton and educate the black men and women working in the fields in what became known as the Port Royal

Experiment. For the first years of the war, however, the permanent status of the growing population of human "contraband" and "abandoned property" remained unsettled.

By the fall of 1862 a number of developments persuaded President Lincoln to adopt a policy of emancipation. When it became clear that the war would last for years rather than months, Northerners increasingly favored completely destroying the Southern slave system. Emancipation, Northerners knew, would also lead to black enrollment in the Union army, thereby relieving the enlistment pressure on Northern whites. European diplomacy played a role as well. Lincoln was aware that the North's official neutrality over slavery hampered U.S. diplomatic efforts to prevent European aid to the South. By issuing the preliminary Emancipation Proclamation in the fall of 1862, Lincoln altered the aims of the war and turned Union forces, which would soon include dozens of black regiments, into an army of liberation.

It quickly became clear that emancipation raised as many questions as it settled. Many members of the Republican Party hoped that emancipation would be only the first step in a permanent and fundamental remaking of Southern society into one in which African Americans would have the same political and economic opportunities enjoyed by whites. Some Republicans advocated a program of land redistribution, in which the property of former Confederates would be divided in small landholdings and given to freed slaves.

Many elements of this reform agenda were carried out. In 1865, Congress established the Freedmen's Bureau to assist former slaves, and ratified the Thirteenth Amendment, which permanently outlawed slavery everywhere in the nation. When Southern states enacted Black Codes that reinstituted many features of slavery, Congress passed a series of Civil Rights Acts, which declared all persons born in the United States to be citizens with equal rights to enter into contracts, hold property, and receive protection from the government. The Fourteenth Amendment, ratified in 1868, prohibited any state from abridging the privileges and immunities of citizens or depriving any person of life, liberty, or property without due process. Finally, the Fifteenth Amendment, ratified in 1870, declared that the right to vote could not be denied on account of race.

These reforms led to impressive gains in the South for African Americans in the decades after the Civil War. Thousands became landowners, and black men could be found holding local office, serving in Southern statehouses, and representing their districts in the halls of the U.S. Congress. Black men and women established thousands of schools and churches, often with the help of the Freedmen's Bureau or private freedmen's relief organizations. African Americans rebuffed white landowners' attempts to force former slaves into year-long labor contracts. Landowners and landless blacks instead settled on a system of sharecropping in which tenants lived and worked on plots of land and gave the owner a large share of their crop in exchange.

Still, the change was neither as fundamental nor as permanent as many reformers had wished. Sharecropping tended to ensnare African Americans in a cycle of debt. A series of Supreme Court decisions weakened the guarantees of the Fourteenth Amendment and gave Southern states the go-ahead to enact discriminatory legislation. Constitutional conventions across the South curtailed access to the ballot box through measures such as the poll tax and literacy tests, and black voting and officeholding fell dramatically.

Today, Americans are seeking to come to terms with the legacy of slavery and emancipation by learning about life during those times. Many are finding excellent research materials on the World Wide Web, and some are creating their own sites for the benefit of other researchers. By allowing people to read about slavery through the eyes of slaves, slaveholders, military commanders, and Freedmen's Bureau officials, the Internet has put the raw materials of history into the hands of the general public.

 EB SITE REVIEWS

The African American Odyssey: A Quest for Full Citizenship

http://lcweb2.loc.gov/ammem/aaohtml/exhibit/aointro.html

Part of the Library of Congress's extensive American Memory project, the African American Odyssey site tells the story of slavery and emancipation through important Library of Congress documents and explanatory narrative.

The section titled Slavery—The Peculiar Institution shows various liberation strategies employed by slaves as well as white reactions to them. The discussion of Nat Turner's 1831 rebellion features Virginia governor John Floyd's explanation of the forces behind the uprising. In his letter to South Carolina governor James Hamilton, which has been partially transcribed, Floyd blamed the rebellion on "Yankee pedlers and traders" who "began first by making them religious" and then by telling slaves "that all men were born free and equal." The section also describes how slaves sought freedom by running away and features a runaway notice offering a reward for the return of an entire slave family that has left its master.

The African American Odyssey site conveys a sense of the promise of Reconstruction as well. Digitized magazine illustrations show African American men at the voting booth, in the South Carolina legislature, and in the U.S. Congress.

Documents about numerous freedmen's schools established after the Civil War give a vivid sense of the importance that former slaves placed on education.

Web visitors proceed through each section of this site as they would through a museum exhibit. Most documents have been digitized but not transcribed, and researchers who wish to conduct more in-depth research will be better served at other sites. The material is arranged along a chronological narrative, and each section opens with several paragraphs of background information. The featured documents are accompanied by explanatory text describing their context and significance.

The site's material on slavery and emancipation, although not extensive, makes it a good starting point, especially in the areas of slave resistance and Reconstruction.

CONTENT	★ ★ ★ ★
AESTHETICS	★ ★ ★ ★ ★
NAVIGATION	★ ★ ★ ★ ★

African American Women: On-line Archival Collections

http://scriptorium.lib.duke.edu/collections/african-american-women.html

This Duke University Library site consists of entirely transcribed texts as well as digital images of the documents themselves. With letters from slave women to their owners and members of their families, this site makes an extremely valuable contribution to the body of online material about slavery.

One letter, from Vilet Lester to Patsey Patterson, her former owner, is a heartbreaking testament to the suffering brought about by the slave trade. After being sold away from the Patterson family, Lester had at least four different owners. In her letter, she longs to see the family she was forced to leave behind: "I have thaugh[t] that I wanted to See mother but never befour did I [k]no[w] what it was to want to See a parent and could not. . . . I wish to [k]now what has Ever become of my Presus little girl. I left her in goldsborough with Mr. Walker and I have not herd from her Since."

The site also features a collection of letters written by two slave women to their owners and family members living in far-off Richmond. Left in charge of running the western Virginia household while their owner, John Campbell, served his term as Virginia governor, Hannah Valentine and Lethe Jackson expressed longing to see their owners as well as their own family members taken by the Campbells to Richmond.

CONTENT	★ ★ ★ ★ ★
AESTHETICS	★ ★ ★
NAVIGATION	★ ★ ★ ★ ★

American Slave Narratives: An Online Anthology

http://xroads.virginia.edu/~HYPER/wpa/wpahome.html

In the 1930s writers working for the Works Progress Administration (WPA) interviewed thousands of former slaves. These interviews have provided historians with rich material for the study of slavery, and historian Bruce Fort, while a graduate student at the University of Virginia, assembled an excellent sample of these narratives and made them available to the public over the World Wide Web.

American Slave Narratives: An Online Anthology contains transcriptions of thirteen WPA interviews. A useful index page summarizes the interviews and provides thumbnail photographs of the subjects, when available. The interview with Fountain Hughes is accompanied by sound files of the recording taken during the interview. Hughes described his memories of slavery: "We were slaves. We belonged to people. They'd sell us like they sell horses an' cows an' hogs an' all like that. Have a auction bench, an' they'd put you on, up on the bench an' bid on you jus' same as you bidding on cattle you know." After the war, Hughes's family was homeless and destitute, and his mother hired him out to white employers for one-year contracts. Hughes lived with these employers, and his mother would come by once a month to collect the money. "We didn' have no property. We didn' have no home. We had nowhere or nothing. We didn' have nothing only just, uh, like your cattle, we were jus' turned out. An,' uh, get along the best you could."

Mary Reynolds's memories testify to slavery's effect on families. Her father, a free black man traveling in the South, sought to buy Reynolds's mother and marry her, but her owner refused. To stay with his bride, Reynolds's father lived and worked on the plantation as a slave. Reynolds's mother nursed the owner's daughter along with Mary, and the two girls spent their first years side by side and formed a lifelong bond. When she was old enough, Reynolds was taught to hoe. Summoned to the fields before sunrise by the blowing of a conch shell, she worked in fear of the brutal driver, who would whip slaves until their bones were exposed. She also recalled secret nighttime prayer meetings, in which the preacher told the slaves that the day was coming when they would be slaves only of God.

In general, the men and women interviewed by the WPA had not spent any of their adult lives as slaves, so their experiences under the institution were limited. The transcriptions can be difficult to read because the interviewers attempted to capture their subjects' dialect. Despite their limitations as historic sources, the WPA slave narratives are essential reading for anyone seeking an understanding of slavery.

CONTENT   ★ ★ ★ ★ ★
AESTHETICS   ★ ★ ★ ★
NAVIGATION   ★ ★ ★ ★ ★

"Been Here So Long": Selections from the WPA American Slave Narratives
http://newdeal.feri.org/asn/

"Been Here So Long": Selections from the WPA American Slave Narratives is a part of the New Deal Network, an online project dedicated to teaching the legacy of the public works projects carried out during the New Deal. The seventeen narratives reproduced on this site are accompanied by explanatory essays and three lesson plans suitable for secondary school history classes. The site offers two gateways to the narratives: one lists the interviews by subject, the other by topic.

As with the American Slave Narratives site reviewed above, the interviews here allow researchers to construct a sense of the African American experience during slavery, emancipation, and Reconstruction. Especially helpful for researchers is this site's topical index, which provides subject links directly to the appropriate section of each relevant interview. Under the heading Runaways, for example, are links to particular passages in five separate interviews. Some interviewees remembered the sound of hounds chasing runaways in the woods. Scott Bond recalled that "when you went to bed at night you could hear the blood hounds, and in the morning when you would wake up, you could hear them running colored people. The white folks said the music they made was the sweetest music in the world."

Several of the former slaves recalled the day when they were told that they were free. Andy Anderson's owner gathered his slaves and announced that they were free but assured them that they could stay on the plantation and work for shares or wages. Anderson remembered his response: "I's says to myse'f, not loud 'nough fo' anyone to heah, I's thinks, but de Marster heahs me w'en I's says, 'Lak hell I's will.' Now, I's don't mean anything 'gainst de Marster. W'at I's mean am dat I's gwine to take my freedom, but he took it to mean something else."

Jerry Moore recalled the political strength enjoyed by African Americans during Reconstruction: "The 'publican party had a 'Loyal League' for to protect the cullud folks. First the Negroes went to the league house to get 'structions and ballots and then marched to the court house, double file, to vote. My father was a member of the 11th and 12th legislature from this county." But James Green pointed out that few things actually changed: "No great change come about in de way we went on. We had de same houses, only we all got credit from de store and bought our own food. We got shoes and what clothes we wanted, too. Some of us got whipped just de same but nobody got nailed to a tree by his ears."

Extremely well designed, "Been Here So Long" is a valuable site for teachers and researchers at all levels.

CONTENT   ★ ★ ★ ★ ★
AESTHETICS   ★ ★ ★ ★
NAVIGATION   ★ ★ ★ ★ ★

Documenting the American South: North American Slave Narratives
http://docsouth.unc.edu/neh/neh.html

In contrast to the WPA slave narrative sites, Documenting the American South: North American Slave Narratives consists of written works by former slaves published up to 1920. According to the essay that accompanies this collection, until 1930 slave narratives outnumbered any other type of African American literature.

The collection contains widely known works such as the *Narrative of the Life of Frederick Douglass, an American Slave*, Harriet Ann Jacobs's *Incidents in the Life of a Slave Girl*, and Booker T. Washington's *Up from Slavery*. In addition, the site includes accounts not well known today, such as *The Life of Isaac Mason as a Slave*.

Mason's *Life* includes a dramatic story of his escape from slavery. He and two other men paid a free black man twelve dollars for helping them get to Pennsylvania. Their escape would not have been possible had it not been for a network of safe havens provided by sympathetic whites and blacks. Mason found work as a farmhand in New Jersey and married. When his master, armed with the terms of the newly passed Fugitive Slave Law, arrived at his new home, Mason and his wife fled to Massachusetts. Later, Mason took part in an ill-fated scheme in which several thousand black men and women emigrated to Haiti. Mason became extremely ill there, quickly recognized that the emigrants had been duped by their leader, and returned to Massachusetts. He published an account of the misadventure in several newspapers, and the Haiti scheme collapsed as a result.

As testaments to the humanity of the slaves, the horrors of slavery, and the fruits of full U.S. citizenship, slave narratives such as Mason's fueled the antislavery and freedmen's aid movements and constitute an important body of American protest and reform literature. As with all of the Documenting the American South collections, the North American Slave Narratives is a true digital library. Apart from one scholarly essay, the site contains no annotations or explanatory material. Users not familiar with the authors or the genre of slave narratives may be overwhelmed by the long list of works to choose from. But with the largest online collection of material written by African Americans, this site is extremely valuable.

CONTENT ★ ★ ★ ★ ★
AESTHETICS ★ ★ ★ ★
NAVIGATION ★ ★ ★

NEW **The Dred Scott Case**

http://library.wustl.edu/vlib/dredscott/

Dred Scott's legal battle for freedom began more than ten years before the famous 1857 U.S. Supreme Court decision that bears his name. Scott and his wife Harriet first sued their owner in 1846, arguing before the St. Louis Circuit Court that the twelve years they served their master in free states and territories rendered their slave status invalid. The jury in this trial ruled against Scott and his wife, but the jury in a second trial in the same court sided with them. The Scotts' owner appealed the ruling to the Missouri Supreme Court, which overturned the second Circuit Court decision in 1852 and returned Dred and Harriet Scott to slavery.

The result of a collaboration between Washington University in St. Louis, the Missouri State Archives, and the St. Louis Circuit Clerk's Office, this web site features eighty-five legal documents filed during these court battles. For each document, users can view a small image of the document, a larger (and more readable) image, an image that is even larger, and full text transcriptions in both HTML (readable through any browser) and Microsoft Word.

The documents are not accompanied by explanatory material, and researchers unfamiliar with the legal system will find themselves struggling through the procedural language. Fortunately for novices, the site features a useful chronology that outlines the main events of Scott's life. Also helpful is the page titled "Background of slave freedom suits in Missouri." (The link to this page is buried in the "related links" at the end of the chronology.) This page explains that the Scott case was the last of many suits filed by slaves in St. Louis for their freedom. In fact, precedent stood with the Scotts—the court had ruled in 1824 that if an owner took a slave to a free state and set up residence there, the slave would be free as a result. But as the site makes clear, the legal system was in different hands some twenty years later.

CONTENT ★ ★ ★
AESTHETICS ★ ★ ★
NAVIGATION ★ ★ ★

Excerpts from Slave Narratives

http://vi.uh.edu/pages/mintz/primary.htm

This course web site developed by University of Houston history professor Steven
   Mintz contains transcriptions of forty-six previously published firsthand accounts
   of slavery in the public domain. The narratives are listed under eleven subject
   headings: Enslavement, the Middle Passage, Arrival, Conditions of Life, Child-
   hood, Family, Religion, Punishment, Resistance, Flight, and Emancipation.

Many of the documents are not true slave narratives but are valuable nonetheless. One is a transcription of an 1863 magazine article about Harriet Tubman,
   which is found in the Flight category. The Emancipation documents include a
   wonderful 1865 letter from Jordan Anderson to his former master in Tennessee,
   who has asked Anderson and his wife to return to the old plantation. Anderson writes, "[W]e have concluded to test your sincerity by asking you to send
   us our wages for the time we served you. This will make us forget and forgive
   old scores, and rely on your justice and friendship in the future. I served you
   faithfully for thirty-two years and Mandy twenty years. At $25 a month for me,
   and $2 a week for Mandy, our earnings would amount to $11,680." It is unlike-
   ly that Anderson returned to Tennessee.

Free of images, frames, and menu bars, this simple site would serve as a good
   starting point for students of slavery. The documents are well chosen, carefully excerpted, and clearly presented.

CONTENT   ★ ★ ★ ★
AESTHETICS   ★ ★ ★
NAVIGATION   ★ ★ ★

Freedmen and Southern Society Project

http://www.inform.umd.edu/ARHU/Depts/History/Freedman/home.html

The Freedmen and Southern Society Project, based at the History Department at
   the University of Maryland, is editing a nine-volume documentary book series
   titled *Freedom: A Documentary History of Emancipation, 1861–1867*, published
   by Cambridge University Press. The primary purpose of this site is to promote
   the book, but the volume and quality of the material made available here make
   it a complete site in its own right.

The section titled Chronology of Emancipation During the Civil War provides
   a timeline in which key events and terms are linked to explanatory material
   and documents on other pages. The timeline traces the federal government's
   halting steps toward full-scale emancipation. It includes the proposal of a constitutional amendment (not passed), which forbade the federal government to

interfere with the institution of slavery, and the first Confiscation Act of 1861, which nullified Confederate owners' claims to slaves who abandoned their plantations for Union army lines. The second Confiscation Act, passed in July 1862, freed the slaves of owners who were assisting the Confederate government. The next step was Lincoln's Emancipation Proclamation, which freed all slaves in areas still under Confederate control. The timeline concludes with the ratification of the Thirteenth Amendment, which abolished slavery in all parts of the United States.

The Sample Documents page consists of a list of annotated links to documents selected from the book series. In one, Maryland slave Annie Davis impatiently demands that President Lincoln clarify the status of slaves there (because Maryland was not part of the Confederacy, the terms of the Emancipation Proclamation did not apply): "Mr president[,] It is my Desire to be free. to go to see my people on the eastern shore. my mistress wont let me[.] you will please let me know if we are free. and what i can do. I write to you for advice. please send me word this week. or as soon as possible and oblidge." Other documents include the full text of federal measures such as the Conscription Acts and Emancipation Proclamation as well as General William T. Sherman's remarkable 1865 order to distribute thousands of acres of seized land to African American families.

The timeline and document collection make the Freedmen and Southern Society Project site a valuable aid for researchers seeking a sense of the complex story of emancipation and its aftermath.

CONTENT ★ ★ ★ ★ ★
AESTHETICS ★ ★ ★ ★
NAVIGATION ★ ★ ★ ★

Jesuit Plantation Project: Maryland's Jesuit Plantations, 1650–1838

http://www.georgetown.edu/departments/amer_studies/jpp/coverjpp.html

This is a challenging site for anyone not already familiar with the history of the Jesuit-owned Maryland plantations, but the material on it is truly fascinating. The site consists primarily of diaries and correspondence of the Jesuit priests who oversaw six plantations in eastern Maryland. The story that unfolds from these documents illustrates the fundamental paradox of slave owner paternalism: how could a good Christian participate in an institution that deprived people of their very humanity?

The earliest documents on the site give a sense of the dissatisfaction some priests felt over the Jesuit practice of owning slaves. Although one of the priests

defended the institution and portrayed abolitionism as just another heresy propagated by Protestants, he later argued that the Jesuit plantations should rid themselves of their troublesome human property: "1st Because we have their souls
to answer for—2nd Because Blacks are more difficult to govern now, than formerly—and 3rd Because we shall make more & more [profit] to our satisfaction." Seeking to establish uniform and just practices for their plantations that
would still be in line with Catholic teachings, the corporation issued regula-
tions for the treatment of slaves. They included "5. That this chastise[ment]
should not be inflicted on any female in the house, where the priest lives—
sometimes they have been tied up in the priests own parlour, which is very
indecorous"; and "7. To devise more effectual means to promote morality & the
frequentation of the sacram[ents]."

In 1838, when the Jesuits of Maryland opted to sell all their slaves to owners
in Louisiana, paternalism was put to the test. The priests set strict conditions
on their sale. Their new owners had to promise that the slaves would be able
to practice Catholicism with the assistance of a priest and that families would
not be separated. The slaves' new owners did not keep their obligations, however, and a Jesuit priest in Louisiana wrote his brothers in Maryland asking for
funds to set up a church for their former slaves: "I am taking the liberty to write
to you again to pledge the cause of these poor negroes, who used to belong to
your Province and who find themselves now deprived of almost any religious
(support) in Louisianna. I might be wrong, but it appears to me that the province
of Maryland is morally obliged to provide them with this support and to make
some sacrifices for this purpose."

Not designed for the lay researcher, the site has extremely confusing navigation. Visitors would be best served by going to the Resource Chronology page,
which lists all the documents in chronological order. Despite the site's weak
navigation, the designers should be congratulated for making these Georgetown
University Library manuscripts available to the general public.

CONTENT   ★ ★ ★ ★
AESTHETICS   ★ ★ ★ ★
NAVIGATION   ★ ★

Levi Jordan Plantation Project
http://www.webarchaeology.com

Focusing on the period from 1848 to 1900, the Levi Jordan Plantation Project site
invites visitors to participate in an archaeological project to reconstruct the lives
of the black and white residents of a Texas plantation before and after emancipation. The site represents the work of a unique collaboration of university
scholars, local historians, and genealogists.

Census manuscripts and plantation papers indicate that the Levi Jordan plantation was home to 150 slaves in 1862 and that many of these individuals remained there as tenants at least until the 1890s. A variety of findings, such as a shell carved with a Kongo symbol and an intricately decorated staff, suggests that the black residents on the plantation maintained strong African traditions. Additional evidence of direct African influence is provided by 1870 census manuscripts, which list Africa as the birthplace of several of the plantation's tenants.

Visitors to the site can examine small photographs of dozens of objects uncovered by the excavation, such as tools, eyeglasses, eating utensils, and decorative shell and bone carvings. Transcriptions of personal papers have also been made available by Levi Jordan's descendents. The site is dominated not by the archaeological findings or historic documents but by papers, interviews, and other material prepared by the scholars engaged in the research. In fact, the site is as much about the process of archaeological inquiry as it is about the plantation and its residents.

Archaeology provides an important window into the world of slaves and former slaves, and the Levi Jordan Plantation Project makes this window available to the general public.

CONTENT ★ ★ ★ ★
AESTHETICS ★ ★ ★
NAVIGATION ★ ★ ★

Third Person, First Person: Slave Voices from the Special Collections Library
http://scriptorium.lib.duke.edu/slavery/

This web version of a physical exhibit at Duke University's Special Collections Library contains fascinating documents that capture the complexities of the master–slave relationship. One section, titled Caesar, contains the 1785 bill of sale of a slave named Caesar to William Gibbons of Georgia. In a document dated 1794, Gibbons authorized an agent to retrieve Caesar, who had run away. He was found in Connecticut, and the person he was living with told Gibbons that Caesar would return if he were allowed to work on his own time and earn money to buy his freedom. A plantation document from several years later showed that Caesar had returned to the Gibbons plantation, but whether his terms were met is unknown.

The section titled Black Southerners in the Old South—The Slave Community features the records of slave owner Louis Manigault, in which he lists the cholera deaths among his slaves and describes the remedy he gave to slaves suffering from the disease (alternating doses of castor oil with a mixture of calomel and opium).

An online exhibit rather than an archive for researchers, Third Person, First Person does not contain full transcriptions of the documents, and only the description is given for some of the items due to the fragility of the original documents.

CONTENT   ★ ★ ★ ★
AESTHETICS   ★ ★ ★ ★ ★
NAVIGATION   ★ ★ ★

NEW Toward Racial Equality: *Harper's Weekly* Reports on Black America, 1857–1874
http://blackhistory.harpweek.com/

*H*arper's *Weekly* was read by more Americans than any other single publication in the late nineteenth century. Its cartoons and illustrations, many by the famous Thomas Nast, are still familiar today. HarpWeek, a privately funded venture offering institutional subscribers full access to the complete, digitized *Harper's Weekly* from 1857 to 1912, has made scores of articles, illustrations, and cartoons pertaining to African American history available on this free, excellent web site.

As an essay on the site explains, the magazine was conservative on racial issues prior to the Civil War. Careful not to offend its Southern readership, editorial writers tended to blame "extremists" and "misunderstandings" for sectional strife. The magazine minimized the ramifications of the Dred Scott opinion and predicted that the states of the Upper South would abandon slavery of their own accord. Slavery was portrayed as a benign institution, with slaves generally content with their lot. A cartoon printed after John Brown's attack on Harpers Ferry showed a planter arming his loyal slaves, who were eager to defend their master's home against abolitionist violence.

Once the war began, *Harper's Weekly* changed its tone. Its editorials argued for full emancipation and for the creation of black fighting units in the Union army. Illustrations began to emphasize the brutality of slavery, showing the effects of whipping and other means of torture. The courage and heroism of black troops and their horrific treatment when captured behind Confederate lines became common themes in the magazine. After the war, *Harper's Weekly* applauded black suffrage and the election of black men to Congress, and it decried mob violence carried out by organizations such as the Ku Klux Klan.

But its editors and artists were not above employing racial stereotypes that most Americans would find objectionable today. Although the magazine's harshest words and images were used to depict urban Irish Catholics, HarpWeek is so concerned about the negative portrayal of African Americans that it places a prominent warning on the home page and showcases an essay by Harvard law professor Randall Kennedy on the use of racially derogatory language.

The site features several elements designed for students and educators. Three timelines (slavery, the Civil War, and Reconstruction) are sufficiently detailed to serve as a review for the average high-school history class. The Reconstruction simulation game is a creative set of lesson plans for advanced high-school students that makes excellent use of the *Harper's Weekly* material and helps students understand both the promise and limitations of Reconstruction.

CONTENT ★ ★ ★ ★ ★
AESTHETICS ★ ★ ★ ★ ★
NAVIGATION ★ ★ ★ ★

NEW **Uncle Tom's Cabin and American Culture: A Multi-Media Archive**
http://jefferson.village.virginia.edu/utc

Created by University of Virginia English professor Stephen Railton, Uncle Tom's Cabin and American Culture employs scores of transcribed documents and artifacts to place Harriet Beecher Stowe's famous antislavery novel in the context of the literary, political, and religious conventions of midnineteenth-century America. This challenging site is likely to be used primarily by advanced scholars and teachers of American literature and culture, but anyone seeking to understand the enduring power of Stowe's novel will find powerful and surprising material here.

Railton divides the documents into three categories. PreTexts includes Christian writings, articles on home and family, antislavery texts, and minstrel shows—all of which both influenced Stowe's work and shaped Americans' response to her novel. "The Sinless Child," a poem published in *The Southern Literary Messenger* in 1843, shows remarkable parallels to Stowe's pious Little Eva. Stowe pointed to *The Life of Josiah Henson*, a slave narrative published in 1849, to prove that Uncle Tom's obedience and profound Christianity were indeed realistic. PreTexts also includes articles in support of sending freed slaves to Africa—a popular position among antislavery whites and one that Stowe seemed to partially endorse by having her darkest-skinned characters go to Africa at the end of the novel. Reviews of minstrel shows in leading national publications show how minstrelsy's representations of black dialogue and singing made Stowe's characters seem familiar to the book's readers.

The second category, titled Stowe's Uncle Toms, features the full text of the novel along with prefaces and addresses written and delivered by Stowe between 1852 and 1882. In this section, users can also listen to performances of eight hymns that Stowe's slave characters sang in the novel. They may examine illustrations and covers from various editions of the book, including the first 1852 edition, the Yiddish-language edition published in 1911, and the edition published as part of the publicity for the 1927 Hollywood movie based on the novel.

The documents in the Response category show how the novel's characters became ingrained into the American imagination in song, theater, advertising, and even as collectible figurines. Vaudeville stars Rosetta and Vivian Duncan retold the story of Uncle Tom's Cabin in "Topsy and Eva," a huge commercial success. The Response documents also include an advertisement for Topsy Tobacco, which shows a jolly Topsy smoking a pipe, saying "I is so wicked!" Well into the midtwentieth century, Uncle Tom-like images were used to sell Cream of Wheat cereal, root beer, brooms, and writing pens.

Uncle Tom's Cabin remains by far the most powerful literary challenge ever written to an entrenched American institution. As the site makes clear, the novel's power stemmed in part from how easily its characters and story fit into 1850s images of domesticity, religion, and race. Ironically, within decades of the book's publication, the novel had become so familiar to Americans that its characters and story could be easily appropriated by entertainers, manufacturers, and advertisers in a way that reinforced the myths of white supremacy and the benign nature of slavery.

CONTENT   ★ ★ ★ ★ ★
AESTHETICS   ★ ★ ★
NAVIGATION   ★ ★ ★

The Valley of the Shadow: Two Communities in the American Civil War
http://jefferson.village.virginia.edu/vshadow2/

Created at the University of Virginia by the Virginia Center for Digital History, the Valley of the Shadow explores the world of slaves and slave owners in Augusta County, Virginia, just before, during, and after the Civil War. The site's geographic focus allows researchers to get a sense of how slavery and its demise shaped and in turn were shaped by its larger community.

Part I: The Eve of War, Public Records, includes the 1860 Augusta County Slaveowner Census, which can be searched by the names of owners and employers and by the numbers of slaves owned. (Unfortunately for researchers, census takers did not record the names of any slaves.)

The Newspaper section of Part I features the transcriptions of dozens of newspaper articles pertaining to slavery. One, titled "Desperate Negro Woman," reports on an Augusta County slave who chopped off three of her fingers to prevent her sale. Newspapers rarely provided such unblemished accounts of slavery and more typically served to bolster white Southerners' confidence in the institution. Papers gleefully reported instances of freed and runaway slaves who voluntarily returned to their masters after suffering terribly in Northern states.

The Letters section of Part I contains several powerful documents from manuscript collections at the University of Virginia, Yale University, and other sources. In one document, a slave residing in a nearby county wrote to her husband that she and her children were about to be sold to a trader. She begged her husband to find someone else to purchase them instead: "Dear Husband, I write you a letter to let you know of my distress. My master has sold Albert to a trader on Monday court day and myself and other child is for sale also." The McCue Papers, a collection from the University of Virginia Library's Special Collections, show how slavery was woven into the business and personal lives of an extended family in Augusta County. This collection includes contracts for the hiring of slaves as well as letters between family members concerning their blacks' behavior. One such letter reports on a slave who has run away: "Dear John, I write this evening, to inform you that Wilson has run off.... You know he is such a sly negro that he may have more in his head than we know of.... [H]e was once taken up in Augusta and has so many acquaintances that he may be harbored ... or perhaps may aim for a free state." For most of the documents in this collection, only the transcriptions are available, although a few have been scanned.

The documents in Part II: The War Years illustrate the disintegration of slavery over the course of the Civil War. The Newspaper section features an 1863 article arguing that the high price of slaves confirmed that the institution was as strong as ever. The frequent runaway notices in the same paper, however, suggest a different story. The Freedmen's Bureau, one of the exhibits in the Student Projects section, is a site unto itself. It uses transcribed newspaper articles and Freedmen's Bureau Records to document how former slaves in Augusta County worked with federal officials to fight for fair wages, reunite their families, build churches and schools, and protect themselves from violence. The newspaper transcriptions in this exhibit are filled with notices about freedmen's fairs to raise money to start churches and schools as well as the following Freedmen's Bureau notice to whites regarding labor contracts with former slaves: "It is a fact which all should bear in mind, that contracts for service between white and colored persons for any time longer than two months are required to be in writing, signed by both parties, and acknowledged before a justice, notary public, or two witnesses, who shall certify, on their oaths, that the contract was read and explained to the colored parties." The exhibit also contains correspondence between the local Freedmen's Bureau agent and his superiors.

CONTENT ★ ★ ★ ★ ★
AESTHETICS ★ ★ ★ ★
NAVIGATION ★ ★ ★ ★

NEW **Virginia Runaways Project**
http://www.uvawise.edu/history/runaways/

Largely the work of the University of Virginia's College at Wise history professor Thomas Costa, this innovative web site features a digital database of over 2,000 advertisements for runaway and captured slaves, servants, and military deserters from eighteenth-century Virginia newspapers. The records are searchable, browsable, and have excellent accompanying material, making this site a very valuable resource for academic researchers, students, and teachers alike.

Owners often provided the birthplace of their runaway property in their advertisements, and searching the database for slaves cited as born in Africa, Angola, and Madagascar yields dozens of matches. In a notice posted on January 30, 1752, Benjamin Scott described his missing slave as "a short well-set Fellow, with a small Scar on his right Cheek, and a Parcel of small Scars on his Forehead, which is suppos'd to be his Country Mark." The advertisement noted that he had been transported on the slave ship *Williamsburg*. Searching the database for other runaways who came to Virginia on the *Williamsburg* shows one additional advertisement, posted in 1751. The owner reported ruefully that "The little Time I had him he went by the Name of David tho' he may not now remember it."

The advertisements also highlight the importance of slave labor in the colony. Owners frequently described the skills of the slaves in question so as to aid in their identification. Searching the runaway slave database for the skill or occupation "cooper" yielded forty-one matches, and searching for all carpenters yielded fifty-eight. One multitalented slave was described as "a Carpenter, Sawyer, Shoemaker, and Cooper."

As the web site makes clear, slavery was not the only type of forced labor in eighteenth-century Virginia. The database includes hundreds of notices regarding indentured servants born in various parts of Europe. One notice appearing in 1736 reported the loss of a male servant from Ireland, a "North-Country" convict, and a Dutch woman who "talks broken English." Like the runaway slaves, indentured servants generally headed toward Virginia's seaports, where they would try to obtain passage far from their masters' homes. Occasionally, slaves and indentured servants would run away together.

Advanced researchers familiar with slavery in Virginia will particularly appreciate the database's search function, which permits users to search the records by the places the slaves ran away from, by occupation or skill, by ethnic origin or birthplace, and by ships' names. This level of searching will allow researchers to consider questions such as whether slaves from some counties were more likely to run away than others, or whether slaves born in captivity were more likely to run away than those captured in Africa.

Those researchers who need a little help getting started will be grateful for the excellent accompanying material found on the "Help with the database" page. This page provides suggestions for searches, and the section titled "Samples" provides a wonderful example of how the sources can help students and others to answer interesting historical questions. The "Supporting Material" page features transcriptions of slave owners' correspondence, a slave's description of the Middle Passage, and the following poem by a indentured convict servant who returned to London after his term was up:

> My countrymen, take warning e'er too late,
> Lest you shou'd share my unhappy fate,
> Altho' but little crimes you here have done,
> Think of seven or fourteen years to come.
> Forc'd from your friends and country to go,
> Among the Negroes to work at the hoe,
> Indifferent countries void of all relief,
> Sold for a slave because you prov'd a thief.

CONTENT ★ ★ ★ ★ ★
AESTHETICS ★ ★ ★ ★
NAVIGATION ★ ★ ★

SUGGESTED READINGS

Berlin, Ira, Barbara J. Fields, Thavolia Glymph, Joseph P. Reidy, and Leslie S. Rowland, eds. *The Destruction of Slavery*. New York, 1985.

Blassingame, John W. *The Slave Community: Plantation Life in the Antebellum South*. Rev. and enl. New York, 1979.

Elkins, Stanley M. *Slavery: A Problem in American Institutional and Intellectual Life*. 3d ed., rev. Chicago, 1976.

Fogel, Robert W. *Without Consent or Contract: The Rise and Fall of American Slavery*. New York, 1989.

Fogel, Robert W., and Stanley L. Engerman. *Life on the Cross: The Economics of American Negro Slavery*. Boston, 1974.

Foner, Eric. *Reconstruction: America's Unfinished Revolution*. New York, 1989.

Fox-Genovese, Elizabeth. *Within the Plantation Household: Black and White Women of the Old South*. Chapel Hill, NC, 1988.

Franklin, John Hope, and Loren Schweninger. *Runaway Slaves: Rebels on the Plantation*. New York, 1999.

Genovese, Eugene. *The Political Economy of Slavery*. New York, 1965.

———. *Roll, Jordan, Roll: The World the Slaves Made*. New York, 1974.

Gutman, Herbert G. *The Black Family in Slavery and Freedom*. New York, 1976.

Lane, Ann J., ed. *The Debate over Slavery: Stanley Elkins and His Critics*. Urbana, IL, 1971.

Litwack, Leon F. *Been in the Storm So Long: The Aftermath of Slavery*. New York, 1979.

McFeely, William S. *Frederick Douglass*. New York, 1995.

Rose, Willie Lee. *Rehearsal for Reconstruction: The Port Royal Experiment*. Athens, GA, 1999.

Stampp, Kenneth M. *The Peculiar Institution: Slavery in the Ante-Bellum South*. New York, 1956.

CHAPTER 7

WOMEN IN THE CIVIL WAR

Women were barred from the polls in the midnineteenth century, but most had strong partisan and regional attachments, and they followed closely the political developments that precipitated the secession crisis. When the war began, women fought for victory by organizing soldiers' aid societies and serving as nurses in military hospitals. More adventurous women served as spies, disguised themselves as men to enlist in the army, and moved south to teach freed slaves. In Maryland, Pennsylvania, and most of the South, women did not need to travel to the war; the war came to them. Standing at their doorsteps, they saw wounded soldiers by the thousands staggering away from battlefields, and many women were forced to live under enemy occupation. The lives of slaveholding women, left first to manage their slaves on their own and then to see their slaves emancipated, were fundamentally and irreversibly altered. Until recently, to explore the varied experiences of Civil War women in their own words, researchers had to comb through manuscripts and academic books. Today, they can turn to the World Wide Web, where they will find a variety of excellent material.

It is possible that there were dozens of women who disguised themselves as men and fought with the military. Searching the Compiled Military Service Records in the National Archives, historian DeAnne Blanton has found discharge orders for several soldiers who had been discovered to be female. She has also located nineteenth- and early twentieth-century newspaper accounts of six other women who enlisted, either on their own or to accompany their husbands. One woman,

Sarah Emma Edmonds, deserted from the 2nd Michigan Infantry to avoid discovery when she contracted malaria after serving more than two years. After the war, Edmonds received a veteran's pension for her service. Private Albert D. J. Cashier of the 95th Illinois lived as a man until an accident in 1910 led to the discovery of her gender. It is entirely likely that there are dozens of additional women who assumed male identities and enlisted in the military.

Women also served as spies during the Civil War. Informal social networks made women well positioned to glean secret military information, cross military lines, and pass the information on to friendly ears. Rose O'Neal Greenhow, a well-connected Washington hostess, organized the network that informed General P. G. T. Beauregard of the Union advance on Manassas Station in the summer of 1861. Beauregard reinforced his lines in time to ensure a Confederate victory. Imprisoned in her home and in a Washington jail for several months, Greenhow was released to Richmond, where she was given a hero's welcome. Belle Boyd of Front Royal, Virginia, passed on the location of Federal troops to General Stonewall Jackson during the Valley Campaign. Tennessee Unionist Sarah Thompson rode to Union lines with the secret location of famous Confederate cavalry raider John Hunt Morgan. She personally led Union soldiers to his hiding place.

For most women, aiding the war effort did not involve becoming a spy or soldier. Typically, female war work consisted of gathering and manufacturing supplies for the army. Tapping into the strong tradition of antebellum women's voluntary associations, women across the country formed aid societies to knit gloves, sew regimental flags, and procure food and medical supplies.

Women soon realized that local aid societies alone could not improve the health and safety of men in the army. The overburdened military transportation system left soldiers languishing at shipping docks and railway stations for months. Military medical bureaus employed unsanitary and outdated medical techniques. Camps housing thousands of men were built without proper latrines and water supplies. In response, Northern women allied with civilian physicians to form organizations such as the U.S. Sanitary Commission. Its leaders bypassed hostile officers of the Army Medical Bureau, appealed directly to President Lincoln, and were authorized officially to inspect camp conditions and advise on proper sanitary practices. The Commission also trained nurses, arranged for the transport of supplies and nurses to army hospitals, and set up food and medical stations for furloughed soldiers at railway stops. Recognizing the quality of the female nurses trained by the U.S. Sanitary Commission, Surgeon General William Hammond appointed the noted reformer Dorothea Dix to recruit and train women nurses, and he ordered that at least one-third of army nurses be women. According to Civil War historian James McPherson, more than three thousand women worked as paid nurses for the Union army, and thousands more served as volunteers and paid agents for the Commission.

Southern women also mobilized to address the poor care given to sick and wounded soldiers, volunteering as nurses and establishing their own infirmaries. As in the North, the superiority of female volunteers over regular military hospital staff inspired the Confederate Congress to pass a law encouraging the hiring of women as nurses.

As the Union army took over more and more Southern territory, the care and education of freed slaves became a concern for many Northern women. These women, many of whom were veterans of the antislavery movement, sought to ensure that former slaves had the education and skills to provide for themselves and strove to ward off the accusation that black men and women were inherently ill suited for freedom. In 1862 dozens of female volunteers traveled to the Sea Islands of South Carolina to teach the slaves there, in the hopes that their success would spur Lincoln to adopt a policy of emancipation. Other women reformers, such as Josephine Griffin, worked to improve the conditions of freedmen refugees in Washington, DC.

Most women remained in their homes during the war, assuming sole responsibility for running farms and shops in addition to meeting their prewar responsibilities of raising children and keeping house. Southern women on the home front faced particular hardships. By the final year of the war, Confederate currency was practically worthless, and women could acquire needed goods only by barter. As Federal control over Southern territory expanded, women faced the ordeal of life under enemy occupation. Looting and destruction of property, whether the acts of undisciplined troops or the result of official military policy, created extreme hardship as well as intense humiliation.

Slaveholding women were in particularly precarious positions. With husbands, sons, and overseers gone, these women found it difficult to force their slaves to work as they had before. In their diaries, they expressed mortal fear of violent insurrection as well as bitter disappointment at the exodus of many of their slaves to Union lines. Historian Drew Gilpin Faust argues that the ordeal of slaveholding women led to their disaffection with the Confederate cause and helped bring about the Confederate defeat. Faust's interpretation is not universally accepted, but there is no question that female slaveholders faced profound difficulties during the Civil War.

Many women remained active in the public sphere when the war ended. Clara Barton, a nurse in the Union army, headed the national effort to locate and return missing soldiers and later founded the American Red Cross. Other nurses fought for and received government pensions for their wartime services. Many freedmen's teachers remained at their schools for the rest of their lives, often campaigning actively for equal rights and improved education for Southern African Americans.

Women's rights advocates, many of whom had participated actively in aiding the war effort, hoped that the social revolution brought about by the end of slavery would expand to bring about increased rights for women. Bitterly disappointed when the Fifteenth Amendment guaranteed suffrage to black men only, women's rights activists returned to the suffrage campaign with renewed determination. It took more than sixty years of intense activity for the constitutional amendment guaranteeing votes for women to pass.

Thanks to the efforts of historians and archivists across the country, dozens of Civil War women's letters, diaries, and memoirs are available to the public on the web. Online researchers can read about the experiences of nurses, spies, and freedmen's schoolteachers in their own words, and they can examine the private thoughts of Southern women living under enemy occupation.

 EB SITE REVIEWS

Civil War Women: On-line Archival Collections

http://scriptorium.lib.duke.edu/collections/civil-war-women.html

This small online archive, part of Duke University's Digital Scriptorium project, features three significant sets of manuscripts that portray key aspects of women's experience in the American Civil War. All are from the manuscript collection of Duke University Library.

Rose O'Neal Greenhow, one of the better-known spies for the Confederacy, ran a spy network out of her home in Washington, DC. Her messages informed General P. G. T. Beauregard of the Union movements toward Manassas in 1861, enabling him to amass troops and defeat the Northern army there. Imprisoned for her activities, Greenhow still managed to pass on information about Union military and diplomatic activities to the South. After her release and exile to the Confederate states, Greenhow traveled to Britain and France to lobby for their support of the Confederate cause.

The Greenhow collection consists of scans and transcriptions of thirteen documents. Most of the material is correspondence from Greenhow to her Confederate colleagues, much of which was sent from Europe. She describes her impatience with her lack of diplomatic success in many of her letters: "I had the honor of an audience with the Emperor [Napoleon III] . . . and altho the Emperor was lavish of expressions of admiration of our President and cause there was nothing upon which to hang the least hope of aid unless England acted simultaneously—the French people are brutal ignorant and depraved to a degree beyond description and have no appreciation of our struggle they believe it is to free the slaves and all their sympathies are really on the Yankee side." In 1864 the British blockade runner that carried Greenhow home from Europe ran aground off the coast of North Carolina, and Greenhow drowned while fleeing from an approaching Northern gunboat.

Sixteen-year-old Alice Williamson, an ardent Confederate partisan, kept a journal while her town of Gallatin, Tennessee, was under Union military occupation. Her diary records the summary executions and looting carried on by Northern forces under notorious Brigadier General Eleazar Arthur Paine, whom she sarcastically referred to as "our King" and "his lordship." Paine's harsh occupation was later replaced by a Unionist East Tennessee regiment, who directed their hostility not against white civilians, as Paine had, but against freed slaves living in the "contraband camp."

Williamson's journal captures many aspects of Southern women's Civil War experience. As more and more Confederate territory fell under Union military control, Southern women, usually with husbands, fathers, and brothers away fighting, had to conduct their daily lives under enemy occupation. Unable to express openly her hatred of her Unionist occupiers, Williamson poured out her defiance in her diary: "Our king (old Payne) has just passed. I suppose he has killed every rebel in twenty miles of Gallatin and burned every town. Poor fellow! you had better be praying, old Sinner! His Lordship left Tuesday. Wednesday three wagons loaded with furniture came over. I do not pretend to say that he sent them. No! Indeed, I would not. I would not slander our king. . . . He always goes for rebels but invariably brings furniture. I suppose his task is to furnish the contraband camp, i.e. the camp of his angels (colored)."

Other Southern women, such as Sarah E. Thompson, were active Unionists. Thompson spent the first years of the war helping her husband raise Union regiments in Tennessee. After her husband was assassinated by pro-Southern elements in his town, Thompson became a spy for the Union army. Her most notable achievement was in 1864, when she informed Union forces that Confederate general John Hunt Morgan was in Greeneville, Tennessee. According to her personal testimony, she led Union troops to his hiding place, where Morgan was shot and killed. In addition to her spy activity, Thompson also served as a military nurse. After the war she supported herself by giving speeches about her wartime experiences and with occasional Washington, DC, government jobs.

Most of the documents in the Thompson collection consist of postwar correspondence from supporters who sought to award her a government pension for her services. In 1878, Captain S. G. Carter wrote, "She undertook the long and dangerous journey from her love for the cause of the Union and her hatred of the rebellion. . . . I take pleasure in recommending Mrs. Thompson to the favorable consideration of the proper authorities as one who deserves well of her country from her fearless devotion to its interests under circumstances of trial and danger." After decades of effort, Thompson was finally awarded a nurse's pension in 1898.

The manuscripts have been transcribed in full and are also available as high-quality digital images. Links to documents are accompanied by summaries of their contents. Each collection features a biographical sketch of the woman. The names of important people and groups mentioned in Alice Williamson's diary are linked to pages that provide additional background information.

CONTENT   ★ ★ ★ ★ ★
AESTHETICS ★ ★ ★
NAVIGATION ★ ★ ★ ★ ★

Clara Barton: National Historic Site

http://www.nps.gov/clba/

This small National Park Service site chronicles the life of Clara Barton, the founder of the American Red Cross. Presented in the form of a timeline, with no analysis or documents, the site serves as a good introduction to her life and times, although it will not satisfy researchers seeking a deep understanding of this complex woman and her role in the Civil War. The timeline covers her prewar struggles against discrimination as an educator and federal government worker. The section on the Civil War years recounts the assistance she provided out of her home to soldiers wounded in the 1861 Baltimore riots as well as her hospital work in Virginia and South Carolina. In 1865, President Lincoln appointed Barton to lead the effort to locate missing soldiers, an undertaking that lasted four years. Barton established the American Red Cross in 1881, having become aware of the international organization while in Europe aiding soldiers wounded in the Franco-Prussian War. The timeline also includes entries that show Barton's connection with Christian Science and the women's suffrage movement.

CONTENT   ★ ★ ★
AESTHETICS ★ ★ ★
NAVIGATION ★ ★ ★ ★

Documenting the American South

http://metalab.unc.edu/docsouth/

Documenting the American South, sponsored by the University of North Carolina, is a digital collection of more than 300 historic sources on Southern history. Although it does not contain a separate collection pertaining exclusively to women in the Civil War, there are numerous documents that illustrate their varied experiences. These documents are generally in the form of memoirs and diaries, some of which were published in the decades after the war.

A Confederate Girl's Diary, by Sarah Morgan Dawson, gives a vivid account of the home front experience of women. Dawson struggled to assert her identity as an ardent Confederate after her home town of Baton Rouge fell under Union occupation in 1862.

"'All devices, signs, and flags of the Confederacy shall be suppressed.' So says Picayune Butler. Good. I devote all my red, white, and blue silk to the manufacture of Confederate flags. As soon as one is confiscated, I make another. . . . [T]he man who says take it off will have to pull it off for himself; the man who dares attempt it—well! a pistol in my pocket fills up the gap. I am capable, too." As the war progressed, however, Dawson's efforts shifted from maintaining her feminine defiance to ensuring the physical survival of her family as they fled the Union shelling of their home.

Several documents at this site chronicle women's experiences as Civil War spies and soldiers. The archive includes the memoirs of the famous Confederate spy Belle Boyd as well as a fascinating book titled *The Woman in Battle: A Narrative of the Exploits, Adventures, and Travels of Madame Loreta Janeta Velazquez, Otherwise Known as Lieutenant Harry T. Burford, Confederate States Army.*

Documenting the American South consists entirely of full-text digital versions of manuscripts and published works. With no summaries or explanatory background information, the site can be challenging for researchers unfamiliar with Civil War history. Furthermore, there is no easy way to identify which among the more than 300 documents are about women in the Civil War. The best option is simply to scroll through the long lists of authors and titles. The search option is confusing for anyone not familiar with digital archive terminology. Although difficult to use, Documenting the American South is the largest collection of full-text Civil War-era manuscripts, and researchers will find it extremely valuable.

CONTENT   ★ ★ ★ ★
AESTHETICS   ★ ★ ★
NAVIGATION   ★ ★ ★

Hearts at Home: Southern Women in the Civil War
http://www.lib.virginia.edu/exhibits/hearts/

A companion to a former museum exhibit at the University of Virginia Library, the Hearts at Home site contains extensive material on Southern women in the American Civil War. Organized around themes such as spies, war work, patriotism, religion, education, refugees, and slavery and freedom, the site invites online researchers to explore many aspects of Southern women's wartime experience.

The documents feature rare books, letters and diaries, and Civil War-era peri-odicals from the University of Virginia's Special Collections Library. A *Harper's Weekly* cartoon of a uniformed Confederate female spy on horseback shows Northern public indignation against the Southern practice of relying on female spies. The section called Hard Times at Home contains a letter written by a Henry County, Virginia, resident describing the economic upheaval created by the war: "Times are very hard here every thing is scarce and high . . . corn is selling for ten dollars, bacon 45 cents per pound, brandy is selling about here from 4 to 5 dollars per gallon, in Danville it sells for eight dollars. We cannot get a yard of calico for less than one dollar we cannot get a pound of copperas [a sulfate used in making ink] for less than a dollar and 25 cents."

Designed as an online exhibit and not as an archive, the site does not contain full-text transcriptions of any of the items on display, which may frustrate some online researchers. But like a good exhibit, each item is accompanied by explana-tory text that provides context as well as brief excerpts of the document.

CONTENT   ★ ★ ★ ★
AESTHETICS   ★ ★ ★ ★ ★
NAVIGATION   ★ ★ ★

Illinois Alive! Illinois in the Civil War: Private Albert D. J. Cashier (Jennie Hodgers)

http://www.alliancelibrarysystem.com/ IllinoisAlive/files/iv/htm2/ivtxt002.cfm

Among the many stories of women who disguised themselves as men and enlisted in the Confederate and Union armies, Albert D. J. Cashier's story stands out. Born in Ireland with the name Jennie Hodgers, Cashier apparently lived her entire adult life as a man. She enlisted in the 95th Illinois Regiment, which participated in the siege of Vicksburg and the blockade of Mobile. In 1910, Cashier was admitted to a Soldier's and Sailor's Home. Four years later, her gen-der was discovered, and Cashier was discharged to an insane asylum, where she died within a year.

This site, sponsored by the Illinois State Library, features an excellent exhibit on this interesting individual. It contains several photographs, a brief biogra-phy, newspaper articles, and scans of Cashier's military, pension, and hospital records. According to the essay titled "Union Maid," Cashier's grave is marked by a monument with this inscription: "Albert D. J. Cashier, Co. G, 95. Inf., Civil War, Born: Jennie Hodgers in Clogher Head, Ireland, 1843–1915."

CONTENT   ★ ★ ★ ★
AESTHETICS   ★ ★ ★
NAVIGATION   ★ ★ ★

NARA Prologue: Women Soldiers of the Civil War
http://www.nara.gov/publications/prologue/women1.html

In this National Archives publication article, historian DeAnne Blanton tells the stories of women who disguised themselves as men and fought in the Union and Confederate armies. Combing through the National Archives' Compiled Military Service Records, Blanton found discharge records of soldiers whose true gender had been discovered, one of whom was discharged for reasons of "sextual [*sic*] incompatibility." She also recounts the cases of Albert D. J. Cashier and Sarah Edmonds Seelye, both of whom received federal pensions for their military service carried out under false identities. Blanton's article is illustrated with photographs of women soldiers and military documents.

CONTENT   ★ ★ ★ ★
AESTHETICS   ★ ★ ★ ★
NAVIGATION   ★ ★ ★ ★

United States Sanitary Commission
http://www.netwalk.com/~jpr/index.htm

Created by Civil War reenacter Jan P. Romanovich with contributions from a network of volunteers, this extensive web site can be explored for hours. A varied collection of documents and helpful explanatory text make this by far the largest and best site on the U.S. Sanitary Commission and on the role of women in this important organization.

The material includes an 1861 New York City newspaper announcement signed by more than one hundred women on the "importance of systematizing and concentrating the spontaneous and earnest efforts now being made by the women of New York" and for establishing a program of selecting, training, and compensating female nurses to care for wounded soldiers in military hospitals. Other documents consist of camp inspection reports, transcriptions of the *U.S.S.C. Bulletin*, and patterns for making bandages and hospital gowns.

The site also contains excerpts from an 1865 history of the U.S. Sanitary Commission. Describing the Commission's work at Shiloh, the author of the publication made special mention of the crucial role women played there: "After the battle, the Commission established a depot at the Landing. . . . [T]he stores issued from this depot amounted in all to 160,143 articles. . . . During the period that this depot was kept open, a great service was rendered to the Sanitary Commission by two women who volunteered for the work, and to whom its thanks are due. (One of whom is familiarly known among the soldiers as 'The Cairo Angel.')"

With its large collection of transcribed documents, Romanovich's United States Sanitary Commission site is of immense value to anyone seeking to understand the experience of Northern women's war work during the American Civil War. The site would benefit from an index that provides a little information about what lies behind each link and from a more careful documentation of sources.

CONTENT   ★ ★ ★ ★
AESTHETICS   ★ ★ ★ ★
NAVIGATION   ★ ★ ★

The Valley of the Shadow: Two Communities in the American Civil War

http://valley.vcdh.virginia.edu/

Created by historians at the University of Virginia, this site assembles a wide variety of documents from one Northern county and one Southern county. With its rich archival content, the Valley of the Shadow allows visitors to get a broad sense of how women worked within their communities in the midst of war.

The War Years Letters and Diaries section contains several documents that cast light on women's home front experience. Nancy Emerson, an unmarried woman living in her brother's home in Augusta County, Virginia, sadly recorded news of casualties from distant and not-so-distant battles. Emerson wrote of the humiliations she and her sister-in-law endured when the war came to her doorstep in the form of occupying Union soldiers in 1864. Anna Mellinger, a young Mennonite woman living in Franklin County, Pennsylvania, during the war, wrote of hiding her family's livestock from approaching Confederate raiders in the summer of 1864. Both of these documents are transcribed and searchable, and beautiful scans of the originals are also available.

Aid societies in both counties assembled supplies to send to the war front, which was never very far from home, and women frequently cared for wounded and hungry soldiers in their own houses. Both counties' newspapers gave complimentary reports of women's war work, and these can be read by clicking Newspapers: Transcriptions by Topic and Date.

With its deep, varied archival content on two counties, the Valley of the Shadow site allows online researchers to gain a sense of how women's war work took place in a society that saw respectable women's lives as properly suited for the domestic sphere only. Articles reporting on women's active relief work were accompanied by pieces such as this one, titled "A Wife!": "A wife! she must be the guardian angel of his footsteps on earth, and guide them to Heaven; so firm in virtue that should he for a moment waver, she can yield him support and place him upon its firm foundation; so happy in conscious innocence that, when from the perplexities of the whole world, he turns to his home, he may never find a frown where he sought a smile." These women, supposedly "so happy in conscious innocence," labored all day to care for wounded and hungry men and faced enemy soldiers at their doorsteps.

The population census database in the section titled The Eve of War provides another means to explore women's experience during the war. With occupational and economic data on every Augusta and Franklin County woman recorded in the 1860 census, this database can be searched by first or last name, race, gender, age, occupation, wealth, and birthplace.

The newspapers, letters and diaries, and public documents on the Valley of the Shadow site allow visitors to explore the Civil War experiences of women from a number of different perspectives. The content is largely archival, with material taken from microfilmed newspapers, documents in the University of Virginia Library, and local historical societies. There is little explanatory material, so some visitors may initially find the site overwhelming. But patient exploring will be rewarded with an excellent sense of women's Civil War experience.

CONTENT   ★ ★ ★ ★ ★
AESTHETICS   ★ ★ ★ ★ ★
NAVIGATION   ★ ★ ★ ★

Women and the Freedmen's Aid Movement, 1863–1891
http://womhist.binghamton.edu/aid/intro.htm

Part of the excellent site titled Women and Social Movements in the United States, 1830–1930, Women and the Freedmen's Aid Movement is the work of SUNY Geneseo history professor Carol Faulkner. The site opens by posing a question: "How did white women aid former slaves during and after the Civil War and what obstacles did they face?" Visitors are then invited either to read the introductory essay, which provides useful background information and many thought-provoking questions, or to proceed directly to an annotated list of eighteen documents. The documents are from the Freedmen's Bureau Records in the National Archives and from the Josephine White Griffing Papers at Columbia University.

Included in the documents is the 1864 appeal made by Freedmen's Bureau agent Josephine Griffing in the *Liberator* and other reform papers. In it, she described in vivid detail the suffering of thousands of freed people living as refugees in Washington, DC. The documents that follow trace the response of the Freedmen's Bureau to this unwelcome publicity. Jacob R. Shipherd of the Freedmen's Aid Commission wrote to the head of the Bureau, "Mrs. Griffing is simply irrepressible: & yet she must be repressed, so far as you & I have to do with her, or else we must bear the odium of her folly. She still represents the '20,000 utterly destitute' as needing outright support from northern charity. Located as she is, & endorsed by the head of the Bureau, she sends her appeal everywhere, to the glee of the copperheads, who want no better reading to confirm their 'I told you so!'" Alarmed at the public suggestion that the efforts of the Bureau and its allies were inadequate, the Bureau removed Griffing from its ranks and publicly denied her allegations.

The postwar letters between Griffing and Lucretia Mott express the women's frustration at their exclusion from freedmen's aid efforts. Mott described an argument she had had with the organizer of the "Reconstruction Union" being formed by Northern reformers: "I told him it was objected, that woman was ignored in their new organization, and if it really were a reconstruction for the nation, she ought not so to be, and that it would be rather humiliating for our anti-slavery women and Quaker women to consent to be thus overlooked." Other postwar documents include reports from Caroline Putney, a freedmen's teacher who remained in Virginia after the war to help African Americans there.

This site, with its excellent background material, well-chosen documents, and central unifying question, has immediate applications to the high-school and college-level classrooms. It is also of immense value to anyone seeking an understanding of how the Civil War gave women opportunities to play a role in public life at the same time that it reminded them of the limits to their influence.

CONTENT   ★ ★ ★ ★ ★
AESTHETICS   ★ ★ ★ ★
NAVIGATION   ★ ★ ★ ★ ★

SUGGESTED READINGS

Attie, Jeanie. *Patriotic Toil.* Ithaca, NY, 1998.

Clinton, Catherine, and Nina Silber, eds. *Divided Houses: Gender and the Civil War.* New York, 1992.

Faust, Drew Gilpin. *Mothers of Invention.* New York, 1997.

Ginzburg, Lori D. *Women and the Work of Benevolence: Morality, Politics, and Class in the Nineteenth-Century United States.* New Haven, CT, 1990.

Leonard, Elizabeth. *Yankee Women: Gender Battles in the Civil War.* New York, 1994.

———. *All the Daring of the Soldier: Women of the Civil War Armies.* New York, 1999.

Rable, George. *Civil War: Women and the Crisis of Southern Nationalism.* Urbana, IL, 1991.

Rose, Willie Lee. *Rehearsal for Reconstruction: The Port Royal Experiment.* Athens, GA, 1999.

CHAPTER 8

CIVIL
WAR
REGIMENTS

In the film *Gettysburg*, based on Michael Shaara's Pulitzer Prize–winning novel *The Killer Angels*, the 20th Maine almost single-handedly changes the course of the battle of Gettysburg. Americans love the idea that one regiment can make a decisive difference in the outcome of so large a battle as Gettysburg, which took place over three days of hard fighting and twenty-five square miles of ground. The idea appeals to our natural sense that a close band of soldiers might break through the chaos of a modern battle and that the smaller unit—the regiment—harbors our aspirations and glories.

The regiment was the basic fighting unit in the Civil War and its members often came from the same locality. In 1861 men rushed to sign up and join regiments that were forming in their area. Most expected a short war, full of quick glory and limited opportunity. These vigorous volunteers did not want to be left out of the fight. Volunteer and militia units went into service already organized. They boasted nicknames from before the war, such as the Palmetto Guards, the Fire Zouaves, the Floyd Rifles, and the Chambers Artillery. Often, the newly formed regiments took the name of their organizing captain or colonel. Regiments were sometimes formed by ethnicity in both North and South, as volunteers took great pride in their heritage. Examples include the fiery 6th Louisiana Irish Regiment and the stout 69th New York, which was a mostly Irish regiment.

Some states, particularly those along the border between the North and South, produced regiments for both the Confederacy and the

Union. Divided loyalties in an area were common. Virginia raised hundreds of regiments for the Confederacy, second in the Confederacy only to North Carolina in its proportion of white men enlisted in the army. Almost twenty regiments of Virginia soldiers fought for the Union, however. They came from the western areas of Virginia where unionism ran strong. The pattern was similar in Missouri, Kentucky, Maryland, Tennessee, and Illinois.

Each Civil War regiment consisted of approximately 1,000 men in ten companies, but units rarely fought at full strength. By the middle of the war, many regiments in both the Union and Confederate armies went into battle with fewer than 500 men. Diseases such as dysentery hospitalized and killed many new recruits, while medical discharges, leaves, and battle deaths further reduced the ranks in a short time.

Initially, officers of the regiment were elected in both Union and Confederate forces. A colonel commanded the regiment and a lieutenant colonel served as second in command. Each regimental commander had a staff of officers, including a surgeon, a chaplain, adjutants, quartermasters, and musicians. Captains commanded each of the ten companies in a regiment, and lieutenants served under them. The regiment fought as a part of a larger unit, the brigade, which was made up of four or five regiments. Three or four brigades formed a division, and two or more divisions constituted an army corps.

Enlistment in regiments ran high in the first year of the war, but began to slow as the war became perceived as less of a freewheeling jaunt and more of a hellish duty. The Confederacy was the first to use conscription to raise regiments. It declared that all able-bodied men between the ages of eighteen and thirty-five were required to serve three years. The volunteers who had already served a year had to remain in the army for two more. Some exemptions to the draft were allowed: state and Confederate officials, railroad employees, clergy, teachers, and eventually overseers of plantations. Substitutes were allowed as well, so richer men could pay another to serve, although the practice was outlawed in the Confederacy after a year. The North enacted a conscription law a year after the South did. The main purpose of these laws was to stimulate volunteering with the threat of a draft.

The regiments that were formed after 1862 differed markedly from their volunteer predecessors. In the North, draftees and new volunteers were brought into new units, not mixed in with depleted veteran units. These new units went into battle green and untested without experienced veterans among them to lead and guide them. In the South, however, the opposite practice developed. New recruits were interspersed with the remaining veterans in old units, bringing depleted units up to full strength. The practice of electing officers was abandoned, and the regiments became more professional.

Regimental histories of the war abound. Veterans published many memoirs, regimental accounts, diaries, and histories. Veterans' associations commissioned many histories as a way of ensuring the preservation of their unit's record. Sons of veterans followed these with regimental histories and edited accounts. Some examples of the wide range of regimental histories include Sam Watkins's fascinating *Co. Aytch*, John B. Gordon's overblown *Reminiscences of the Civil War*, and John Obreiter's turgid *The Seventy-seventh Pennsylvania at Shiloh*.

These veterans and writers might be surprised by how little their work is read or taken seriously by academics. Regimental histories, especially those commissioned by associations, tended to offer bland accounts of movement and abbreviated, generic battle descriptions, punctuated by lively, humorous stories of camp life or buffoonery on the march. Rarely did these histories cover tactics, overall strategy, the exact movement of troops in battle, or the emotions of the men involved in the actions. These histories had little to offer scholars of military history and even less to scholars of social history. As a result, regimental histories as a source of information and as a means of viewing the war have languished on library bookshelves, rarely checked out or loaned.

The World Wide Web offers a rich collection of regimental sites. Indeed, it has revived the genre of regimental history. Followers of a particular unit's history have produced online versions of what once were commonplace volumes. Surprisingly, sites for hundreds of units can be found online, with the obscure far outnumbering the well known. Individuals maintain most of these sites, which consequently vary in quality and sophistication. As a group, the sites impress any researcher with their dedication, attention to detail, and care for their subject. More significantly, most have moved beyond the limited usefulness of the old regimental histories and instead have created complex social and military histories.

 EB SITE REVIEWS

MASSACHUSETTS

The Harvard Regiment: 20th Regiment of Massachusetts Volunteer Infantry, 1861–1865

http://harvardregiment.org/

This site was created by an independent researcher at the University of Virginia to honor the men of the 20th Massachusetts Volunteer Infantry, which was known as the Harvard Regiment because of the preponderance of Harvard graduates among its officers. The 20th Massachusetts played a prominent role in most of the major battles of the eastern theater, including Fair Oaks/Seven Pines, Antietam, Fredericksburg, Chancellorsville, Gettysburg, and the Wilderness, and it lost more men than any other regiment from its state.

Secondary accounts of the 20th Massachusetts on this site include excerpts from William F. Fox's *Regimental Losses in the Civil War* and Frederick H. Dyer's *Compendium* as well as a summary of the unit's history written by the site designer. Key details in the summary are linked to explanatory notes elsewhere in the site. As the summary explains, the unit is most renowned for its contribution in two battles. At Fredericksburg, the regiment led a deadly advance through the streets of the town while under fierce fire from Confederate sharpshooters. At the Battle of Gettysburg, men of the 20th formed the front line against Confederate general George E. Pickett's famous July 3 charge. In addition to the general overviews, the site features biographical sketches of many of the officers, including future Supreme Court justice Oliver Wendell Holmes Jr., and Paul Revere, the grandson of the midnight rider.

The site also contains extensive primary sources. Many of these sources, such as *Official Records*, are in the public domain, and others come from manuscripts housed in the Boston Public Library that have been transcribed by the site's designer. The Letters page contains links to a variety of correspondence, including a letter written by General Robert E. Lee to thank Colonel W. Raymond Lee of the 20th Massachusetts for returning the sword of a Confederate officer who had died while in the custody of the 20th: "I have caused your kind and considerate communication to be transmitted to the father of the deceased, to whom I doubt not it will afford a great satisfaction to know that his son, in his last moments, enjoyed the care and attention of a humane and generous enemy." The documents also include several famous Memorial Day speeches given by Oliver Wendell Holmes Jr. after the war. In one, Holmes made his famous pronouncement about the men who fought for the Union: "The generation that carried on the war has been set apart by its experience. Through our great good fortune, in our youth our hearts were touched with fire."

The Battles page contains links to a variety of documents and secondary accounts about Ball's Bluff, Yorktown, Fair Oaks, Antietam, Chancellorsville, and Gettysburg, but the most dramatic accounts are of the Battle of Fredericksburg. A. W. Greeley, a member of the 19th Massachusetts who witnessed the 20th's desperate advance toward Caroline Street, wrote, "Thrown into platoon fronts I saw the 20th make this desperate march, with no definite end in view as far as anyone could see, into the most useless slaughter I ever witnessed. It was a wonderful display of orderly movement by a body of men of unsurpassed courage and coolness."

The Harvard Regiment web site does an excellent job of conveying the heroism and sacrifice made by the men of this famous unit.

CONTENT   ★ ★ ★ ★ ★
AESTHETICS   ★ ★ ★
NAVIGATION   ★ ★ ★ ★

28th Massachusetts Volunteer Infantry
http://www.28thmass.org/

A predominantly Irish regiment when it was raised in the fall of 1861, the 28th Massachusetts served in the Sea Islands of South Carolina and Georgia before engaging in its first major battle at Manassas in August 1862. At Fredericksburg, while attacking Marye's Heights, the regiment lost 38 percent of its men. By the end of the war, having participated in every major battle in the Eastern theater after the Peninsula Campaign, the 28th had suffered enough casualties to qualify for designation as one of the "Fighting 300" in historian William F. Fox's *Regimental Losses in the Civil War*.

In addition to a concise regimental history, this web site features the complete rosters for the regiment, providing name, occupation, enlistment date, and remarks for each man. The selected *Official Records* contained in the section titled Life in the 28th gives a sense of the regiment's combat experience, and a small collection of letters allows researchers to explore the stories of the men of the 28th in their own words. Private Dennis Ford's letter to his wife and neighbors shows how ethnic identity shaped the soldiers' sense of themselves and their regiment: "Do pray for us, we look shabby and thin, though we were called a clean regiment. I saw a great deal [of] shot and wounded. . . . Our regiment stood the severest fire that was witnessed. . . . [W]e ran through what we did not shoot. We bayoneted them. One man begged and got no mercy, a yankee ran him through. Thank God it was not an Irishman [who] did it." According to the notes accompanying the letter, Ford survived many more battles and spent several months as a prisoner of war. He returned to Massachusetts after his enlistment expired in December 1864.

One of the several impressive features of this site is the careful analysis of Irish-born Americans and the Civil War. The designer has devoted an entire section to this topic, describing immigration, Democratic Party allegiance, and the uneasy relationship between Irish and African American residents in Northern cities before the war. Confounding the expectations of many, Irishmen enlisted in great numbers during the war's early years. But by 1863 Lincoln's emancipation policy combined with general war weariness to create disaffection. Antiwar and antiblack sentiment peaked in the New York City draft riots of the summer of 1863. Still, the 28th Massachusetts and other members of the Irish Brigade fought fiercely through the entire war and made important contributions to the Union victory.

Sponsored by a 28th Massachusetts reenacting organization, this site is one of the few that clearly separates historic material from reenactment news. Easily navigated, it is a beautifully designed site with a great deal of interesting content.

CONTENT   ★ ★ ★ ★
AESTHETICS   ★ ★ ★ ★ ★
NAVIGATION   ★ ★ ★ ★ ★

MICHIGAN

NEW The Third Michigan Infantry Project

http://www.oldthirdmichigan.org/

This web site offers the user a lively, easily browsable, and informative account of the Civil War experience of the men who served in the 3rd Michigan Infantry— a unit that fought in just about every major campaign in the Eastern theater. The History page provides an excellent, if brief, summary of the wartime experience of this unit. Users who want more detailed information can click links embedded in the text. For example, the History page states that in 1862 the unit fought at Malvern Hill, Second Bull Run, and Fredericksburg. Clicking "1862" opens a new browser window that shows practically every movement taken by the unit in that year. This new window informs the user that early in the Peninsula Campaign, one company was assigned to manufacture lumber in Yorktown and that as the campaign progressed, the 3rd Michigan saw action in the battles of Williamsburg and Fair Oaks as well as Malvern Hill.

The site's designer takes an even more innovative approach in the pages titled "Regiment" and "Men." The Regiment page is simply a series of bullet points with key terms linked to more details. One bullet point states merely that 253 men died. Clicking the word "died," however, opens a window that provides a grim breakdown of this number by year, cause, and battle. If we add the deaths of men who died of wounds after they were discharged or while they were serving in other units (the 3rd Michigan was mustered out in 1864, but many reenlisted), the number rises to a "probable total dead of 382." The Men page presents the information in a series of thirteen questions and answers. Clicking "What were their religious preferences?" opens a pop-up window that reports that of the men for whom they have records, sixty were Protestant, eighteen were Catholic, two were Universalist, one was Jewish, and one was a Christian Scientist.

But it is here that the site will leave many visitors unsatisfied. Who were the eighteen Catholics, and were they concentrated in the same company? What records were consulted to find this information? The site provides no bibliography and no primary sources that would allow the user to delve deeper into the experience of this unit.

This significant drawback aside, this site should still be examined by anyone considering building a web site about a military unit. Its elegant design and lively manner of presenting a daunting amount of information are certainly worth emulating.

CONTENT   ★ ★ ★
AESTHETICS   ★ ★ ★ ★ ★
NAVIGATION   ★ ★ ★ ★ ★

NEW YORK

5th New York Volunteer Infantry: Duryée's Zouaves
http://www.zouave.org/

The 5th New York Volunteer Infantry was one of dozens of Zouave regiments fighting on both sides in the American Civil War. This web site, sponsored by a 5th New York reenacting group, provides both a thorough account of the Zouave craze that swept the divided nation in 1861 and an excellent history of the 5th New York.

According to the site's designer, French Zouave units, inspired by the distinctive garb worn by Algerian and Moroccan fighters, were first formed during the reign of Louis Napoleon. During the Crimean War, these Zouave units received a great deal of coverage in the American press. Illinois politician Elmer Ephraim Ellsworth raised a militia based on the Zouave model that toured the country in the 1850s, inspiring imitators in its wake. At the beginning of the Civil War, Ellsworth raised a new Zouave regiment in New York and led it against secessionist strongholds in Alexandria, Virginia, where he was shot. The first Union officer killed in the war, Ellsworth became an instant martyr, inspiring the creation of numerous Zouave regiments across the Union.

One of these units was the 5th New York Volunteer Infantry, also known as Duryée's Zouaves. Composed of men from New York City, Long Island, and Poughkeepsie, the unit's first major engagement was at Gaines's Mill, part of the Seven Days battles near Richmond. The regiment also faced enemy fire at the Second Battle of Manassas, where more than half the unit was killed or wounded. Replenished with new recruits, Duryée's Zouaves fought at Antietam, Fredericksburg, and Chancellorsville before the men's enlistment terms expired.

In addition to the fascinating history, the 5th New York Volunteer Infantry site features an image gallery, a list of all the men who fought, and an account of the many reunions that took place after the war. Although not strong in terms of documentary content, this is a well-made site that deserves a visit.

CONTENT   ★ ★ ★ ★
AESTHETICS   ★ ★ ★ ★
NAVIGATION   ★ ★ ★ ★ ★

PENNSYLVANIA

77th Pennsylvania Volunteers: On the March

http://jefferson.village.virginia.edu/vshadow2/HIUS403/77pa/main.html

As the only regiment from Franklin County, Pennsylvania, that did not fight in the Eastern theater during the Civil War, the 77th Pennsylvania Volunteers received little of the public attention given to other units from that state. This innovative web site, created as a class project by a group of students at the University of Virginia, corrects this imbalance by making the rich record of this unit available to the public.

Visitors may want to start with the Timeline page, which is divided into The War and The Regiment, because it outlines the larger context of the regiment's activities. The timeline reveals that in the same month (February 1862) that the 77th Pennsylvania was marching through Kentucky on its way to Pittsburg Landing, Jefferson Davis was sworn in as the president of the Confederate States of America. The timeline takes the unit through the entire war and beyond. In May 1865, a month after Lee's surrender at Appomattox, the 77th boarded a steamer for Texas, where the troops were on duty until the beginning of 1866.

The site presents a variety of options for exploring certain aspects of the experience of the 77th Pennsylvania Volunteers in greater detail. The map on the home page serves as a gateway to collections of documents about the unit's activities in those regions. Clicking Chickamauga takes the visitor to photographs, maps, and a list of casualties printed in the unit's hometown newspaper. At the bottom of the home page is a link for the Documents section, which contains letters, newspaper articles, and official military documents. The documents include letters from the Compiled Military Service Records at the National Archives (which have been scanned but not transcribed). One of these letters is an 1866 appeal from Private H. Metchley that his name be cleared of the desertion charges against him. Documents also include the record of death for Adam Lautenschlager, a German-born 18-year-old resident of Chambersburg, Pennsylvania, who was killed by a gunshot wound to the knee at Murfreesboro, Tennessee.

The most sophisticated feature of the 77th Pennsylvania web site is the searchable database, which contains the records of all the men from Franklin County who enlisted in Union regiments. The database can be queried in countless ways. A search for all the men in the 77th whose records indicate that they died of disease resulted in eleven matches, including John Wetzel, who was captured at Chickamauga and who died at Andersonville Prison a year later. Five men in the database died of their wounds, and seven were killed in action, including Captain John A. Walker, shot during the campaign for Atlanta.

This site, drawn largely from local newspapers and National Archives records, successfully portrays the experience of a group of Pennsylvania men drawn far from their homes to defend the Union. With rich material tucked away in every corner, it invites hours of exploration.

CONTENT   ★ ★ ★ ★ ★
AESTHETICS   ★ ★ ★ ★ ★
NAVIGATION   ★ ★ ★

TENNESSEE

20th (Russell's) Tennessee Cavalry
http://home.olemiss.edu/~cmprice/cav.html

The 20th Tennessee Cavalry was formed in late 1863 by West Tennessee veterans whose original terms had ended or who had deserted their infantry regiments, and it fought under Lieutenant General Nathan Bedford Forrest in the Confederate Department of Alabama, Mississippi, and East Louisiana. This thorough online history of the 20th Tennessee Cavalry was created by a professor at the University of Mississippi.

The home page includes a detailed table of contents and a brief summary of the history of the 20th Tennessee Cavalry. Key terms on this page are linked to explanatory notes, maps, and images. From the home page, visitors can choose a number of ways to learn more about the experience of this regiment. The most helpful starting point is the Chronology of Movements and Activities, which lists recruiting and organizational developments along with troop movements and engagements with the enemy. The regiment's first major engagement was in Estenula, Tennessee, in the winter of 1863. The following spring, the 20th participated in the Confederate capture of Fort Pillow. Although the designer of the site does not recount the controversy over the Confederates' firing on retreating Union soldiers, many of whom were African American, the description of Fort Pillow features a link to the National Park Service Battle Summaries site that does present a few basic facts about the controversy. The chronology follows the unit into Mississippi and Alabama, where it engaged in numerous small skirmishes as well as in major attacks on the Union positions in Tennessee at Franklin and Nashville.

The Biographical Notes section covers officers and enlisted men alike. For each member of the regiment, the information from the Compiled Military Service Record is provided. For example, the following is found for D. F. Bullock, of Company K: he enlisted in the 20th Cavalry on May 1, 1863, with a bay horse valued at $1,100. Although present on both muster rolls recorded for 1863, Bullock's name appeared on the list of absentees and deserters made on February 28, 1865.

The site has few images and makes minimal use of colors. But the 20th Tennessee Cavalry site compensates for its utilitarian design with extensive documentary content and careful editing. It is extremely informative and worth a long visit.

CONTENT   ★ ★ ★ ★
AESTHETICS   ★ ★ ★
NAVIGATION   ★ ★ ★ ★

TEXAS

Official Historic Website of the 10th Texas Infantry
http://members.aol.com/SMckay1234/

This site, created by a private historian and reenactor, invites online researchers to construct a history of the 10th Texas Infantry, which saw action in Arkansas, Georgia, and Tennessee in 1863 and 1864. Rosters, letters, and official military correspondence make this one of the best sites for documentary content on a Confederate unit.

Visitors may want to start by going to the Battle Reports section and skimming the contents to see when and where the 10th Texas Infantry operated. Clicking the name of a battle accesses a detailed report of the unit's actions there. One of the more interesting reports is the one for Tunnel Hill, Tennessee, which was defended from attacking Union forces during the Battle of Chattanooga. The anonymous author of the report, which was printed in the *Memphis Daily Appeal*, wrote to exonerate the 10th Infantry and other units in his command from the Confederate disaster there: "To sum up—we lost no prisoners, lost no artillery, held our position against five times our numbers, took two hundred prisoners and five stands of colors, repulsed the enemy and charged them twice from our works, driving them from the field. That night we crossed the Chickamauga, learning . . . every where of our disaster at other points on the line." Other battles covered in the Battle Reports section include Chickamauga, Pickett's Mill, Atlanta, and Franklin. Many of the reports are accompanied by links to additional information about that battle, such as casualty lists, letters, and ordnance records.

The site features an impressive collection of transcribed personal papers that have been assembled in chronological order. Some of the documents in this section have been contributed by descendents of members of the original regiment. Others are previously published works, and still others have been located in different repositories by the site's designer. One letter, written by First Lieutenant Overton F. Davenport to his brother in December 1863, echoes the defensiveness of the Tunnel Hill report that appeared in the *Memphis Appeal*: "I notice that the papers give all the credit of the fight on Missionary Ridge on the right to the 2nd Tenn & 5th Arkansas. I like to see honor given to whom honor is due but our Brigade done the fighting that day on the right the others might have done equally as well if they had been there but they were held in reserve & I never saw them on the field & if they are to receive the honor, I would like for them to share the danger."

Additional contents on the 10th Texas Infantry site include rosters, casualty lists, and ordnance reports. The rosters list the men by company, and since each company was recruited from a particular Texas county, the men in each company were likely to be neighbors. For each man, the rosters provide the rank, age, date of enlistment, and "remarks." The Official Historic Website of the 10th Texas Infantry is one of the few regimental history sites that feature casualty reports that give the name of men killed, wounded, or captured during every engagement. Interesting details from personal papers and published accounts have been inserted into the lists. Ordnance reports, filed by officers after every engagement to record the loss of equipment, allow researchers to see the kinds of rifles and ammunition the men of the 10th used. After the Battle of Tunnel Hill, Captain Jonathan Kennard recorded the following losses:

103 Austrian Rifles, Cal. 54
14 Mississippi Rifles, Cal. 54
204 Rifle Bayonets
104 Cartridge Boxes
112 Cap Boxes
122 Waist Belts & Plates
153 C B Belts
224 Bayonet Scabbards
31 Knapsacks
144 Haversacks
56 Canteens & Straps
8 Ammunition Boxes

Innovative and extensive use of primary sources on this site compensates for distracting background images and proofreading errors. Anyone seeking a deep understanding of the experience of a Confederate infantry unit will be well served by a visit to this interesting site.

CONTENT	★ ★ ★ ★ ★	
AESTHETICS	★ ★ ★	
NAVIGATION	★ ★ ★ ★ ★	

U.S. COLORED TROOPS

5th Regimental Cavalry, United States Colored Troops

http://mywebpages.comcast.net/5thuscc/

See Chapter 5 for a description

WISCONSIN

The 26th Wisconsin Infantry Volunteers

http://www.russscott.com/~rscott/26thwis/

This site, sponsored by the Sons of the 26th Wisconsin Infantry Volunteers, is a compelling documentary account of the 26th Wisconsin Infantry. Composed primarily of German immigrants, the 26th Wisconsin fought at Chancellorsville, Gettysburg, and Atlanta, and it participated in Sherman's March to the Sea. Heavy casualties suffered by the unit during these battles and campaigns led William F. Fox, in his influential *Regimental Losses in the Civil War*, to include the 26th Wisconsin in his "Fighting 300." Only four other units lost a greater proportion of men.

The section titled History opens with an illustrated summary of the 26th Wisconsin's Civil War record, with key terms linked to other pages on the site or to outside sites. Clicking Day to Day History accesses a chronological compilation of excerpts from letters, diaries, reports, and newspaper articles. On August 13, 1862, for example, the *Milwaukee Sentinel* printed this announcement: " 'GERMAN AMERICANS' FOR GEN. SIGEL'S COMMAND. All are invited, without regard to nationality, to serve under that gallant commander. F. C. Winkler, Francis Lackner, Chas. Doerflinger, Louis C. Heide and others are combining their efforts to raise a first rate company. Fall in for the army of Virginia!" On the same day, Karl Karsten wrote in his diary, "I signed up as a solder for the U.S.A. for three years." In addition to this innovative timeline, the material in History also includes a reprint of a regimental history written in 1866, the memoirs of Generals Carl Schurz and Oliver Otis Howard, and descriptions of rifles used by the men of the 26th.

Visitors who choose to go directly to the documents themselves can read the Letters/Diaries, Documents, or Newspaper section. One of the letters was written by Adam Muenzenberger to his wife. Muenzenberger, along with many others in his unit, was captured at the Battle of Gettysburg and held at Richmond's Libby Prison, where he died a few months later. The letters in this section have been transcribed from the originals in the University of Wisconsin Milwaukee Library, the Wisconsin State Historical Society, and other sources. Documents include the *Official Records* for the Battle of Chancellorsville, the Battle of Gettysburg, and the Atlanta and Savannah campaigns. Writing from North Carolina in March 1865, Captain Fred Winkler recorded the damage his Wisconsin men had inflicted on the Southern countryside: "The whole amount taken from the country may be about as follows: Eight hundred pounds of wheat flour, 4,000 pounds of corn meal, 550 bushels of sweet potatoes, 13,000 pounds of meat, 900 pounds of lard, 150 pounds of dried fruit."

The site's newspaper transcriptions show how leaders jealously protected their units' reputations. Major General Franz Sigel wrote to the *Wisconsin Daily* in November 1862 that rumors of the 26th's cowardice at Thoroughfare Gap were entirely false: "The whole story about throwing away arms . . . is a most malicious and infamous missticket [*sic*] misrepresentation and lie, brought up by some treacherous scoundrel."

The 26th Wisconsin site has augmented the traditional rosters featured in most regimental web sites. In addition to providing the rank, company, place enlisted, and "remarks" for every member of the regiment, the Interactive Roster links many men's names to documents, photographs, and biographical narratives. Clicking the name of Henry Fink, a private in Company B, reveals that Fink was a Milwaukee store clerk before the war. After his discharge due to wounds received at Chancellorsville, Fink became a traveling salesman and later was active in state politics and veterans' organizations.

The memoirs linked to Major General Oliver Otis Howard's name in the roster list shed light on the centrality of ethnicity in recruitment and command. Since Howard's appointment as commander of the 11th Corps was accompanied by the demotion of German-born commanders Franz Sigel and Carl Schurz, there was resentment in the ranks. Howard wrote, "The corps . . . had about 5,000 Germans and 8,000 Americans. . . . Outwardly I met a cordial reception, but I soon found that my past record was not known here; that there was much complaint in the German language at the removal of Sigel."

The 26th Wisconsin is an excellent model of a regimental web site. Rich and extensive documents and secondary narrative are creatively linked in ways that invite visitors to explore for hours.

CONTENT   ★ ★ ★ ★
AESTHETICS   ★ ★ ★
NAVIGATION   ★ ★ ★

SUGGESTED READINGS

Driver, Robert J. *The First and Second Rockbridge Artillery.* Virginia Regimental Histories Series. Appomattox, VA, 1987.

——. *Fourteenth Virginia Cavalry.* Virginia Regimental Histories Series. Appomattox, VA, 1988.

——. *First Virginia Cavalry.* Virginia Regimental Histories Series. Appomattox, VA, 1991.

Dyer, Frederick H. *A Compendium of the War of the Rebellion.* 1908. Reprint. Dayton, OH, 1979.

Fox, William F. *Regimental Losses in the Civil War.* 1898. Reprint. Dayton, OH, 1993.

Gaff, Alan D. *On Many a Bloody Field: Four Years in the Iron Brigade.* Bloomington, IN, 1997.

Gordon, John B. *Reminiscences of the Civil War.* 1888. Reprint. Baton Rouge, LA, 1993.

Hagerty, Edward J. *Collis' Zouaves: The 114th Pennsylvania Volunteers in the Civil War.* Baton Rouge, LA, 1997.

Johansson, M. Jane. *Peculiar Honor: A History of the 28th Texas Cavalry, 1862–1865.* Fayetteville, AR, 1998.

Krick, Robert E. L. *40th Virginia Infantry.* Virginia Regimental Histories Series. Appomattox, VA, 1985.

McGowen, Stanley S. *Horse Sweat and Powder Smoke: The First Texas Cavalry in the Civil War.* Texas A & M University Military History Series, no. 66. College Station, TX, 1999.

Miller, Edward A., Jr. *The Black Civil War Soldiers of Illinois: The Story of the Twenty-ninth U.S. Colored Infantry.* Columbia, SC, 1998.

Morris, W. S., L. D. Hartwell, and J. B. Kuykendall. *History 31st Regiment Illinois Volunteers Organized by John A. Logan.* Carbondale, IL, 1998.

Morrison, Marion, and John Y. Simon. *A History of the Ninth Regiment Illinois Volunteer Infantry, with the Regimental Roster.* Carbondale, IL, 1997.

Mullholland, St. Clair A. *The Story of the 116th Regiment: Pennsylvania Volunteers in the War of Rebellion.* New York, 1996.

Norman, Douglas Hale. *The Third Texas Cavalry in the Civil War.* Norman, OK, 1992.

Obreiter, John. *The Seventy-seventh Pennsylvania at Shiloh—History of the Regiment—The Battle of Shiloh*. Harrisburg, PA, 1905.

Overmyer, Jack K. *A Stupendous Effort: The 87th Indiana in the War of the Rebellion*. Bloomington, IN, 1997.

Washington, Versalle F. *Eagles on Their Buttons: A Black Infantry Regiment in the Civil War*. Shades of Blue and Gray Series. Columbia, MO, 1999.

Watkins, Sam R. *Co. Aytch: A Confederate's Memoir of the Civil War*. 1880. Reprint. New York, 1997.

Wilkinson, Warren. *Mother, May You Never See the Sights I Have Seen: The Fifty-seventh Massachusetts Veteran Volunteers in the Army of the Potomac, 1864–1865*. New York, 1990.

CHAPTER 9

GENERAL HISTORY, HISTORIC DOCUMENTS, LINKS, AND ONLINE BOOKSTORE SITES

The previous eight chapters in this book focused on specific topical themes within the broad field of American Civil War studies and reviewed web sites particularly helpful for researching them. This chapter reviews sites that do not fall neatly into any of the earlier categories but that nonetheless deserve commendation. These sites are grouped into four types: general history, historic documents, links primarily to Civil War sites, and online bookstores.

GENERAL HISTORY

Oriented toward the typical history enthusiast, general history sites display neither the quirky individualism nor the scholarly edge that characterizes most of the sites reviewed in this book. The two sites discussed here are made by for-profit organizations and have a distinctly commercial air, with animated banner advertisements for products ranging from Chevy trucks to miniature historical figurines. Covering ancient, medieval, and modern history, the range of these sites is quite broad. Nonetheless, their content on the American Civil War is deep enough to warrant a visit.

WEB SITE REVIEWS

NEW **Ehistory**

http://www.ehistory.com

Clearly lacking the huge financial resources behind the History Channel site (reviewed below), the makers of Ehistory.com have nevertheless embarked on an ambitious undertaking. According to its mission statement, the site consists of "over 130,000 pages of historical content; 4,000 timeline events; 400 battle outlines; 300 biographies; and thousands of images and maps." Certainly, its Civil War content alone would probably make it one of the biggest history endeavors on the web.

The Civil War tab on the horizontal bar near the top of the home page takes users to a page of links to various material, some of which is clearly better than others. A section titled Battles starts with a clickable U.S. map with key states linked to timelines and brief descriptions of the military events there. The format, scholarship, and level of detail in these descriptions vary widely. Some appear to be copied from the National Park Service Battle Summaries site; others are simply short paragraphs with no attribution whatsoever. The *Official Records* section is just that, with the added bonus of a good search function. The Images link on the Civil War page merely takes the user to a search box. Entering the term Manassas yielded eleven photographs of the battlefield, all of which seemed to be scanned from Francis T. Miller's *Photographic History of the Civil War*. Unfortunately, beyond titles such as "The Lost Chance. Confederate Fortifications at Manassas," no explanatory material accompanies the photographs. The Civil War section titled Articles consists of essays on topics such as the 1913 reunion of veterans at the Gettysburg battlefield. They appear to have been written by Ehistory.com's staff of writers as well as by lay historians.

The site's more valuable material can be found in its Letters and Diaries, Glossary, and Civil War Medicine sections. The Follet Collection presents the correspondence of an Illinois family that sent three sons to fight for the Union. All three men saw action in the Western theater, and at least one died of his wounds. Visitors can view high-quality scans, thumbnail summaries, and full-text transcriptions of each letter. Another valuable section of Ehistory's Civil War content is the glossary, which defines military terms such as *brevet* and *epaulement* as well as common nineteenth-century words such as *encomium* and *marplot*. Finally, the site's Civil War Medicine section is a true gem. It features a useful overview of the topic as well as more detailed discussions on dentistry and surgery.

CONTENT   ★ ★ ★
AESTHETICS   ★ ★ ★
NAVIGATION   ★ ★ ★

NEW The History Channel

http://www.historychannel.com

Given the popularity of the American Civil War, it is surprising that the History Channel web site does not feature an easy-to-find, distinct page with an overview of all of its content on the topic. But apparently the only way to locate Civil War material (beyond This Day in Civil War History on the home page) is to use the site's search function.

Typing "civil war" in the search box will provide the user with a list of links, the first of which is labeled simply Civil War. Clicking this link takes the user to a series of essays by James McPherson and Stephen W. Sears, two of the most well-known and highly regarded scholars of the war. Links from their articles take the user to pieces by various authors on more detailed topics such as Robert E. Lee and the U.S. Sanitary Commission. Visitors who have read the Civil War articles in the *Reader's Companion to American History* will find that these essays have a familiar ring—indeed, the site credits this source and has apparently reprinted entire articles from it.

There are no Civil War primary sources on HistoryChannel.com, and the articles read much like the excellent reference book from which they were taken. But what it lacks in originality and depth it makes up for in the scholarly credentials of its contributors and in its selection of topics to discuss. The Civil War essays on this site provide an excellent "state of the scholarship" overview of the conflict. In fact, anyone not already well versed in the field should probably visit this site before embarking on any online (or traditional) research.

CONTENT   ★ ★ ★ ★
AESTHETICS   ★ ★ ★
NAVIGATION   ★ ★

HISTORIC DOCUMENTS

The value of historic documents web sites will be immediately apparent to anyone who has ever embarked on the cumbersome process of historical research in a traditional library or archive. Locating and reading old *New York Times* articles, for example, requires looking up terms in dusty bound indexes for every year of interest and jotting down a list of dates and page numbers. Researchers must then locate the appropriate microfilm roll and thread it through a functioning microfilm reader/printer. Printing articles usually requires toting a small treasury of nickels, dimes, or quarters, since printing is almost never free and change is rarely available. And the quality of the microfilm photography is often so poor that it is next to impossible to read the actual words of many articles.

True manuscript research is even more labor-intensive. Getting to the repository of interest seems always to require at least several hours of travel, so researchers generally set out before sunrise in order to start their work when the repository's doors open. Entrance to the research room requires displaying several pieces of identification and leaving personal possessions in a locker. After submitting the request for documents, researchers must wait quietly at a table with nothing but the dull pencils and colored paper the staff has provided. Eventually, boxes of documents are wheeled over. Under the watchful gaze of the staff, researchers pull the precious and fragile paper from the folders one by one and spend the rest of the day squinting to decipher faded ancient handwriting.

Early web enthusiasts predicted that the Internet would render microfilm obsolete and make every historical document that has been locked away in archives and manuscripts libraries available to anyone with an Internet hookup. But the high cost of scanning, transcribing, and indexing archival material has prevented this vision from becoming a reality. To date, only a tiny fraction of historic American documents has been made available over the Internet. And this is not necessarily bad. Any lover of history would agree that even the most advanced technology could never replace the excitement of real manuscript research, although it is likely that few researchers would miss microfilm.

But lovers of history will also greatly appreciate the sites reviewed here. Professional and casual scholars alike have been greatly served by these efforts by universities and government agencies to place at their fingertips, in the comfort of their own offices and homes, the raw materials of their craft.

WEB SITE REVIEWS

NEW *Congressional Globe*

http://memory.loc.gov/ammem/amlaw/lwcg.html

For the past decade, the Library of Congress has photographed, transcribed, and laboriously indexed hundreds of thousands of historic documents and made them freely available on its American Memory Collection web site. American Memory includes everything from ballroom dance instruction manuals to the papers of Samuel F. B. Morse. Four of its collections are particularly valuable to researchers on the Civil War: Selected Civil War Photographs, the Abraham Lincoln Papers, and the African American Odyssey, all of which are reviewed elsewhere in Part I in this book, and *Congressional Globe*, reviewed here. The *Congressional Globe* is part of a larger collection titled *A Century of Lawmaking for a New Nation*, which also features the *Journals of the Continental Congress*, *American State Papers*, and the *Congressional Record*.

As the official printer of congressional debates from 1833 to 1873, the *Globe* recorded the words of Henry Clay, John C. Calhoun, and Daniel Webster as they argued over the Compromise of 1850, the barbs traded by William H. Seward and Stephen Douglas over the Kansas-Nebraska Act, and the impassioned addresses of Thaddeus Stevens and Charles Sumner as they laid out their plans for reconstructing the defeated South. The *Globe* also contains historically interesting debates on topics now largely forgotten by men barely remembered.

Using this digital version of the *Congressional Globe* is remarkably similar to working with the physical volumes themselves. Researchers are generally best served by first identifying the session of Congress in which they are interested and then starting with the Index to the Debates and the Index to the Appendix. Although fully transcribed, the indexes are only searchable via the browser's find function. Searching the Index to the Debates for the Thirty-first Congress (1849–1850) by the word "slavery" naturally led to numerous matches, one of which was in this entry: "remarks on the petition against the extension of slavery to the Territories, . . . 343." By scrolling up from that obscure entry, one learns that this is a reference to a remark by South Carolina senator Andrew P. Butler. To read the actual address, users must return to the table of contents, click the link for the House and Senate Debates for that Congress, enter the page number (343) into the search box, and wait a few seconds for a scanned page containing Butler's words to appear:

Sir, I have some petitions to offer which require immediate action; for, if they are not acted upon now, or at a very early period, that action will answer no purpose. And yet, every morning the gentleman representing a minority monopolizes the whole time of this Senate by resolutions such as this, producing nothing but mischief, without rebuke, and it would almost seem with the countenance of those who vote for his resolutions. Can this be tolerated? That the time of the Senate, the Legislature of the United States, should be appropriated by mischievous incendiaries, who claim the right of introducing petitions, resolutions, memorials, and propositions of this kind to the Senate?

The most significant navigational advance that this web site has over the paper volumes is the index of page headings. This one-page alphabetical list of links starts with "Abolition and Slavery—Mr. C. Brown (House of Representatives)" and ends with "Wool and Woollens—Mr. Collamer (House of Representatives)." The items on the list are linked to the actual pages of the debates with that heading. Although it seems unfair to criticize such a Herculean effort for not doing even more, one cannot help but regret that the entries on this index of page headings are not accompanied by such minimal additional information as the year or the Congress in which the debate took place.

With neither full-text searchability nor topical indexes with terms familiar to the novice researcher, this site will probably be extensively used only by scholars already familiar with the physical version of the source. But energetic readers of popular Civil War histories may find this site to be a wonderful supplement to their personal libraries. For example, James McPherson's *Battle Cry of Freedom* excerpts two sentences from William H. Seward's famous speech about popular sovereignty in Kansas: "Since there is no escaping your challenge, I accept it on behalf of the cause of freedom. We will engage in competition for the virgin soil of Kansas, and God give victory to the side which is stronger in numbers as it is in right." The bottom of the page cites "CG, 33 Cong., 1 Sess., Appendix, 769." Armed with this citation, readers can go to the *Congressional Globe* site, navigate directly to the beginning of Seward's address, and read the speech in its entirety.

CONTENT   ★ ★ ★ ★ ★
AESTHETICS   ★ ★ ★ ★
NAVIGATION   ★ ★

NEW **Documenting the American South: The Southern Homefront, 1861–1865**
http://docsouth.dsi.internet2.edu/imls/index.html

Intended to help researchers study Southern life during the Civil War, this web site features hundreds of items including poems and novels ("belles lettres"), business records, official Confederate and state government documents, maps, broadsides, illustrations and photographs, letters and diaries, schoolbooks, and sermons and religious tracts.

The sermons are particularly interesting, because they show a conscious effort to imbue the Confederate cause with a moral purpose. On a national day of fasting and prayer, the Reverend Stephen Elliot delivered this prayer from the pulpit of Christ Church, Savannah: "Cover the heads of our soldiers in the day of battle, and send thy fear before them that our enemies may flee at their presence. Establish us in the rights thou hast given us, in our Government and in our Laws, in our Religion, and in all our holy Ministries."

Other interesting documents illustrate Southerners' sense of their emerging nationhood. "The Proceedings of the Convention of Teachers of the Confederate States" resolved to end the South's "dependence for books, for teachers and for manufacturers on those who now seek our subjugation" and "to encourage and foster a spirit of home enterprise and self-reliance." This sense of nationhood was particularly apparent in Richmond. Guides were written to orient Southerners to their new capital, with every office and landmark carefully documented. "The Stranger's Guide and Official Directory for the City of Richmond" promised readers a convenient resource for finding their way around the city. (It also promised would-be advertisers that it would "command the attention of all strangers visiting Richmond, either for pleasure or profit.")

There is far more in this site than would interest most researchers. Although all of the documents date from the Civil War, they are not all about the war per se. But the site's breadth reminds researchers that even in the South, the war did not dominate every aspect of life. Old concerns did not suddenly evaporate, as is shown in "A Controversy Between 'Erskine' And 'W. M.' On The Practicability Of Suppressing Gambling," published in 1862.

CONTENT   ★ ★ ★ ★
AESTHETICS   ★ ★ ★
NAVIGATION   ★ ★ ★

NEW **DOUGLASS: Archive of American Public Address**
http://douglassarchives.org/

Northwestern University has created this online archive primarily for students in its American rhetorical history classes. The site has full-text transcriptions of about one hundred famous speeches from American history, starting with John Winthrop's 1625 "On Liberty" and concluding with George W. Bush's address to the nation nine days after the September 11, 2001, terrorist attacks. Recognizing that students at Northwestern may need a factual background to provide the context for the speeches they are reading, the creators of this site have made the United States Information Office's *An Outline of American History* available on the site as well.

The Civil War collection of speeches on DOUGLASS, while not extensive, provides a good introduction to primary sources of the era. The best way to access the Civil War material is to click "Chronologically" under the "Browse on-site speeches and documents" heading. This link will take the user to an index of documents that includes two speeches from Lincoln's early political career in Illinois as well as the famous 1860 Cooper Institute Address, the Gettysburg Address, and both inaugural speeches. Other documents of interest to Civil War scholars include Frederick Douglass's 1860 "A Plea for Free Speech in Boston" and the following *Richmond Dispatch* item on the first flag of the Confederacy: "We knew the flag we had to fight, yet instead of getting as far from it, we were guilty of the huge mistake of getting as near to it as possible." Each speech is accompanied by a short introduction that explains its significance and provides historical context.

CONTENT   ★ ★ ★
AESTHETICS   ★ ★ ★ ★
NAVIGATION   ★ ★ ★ ★

NEW The Historical *New York Times* Project

http://www.nyt.ulib.org

The Historical *New York Times* Project is part of the Universal Library, an ambitious undertaking based at Carnegie Mellon University. The web site consists of digital reproductions of every edition of the *New York Times* published from 1860 to 1866. By entering a date into the navigation form on the left side of the screen, users can navigate to the first page of the issue they are interested in. A "next page" function then allows users to scroll page by page, as if they were using microfilm or reading the actual paper. A zoom feature (indicated by a magnifying glass) allows users to see a section of the paper at higher magnification.

But users will find themselves straining to decipher the words even at this higher level of detail. The images, apparently photographs of microfilm rather than of the original newspaper, are extremely difficult to read. Fortunately, the site's creators have also made even larger versions of several dozen selected articles, which are indexed both by year (1860–1865) and topic (battles, military, politics, relations among the states, social issues). These selected articles can be read with little effort.

What does the Historical *New York Times* Project give us over the microfilm version of the paper? It is certainly an advance in terms of accessibility. Many public and school libraries do not have the historical *New York Times* on microfilm, so this site might provide the only means for researchers in many areas to read this important source. It is also superior in navigation. Entering the date of the paper of interest is certainly more convenient than locating the appropriate microfilm roll, searching for a working microfilm reader, and rolling through the reel to find the particular issue. Finally, the selected clippings indexed by year and topic make it easy for researchers to quickly locate articles on the key events of the Civil War. Harried students facing tough research assignments would be well served by utilizing this feature.

At the time this review was written, the site had neither a complete index of articles (available in any library that has the microfilm) nor full-text searchability. And there is no easy way to print sections of the full-page scans. These drawbacks, however minor, will still make many researchers prefer a trip to the nearest decent library.

CONTENT   ★ ★ ★ ★
AESTHETICS   ★ ★ ★
NAVIGATION   ★ ★ ★ ★

NEW **Secession Era Editorials Project**
http://history.furman.edu/~benson/docs/

Nineteenth-century newspapers made no pretense of objectivity; in fact, their editors tended to produce some of the most partisan and sectional rhetoric of the antebellum era. The hundreds of transcriptions featured on this site, created by Furman University professor Lloyd Benson, allow researchers to see for themselves how the press fanned the flames of discord in the 1850s.

At times, party trumped geography in determining a paper's position. In its commentary on South Carolina representative Preston Brooks's attack on Massachusetts Republican senator Charles Sumner, the *Democratic Illinois State Register* wrote, "we cannot but believe that the nation will say that Sumner got no more than he deserved." Similarly, several editors blamed John Brown's raid not on Mr. Brown, abolitionists, or slavery, but on the opposing party. The *Evening Journal*, a Republican paper printed in Albany, New York, held the Democrats responsible, asking rhetorically, "Who taught that crazy crew to band together . . . ? The Border Ruffians of Kansas and the Democratic Administration at Washington!" In turn, the Democratic *Nashville Tennessee Union and American* wrote that "the fanatics engaged [at Harpers Ferry] would never have dared the attempt at insurrection but for the inflammatory speeches and writings of Seward, Greeley, and the other Republican leaders."

Yet sectional voices are by far the most evident. Responding to the Dred Scott decision, the *Evening Journal* editorialized that the decision was "a new shackle for the North . . . handed to the servile Supreme Court, to rivet upon us." The pages of the fiery *Charleston South Carolina Mercury* blazed forth in kind, arguing that the decision proved that "every principle on which the North has assailed us and sought to repress us in the exercise of our rights . . . is false in law."

The site's search function shows interesting promise but is ultimately disappointing. Entering the term "California" in the search box yielded a U.S. map with color-coded dots over certain states—apparently those with papers that featured editorials using the term "California." Underneath the map were fourteen links to editorials that used that term, but even after clicking the link it was not possible to determine from what newspaper the editorial was taken.

Still, the organization of Mr. Benson's site more than compensates for its poor searchability. The editorials are grouped under one of four topics: the Nebraska Bill, the attack on Sumner, the Dred Scott decision, and John Brown's raid. Each link informs the reader of the newspaper's state, city, and party affiliation and also provides a useful one-sentence excerpt.

CONTENT   ★ ★ ★ ★ ★
AESTHETICS   ★ ★ ★
NAVIGATION   ★ ★ ★

LINK SITES

The term "Link site" is used to describe a web site whose primary function is to help users locate other web sites with content on particular topics. Most link sites, including many on the Civil War, are of little use to serious students and scholars. Too frequently, the links are simply to other link sites, forcing users to click and click again in search of real content. They generally sacrifice quality for quantity, linking to sites of very little value in order to cover an obscure topic. And the links themselves are generally not accompanied by any descriptive information regarding the site's authorship, sponsorship, intended audience, or purpose.

The two Civil War link sites reviewed here stand out from the rest, however. Frequently updated, their links only rarely prove to be obsolete. Moreover, the links are well indexed and categorized, so researchers can easily locate sites suited to their needs. And, most important, these two link sites have much better quality control—with very few duds and quite a few gems—than the average link site on the Civil War.

WEB SITE REVIEWS

NEW **Richard Jensen's Civil War Guides**
http://tigger.uic.edu/~rjensen/civilwar.htm

Among the dozens of Civil War link sites on the Internet, Richard Jensen's Civil
War Guides is the most oriented toward the needs of academic researchers. Most
of the links are to primary sources and scholarly essays, and each is accompanied by a descriptive annotation. Some of the sites linked to are restricted to
institutional subscribers, but the majority are free and open to the public.

Those new to Civil War studies may be best served by starting with Mr. Jensen's
two essays on the Civil War, which offer a general overview of the war years
and cover everything from developments in weaponry to the Confederate economy. Many of the terms in these essays are linked to sites with additional material, although some of these linked sites are restricted to paid subscribers.

Those already familiar with the basic outline of the Civil War will want to proceed directly to one of Mr. Jensen's three links pages. The most comprehensive of these pages is titled Civil War and Reconstruction. It starts with sites
on the coming of the war, with topics such as Nativism, Bleeding Kansas, and
the Dred Scott decision, and continues with sites on the political crisis of 1860,
secession, the Lincoln administration, the home front, military aspects of the
conflict (with links to sites on major battles), and Reconstruction.

Mr. Jensen's sites fall into three main categories: primary sources, topical web
sites for the lay researcher, and current scholarship. The primary sources sites
include speeches and newspaper editorials, memoirs of Civil War combatants
and civilians, and full-text transcriptions of early histories of the war. Many of
the memoirs and early histories are from Making of America, a huge digitization effort undertaken by Cornell University and the University of Michigan.
Mr. Jensen's selections from Making of America include "Woman's work in the
civil war: a record of heroism, patriotism and patience," by L. P. Brockett and
Mrs. Mary C. Vaughan, published in 1867; and "Enrollment and the Draft," by
J. G. Nicolay and John Hay, published in 1889.

The topical web sites linked from Mr. Jensen's are like many of the sites reviewed
in the first eight chapters of this book: good web sites created by educators, government agencies, and nonprofit organizations to educate the public about particular aspects of the Civil War. Many of Mr. Jensen's battles sites fall in this
category. Among his selections, the topical web sites tend to vary most widely in terms of aesthetics and content.

Current scholarship referenced by the site includes articles, bibliographies,
course syllabi, book reviews, and book excerpts. Although some of the articles

are available to paid subscribers only, Mr. Jensen has found quite a few scholarly pieces that are open to the public for free, such as selections from *Ohio History* and the *Handbook of Texas*. Most of the book reviews are from H-Net, an online community for humanities scholars that Mr. Jensen helped found in the 1990s. Mr. Jensen's site also takes full advantage of one of the hidden gems of the web: first chapters from many books reviewed in the *New York Times*. One of these is the first chapter of Gary Gallagher's *The Confederate War* (1997).

While not as exhaustive as the other link site reviewed here, the combination of academic essays and archival material makes Richard Jensen's Civil War Guides extremely valuable for serious scholars.

CONTENT   ★ ★ ★ ★ ★
AESTHETICS   ★ ★ ★
NAVIGATION   ★ ★ ★

NEW United States Civil War Center Index of Civil War Information
http://www.cwc.lsu.edu/cwc/civlink.htm

The six links on the New York City draft give a sense of the wide range of material indexed by the United States Civil War Center. The sites include a classroom activity prepared by the New-York Historical Society, a page from "The Political & Economic History of New York City" by the McManus Midtown Democratic Association, a description of (and link to buy) a book on the draft riots, a one-paragraph summary of the riots on the New York Police Department site, and two seemingly distinct links that each take the user to the home page of The History Net (which, oddly, contained no reference to the draft riots).

The United States Civil War Center's main value is its broad breadth and impressive level of detail. The site's 500 links for battles, for example, include major battles such as Antietam and Chancellorsville as well as less well-known engagements such as Champion Hill (4 links) and Haw's Shop (1 link.) The site provides ten entries on the topic of Geology and the Civil War. These include links to the United States Geological Survey site's history section and a site on the geology of Virginia made at the College of William and Mary.

Not surprisingly, given its mission to include *all* sites on the Civil War, the United States Civil War Center links to sites of variable quality. Still, the site is quite useful to two main types of users: those seeking a general overview of Civil War material available on the web, and those seeking information on very focused topics.

CONTENT   ★ ★ ★ ★
AESTHETICS   ★ ★ ★
NAVIGATION   ★ ★ ★

ONLINE BOOKSTORES

Few of us have the good fortune to live near a bookstore with both a broad selection of Civil War titles and a staff conversant with the topic. The large chain superstores may have entire sections on the American Civil War, but the chances of finding a salesperson with enough knowledge to help you select among the scores of titles are slim. Smaller, owner-operated stores may be staffed entirely by Ph.D.s, but these shops cannot stock a large inventory, and it is likely that the publication you are looking for will not be on the shelves. It is not surprising, then, that books have proven to be the most common item bought over the Internet. The sales figures at Amazon.com alone demonstrate the appeal of a "store" freed from the limitations of shelf space and filled with useful information about the books browsers are considering.

Of the four online bookstore sites chosen as Best of the Web, two (the History Book Club and the Military Book Club) are best suited for the reader who may be seeking to start a Civil War collection from scratch. The other two, Morningside Bookshop and *War Times Journal* Store, would appeal more to buyers already fairly well read on the Civil War. All four show the incredible convenience of e-commerce, allowing users at any level of scholarship or technical sophistication to build an impressive Civil War library without having to enroll in a college course or look for a parking space.

WEB SITE REVIEWS

 NEW **History Book Club**

www.historybookclub.com

Don't be fooled by the confusing home page. It is possible to enter and browse the History Book Club's offerings without already being a member of the club and without actually joining. Ignore the prominently placed "log in" and "join now" links on the page and click the "get 4 books for $4" banner.

Users who click this link will be taken to a screen with a selection of the $1 books in the center and a menu of subject links to the left. At the time this review was written, clicking "Civil War" on this menu generated a list of sixty-six books that could be purchased as part of the "4 books for $4" offer. Of these sixty-six selections, thirteen were various volumes of Shelby Foote's *The Civil War: 40th Anniversary Edition* (Time-Life Books), and the rest consisted of popular monographs such as Jeffry D. Wert's *Gettysburg, Day Three* and James M. McPherson's *Crossroads of Freedom: Antietam.*

The selection leans toward the military, with most books dealing with battles, campaigns, unit histories, and military leaders. But the list also features several important works on other aspects of the war and its aftermath, such as *Confederate Industry* by Harold S. Wilson, *Our Secret Constitution* by George P. Fletcher, and *Race and Reunion* by David Blight.

History buffs will find it difficult to resist the introductory offer, even after they realize that some of the larger books actually count as two of the four selections and that they will be paying around $12 in shipping and handling charges on top of their $4. Up to four books for $16 is still a good deal, and the added bonus of unlimited access to the online *Oxford English Dictionary* via a link on the club's main page makes the offer even more attractive. History Book Club members are obligated to buy one more book at the regular price from the club within the year.

The browsing experience for existing members differs slightly from that of prospective members. The subject menu does not feature a Civil War link, and clicking the link for 19th-century American History yielded a list of only eleven books. But a keyword search for Civil War would bring the user to the same list of sixty-six books that were viewable when browsing as a nonmember.

Many, but not all, of the books for sale here are accompanied by descriptions and/or reviews. The club has solicited scholarly reviews for some of its books (for example, University of Texas law professor Sanford Levinson commented on *The First Great Triumph* by Warren Zimmerman), but not for any of the Civil War books at the time this volume was written. Instead, the Civil War book reviews seem to have been composed either by the publishers of the books or by club members.

CONTENT   ★ ★ ★ ★
AESTHETICS   ★ ★ ★ ★
NAVIGATION   ★ ★ ★ ★

NEW Military Book Club
http://www.militarybookclub.com

It's not every day that avid readers get to browse through a selection of over one hundred titles with the opportunity to purchase four for 98 cents each, plus a fifth book thrown in for free. But that is the offer that military history buffs will get when they join the Military Book Club.

At the time this review was written, the military history topics on the Military Book Club site ranged from Ancient/Medieval Warfare to Anti-Terrorism. The American Civil War category featured twenty-three books, all of which were new works published since 2000. The list included several prominent historians' works, including *Antietam, 1862*, by James McPherson; *Cold Harbor*, by Gordon C. Rhea; and *Lee's Last Retreat*, by William Marvel. Complementing these traditional academic works were titles such as *Gods and Generals: The Paintings of Mort Kunstler* (the official companion to the movie), and eyewitness watercolor renditions of the war titled *Eye of the Storm*.

Each book on the site is accompanied by a promotional description prepared by Military Book Club writers, and many are also accompanied by reviews submitted by members. Comparing the two types of reviews allows for an interesting illustration of the gulf between Civil War scholarship and many of its consumers. The promotional review of Rhea's *Cold Harbor* praised the book for "avoiding the old myths historians have accepted without question. . . . Rhea reveals Grant as a savvy, sometimes brilliant general, and Lee as far from perfect." But the anonymous reader who submitted a member's review saw the book differently: "The author clearly displays a personal bias in his writing. It is evident he is trying to re-wright history to the Politically Correct genru [*sic*]."

In addition to its military history books, the site offers historic fiction (with a strong showing by Tom Clancy and Stephen Coonts), books in the tradition of the enlisted man's pin-up girls, and military technology manuals such as *Jane's Gun Recognition Guide*.

The Military Book Club site is not a full e-commerce site in that it does not take credit cards. Instead, after selecting their five books, users submit their names, street address, and email address, and the club follows up by sending a membership kit, which presumably contains the five selected books, an invoice, and the next month's catalog. Although this information is not prominently placed, the club charges $5.49 in shipping and handling for the first book plus $2.19 for each additional one—adding $14.25 to the order total. In spite of this rather large hidden fee, the introductory offer is still a good way for military enthusiasts to build their libraries.

CONTENT ★ ★ ★ ★
AESTHETICS ★ ★ ★ ★
NAVIGATION ★ ★ ★ ★

NEW **Morningside Bookshop**
http://www.morningsidebooks.com

The Morningside Books web site offers over 2,000 books on the American Civil War. An entire section of the site is devoted to books—generally large, multivolume sets—published by its own Morningside Press. For $2,650, users can purchase the full 128-volume set of the *Official Records*. Still considered an essential source by military historians, the *Official Records* was originally compiled by the U.S. government in the 1880s and 1890s from dispatches filed by Civil War commanders in the field.

Morningside Press also offers the *Southern Historical Society Papers* (52 volumes for $1,500). Founded by former Confederate leaders in 1869 with the aim of preserving the history of the wartime South, the Southern Historical Society was first led by illustrious Confederates such as Jubal Early, Robert E. Lee, and Alexander Stephens, and later by well-known historian Douglas Southall Freeman. The Society's voluminous publications, with their unmistakably pro-South point of view, profoundly shaped views of the war for generations. In addition to these large multivolume sets, Morningside Press also publishes and offers for sale individual monographs such as *Grappling with Death: The Union Corps Hospital at Gettysburg* by Rowland Maust (almost 1,000 pages) and *The History of the 16th Michigan Infantry* by Kim Crawford.

To access the site's full offerings, which include books by a range of publishers, click the Bookstore tab. This link takes the user to two search forms: one with free text boxes for author, title, keywords, and book number, and the other with drop-down menus of authors and subjects. Selecting "Cavalry" from the subject drop-down menu yields a list of 105 books, most of which appear to be histories of cavalry units. There were thirty matches for "Sherman, Gen. William T." (although not all of them were actually about General Sherman).

A handful of the books offered for sale on the site are accompanied by descriptions provided by the authors or publishers or excerpted from David J. Eicher's *The Civil War in Books: An Analytical Bibliography* (1996). For most books, however, the only information offered is title, author, and number of pages.

Researchers seeking to learn a little about the Civil War before buying any books will appreciate the free material that Morningside Press has made available on its web site. At the time this review was written, eight articles from Morningside Press's *Gettysburg Magazine* and six articles from *Morningside Notes* could be read on the site. These articles include "Union City: Philadelphia and the Battle of Gettysburg," by John Reid Seitter, and "Forrest Gets the Bulge on Sooy Smith," by Edwin C. Bearss.

CONTENT   ★ ★ ★ ★ ★
AESTHETICS   ★ ★ ★
NAVIGATION   ★ ★ ★

NEW   **The *War Times Journal* Store**
http://www.wtj.com/store/

The *War Times Journal* is one of the few web initiatives that combine e-commerce with free archival material. In fact, its online memoirs of five Civil War generals and its documents on Civil War navies merit the *War Times Journal's* inclusion as Best of the Web sites in both the Political and Military Leaders and Naval Operations chapters of this book.

The *War Times Journal* Store is divided into two sections: Game Shops, with products that can be purchased on the *War Times Journal* site itself; and Books & Movies, which uses Amazon.com to sell its selections. At the time this review was written, the Civil War list featured almost fifty books, including four by Shelby Foote, three by Edwin C. Bearss, and two by Alan T. Nolan. In addition to the standard Civil War topics (the main categories are "Campaigns," "Troops," "Naval," and "People"), the list includes a book on re-enacting as well as *The Myth of the Lost Cause and Civil War History*, edited by Nolan and Gary W. Gallagher.

In some ways it is a shame that the *War Times Journal* site does not include its own editorial and reader reviews of the books on the list. But the Amazon.com reviews give a good sense of the books as well as the reaction to them among readers. Amazon.com reprinted the American Library Association's *Booklist* review of *The Myth of the Lost Cause*, which praised the collection of essays for showing "how the myth was consciously propagated by southerners, often in an attempt to rationalize the physical and social carnage left by the war." Not so, responded a critic from North Carolina, who argued that the book merely "displays the author's jealousy of being products of a bankrupt culture: Yankee."

The passion that the American Civil War still inspires nearly 150 years after it ended will ensure that books and web sites on the war will continue to be created, consumed, and discussed. The *War Times Journal* has done an admirable job of tapping into this passion without commercializing or trivializing the conflict.

CONTENT   ★ ★ ★ ★
AESTHETICS   ★ ★ ★
NAVIGATION   ★ ★ ★

PART II

SITES
WORTH
A VISIT

A

TOPICAL

INDEX

B ATTLES AND CAMPAIGNS

GENERAL SITES

American Military History: The Civil War

http://www.army.mil/cmh-pg/online/Bookshelves/CW.htm

Relevant chapters from the U.S. Army official textbook, used by the ROTC.

The Civil War Artillery Page

http://www.cwartillery.org

Extremely thorough explanation of artillery technology, organization, and strategy, with excellent diagrams and other illustrations.

Civil War Battles by State

http://americancivilwar.com/statepic/

Very useful maps of each state, with brief reports of each battle. Excellent starting point.

Civil War Sites Advisory Commission Battle Summaries

http://www2.cr.nps.gov/abpp/battles/tvii.htm

National Park Service site; provides brief summaries of hundreds of Civil War battles divided into campaigns and listed in chronological order. Updated 1997.

Confederate States Armory Homepage

http://www.geocities.com/Athens/Delphi/1880/csarmory/csarmory.html

Brief history of Confederate armories; links to sites about armories in Macon, Columbia, and Fayetteville; biographical sketches and drawings.

TheHistoryNet

http://militaryhistory.about.com/cs/americancivilwar2/

Popular articles on forts, logistics, battles, personalities.

Military History of the Civil War

http://tigger.uic.edu/~rjensen/cw-1.htm

Original essay by historian Richard Jensen, with links to numerous primary documents and maps.

Selected Civil War Photographs in the American Memory Collection

http://memory.loc.gov/ammem/cwphtml/cwphome.html

Over 1,100 photographs taken by Matthew Brady and other notable photographers; many vivid battlefield scenes. Some shots were staged. From the Library of Congress's American Memory Project.

Shotgun's Home of the American Civil War: Battles

http://www.civilwarhome.com/records.htm

The most comprehensive single online source for Orders of Battle, *Official Records*, and other firsthand accounts of practically every major Civil War battle.

This Week in the Civil War

http://www.civilweek.com/

Presents events that happened each week in the first years of the Civil War. Features excerpts from *Official Records* and other documents.

United States Civil War

http://www.us-civilwar.com/

Provides a timeline of major military events in the Civil War.

The Valley of the Shadow: Two Communities in the American Civil War—The War Years

http://jefferson.village.virginia.edu/cwhome.html

University of Virginia site; contains an interactive theater-level map showing battles fought by regiments from two counties, one in the North and one in the South, with each battle linked to information about that unit's experience there. Also features newspapers, letters, and diaries, *Official Records*.

BOOKS AND ARTICLES ON BATTLES AND CAMPAIGNS PUBLISHED 1861–1920

The Civil War Home Page

http://www.rugreview.com/cw/cwhp.htm

Features illustrated articles from *Harper's* and *Century* magazines on First Bull Run, Fort Donelson, the Western Flotilla, Shiloh, the *Monitor* and *Merrimac*, New Orleans, and the memoirs of a Yankee private.

Ehistory: Battles and Leaders of the Civil War

http://www.ehistory.com/uscw/library/books/battles/index.cfm

In the 1880s the *Century* magazine commissioned battle reports from leading generals; they were also published in four volumes, which have often been reprinted. This is an invaluable resource, and essential reading on every major battle.

A History of the Civil War

http://www.ehistory.com/uscw/library/periodicals/ahotcw/index.cfm

1912 popular book by Benson J. Lossing; illustrated with Brady photographs.

James Ford Rhodes, History of the Civil War, 1861–1865 (1918)

http://www.bartleby.com/252/

This is the best of the older histories of the war years; it covers military and civilian topics. Rhodes is especially strong on politics and character analysis of leaders.

The War of the Rebellion: A Compilation of the Official Records of the Union and Confederate Armies

http://www.ehistory.com/uscw/library/or/index.cfm

After the war, Washington compiled all the official battle reports, for the Union and the Confederacy, and published them in 128 large volumes, which are usually called *Official Records*, abbreviated *O.R.* They are absolutely basic for all serious research. Many of the sites listed below contain excerpts. Inexpensive CD-ROM versions are also available.

CIVIL WAR MAPS

Civil War Maps

http://lcweb2.loc.gov/ammem/gmdhtml/cwmhtml/cwmhome.html

Excellent collection of 2,200 original maps from the Library of Congress, together with a history of wartime cartography.

Hargrett Rare Book and Manuscript Library Rare Map Collection: The American Civil War

http://www.libs.uga.edu/darchive/hargrett/maps/civil.html

Dozens of maps of battlefields and campaigns, most drawn during the Civil War.

Maps of the American Civil War

http://www.dean.usma.edu/history/dhistorymaps/AcivilwarPages/ACWToC.htm

Superb *West Point Atlas* of the war; 58 maps drawn by Edward J. Krasnoborski in recent decades (these are not the maps used during the war).

Maps of the Civil War

http://www.ehistory.com/uscw/library/maps/group1.cfm

A selection of maps actually used during the war.

CIVIL WAR MILITARY MANUALS

A treatise on field fortification, containing instructions on the methods of laying out, constructing, defending, and attacking intrenchments, with the general outlines also of the arrangement, the attack and defence of permanent fortifications. By Dennis Hart Mahan.

http://www.hti.umich.edu/cgi/t/text/text-idx?sid=26ccecb532c18c6d&c=moa&idno=AJR7399.0001.001&view=toc

This is the textbook that taught pre-Civil War West Pointers their technique. Dennis Mahan's son was the famous naval historian Alfred Thayer Mahan.

U.S. infantry tactics for the instruction, exercise, and manœuvres of the United States infantry, including infantry of the line, light infantry, and riflemen. Prepared under the direction of the War department, and authorized and adopted by the secretary of war, May 1, 1861.

http://www.hti.umich.edu/cgi/t/text/text-idx?c=moa;idno=AJS4261

Full text of the Union Army's bible of tactics.

ANTIETAM/SHARPSBURG

Antietam: The Bloodiest Day

http://www.alleghenymountain.org/antmain.htm

Created by a local historian and part of a larger site on the Civil War in the Allegheny Highlands; contains an illustrated summary of the battle and an animated map.

Antietam National Battlefield

http://www.nps.gov/anti/home.htm

National Park Service site; provides a brief overview of the Battle of Antietam, with emphasis on the battle's role in Lincoln's Emancipation Proclamation.

Brian Downey's Antietam on the Web

http://www2.ari.net/brdowney/index.html

Well-designed site; provides in-depth analysis as well as interesting primary sources.

APPOMATTOX

See also Richmond

The Battle of Appomattox Court House (April 9, 1865)

http://www.civilwarhome.com/appomatt.htm

Primary sources regarding the surrender.

ATLANTA

The Atlanta Campaign, 1864

http://ngeorgia.com/history/atlcamp.html

Timeline with summaries of maneuvers and battles and maps, and a distinct Confederate point of view.

The Atlanta Campaign, May 1–September 8, 1864

http://www.civilwarhome.com/atlantarecordspage.htm

Includes primary sources and later historical accounts.

Grant's Analysis

http://members.aol.com/_ht_a/historiography/grant4.html#Ch-49

This excerpt from Grant's memoirs gives his perceptions of Sherman's campaign.

Sherman's Narrative

http://www.sonshi.com/sherman.html

Chapters 16–20 of Sherman's *Memoirs*.

CHANCELLORSVILLE

See also Fredericksburg

The Battle of Chancellorsville (May 1–3, 1863)

http://www.civilwarhome.com/chancell.htm

Primary source documents and later historical accounts of Lee's greatest victory; maps.

Fredericksburg and Spotsylvania National Military Park: Chancellorsville Battlefield

http://www.nps.gov/frsp/cville.htm

National Park Service guide to the battlefield and history of the battle.

The Red Badge of Courage: An Episode of the American Civil War

http://xroads.virginia.edu/~HYPER/CRANE/chancellorsville/section2.html

A student site that explains Stephen Crane's use of the battle in his famous novel.

Rumble on The Rappahannock

http://members.tripod.com/~Andrew_Dehart/

A short popular history of the battle by Andrew Dehart.

CHICKAMAUGA, CHATTANOOGA, AND LOOKOUT MOUNTAIN

Chickamauga Battlefield

http://scarlett.libs.uga.edu/darchive/hargrett/maps/1895m2.jpg

The map was created by a military historian in the 1890s.

The Chickamauga Campaign

http://www.civilwarhome.com/chickama.htm

Primary documents and later historical accounts of one of the last Confederate victories in the West.

An SR Books
BEST CIVIL WAR SITE
Selection

Chattanooga: A Road Trip Through Time

http://www.mediaalchemy.com/civilwar/

Award-winning photo-documentary site; contains an excellent narrative, artistic photographs, and informative maps.

Grant's Memoirs

http://members.aol.com/_ht_a/historiography/grant3.html#Ch-41

Grant's account of how he took control of a bad situation and won a stunning victory.

COLD HARBOR

See also Richmond

North Anna and Cold Harbor (May 21–June 3, 1864)

http://www.civilwarhome.com/Cold%20Harbor.htm

Includes primary sources and later historical accounts.

Richmond National Battlefield

http://www.nps.gov/rich/ri_cold.htm

Summary of Cold Harbor and related campaigns.

CORINTH

See Western Theater

FLORIDA

Battle of Olustee

http://extlab1.entnem.ufl.edu/olustee

A battlefield preservationist provides a capsule history as well as a detailed analysis, primary documents, and regimental histories.

Florida in the Civil War

http://dhr.dos.state.fl.us/museum/civwar/

Comprehensive coverage provided by state agency.

FREDERICKSBURG

Battle of Fredericksburg

http://members.aol.com/lmjarl/civwar/frdrksburg.html

Comprehensive description of Lee's great victory over Burnside and its effect on the Union command.

The Battle of Fredericksburg (December 13, 1862)

http://www.civilwarhome.com/fredrick.htm

Includes primary sources and later historical accounts.

Fredericksburg and Spotsylvania National Military Park Visitor Center

http://www.nps.gov/frsp/vc.htm

National Park Service site; has good overviews and excerpts of firsthand accounts of the four major battles fought around the Fredericksburg area.

GEORGIA

See also Sherman's March

The Great Locomotive Chase: The Definitive Story of the Andrews Raid, April 12, 1862

http://www.andrewsraid.com

Illustrated account of this strange event, along with an interesting analysis of the raid's memorialization in print and film.

GETTYSBURG

The Battle of Gettysburg (July 1–3, 1863)

http://www.civilwarhome.com/gettysbu.htm

Includes primary sources and later historical accounts.

Carl Reed's Gettysburg Revisited

http://home.sprynet.com/~carlreed/

Well-designed, privately made site; contains interesting essays, *Official Records*, and excerpts of previously published accounts.

Gettysburg Discussion Group

http://www.gdg.org

Created by a Civil War history association; consists of essays and articles by association members as well as a small collection of primary sources.

Gettysburg National Military Park

http://www.nps.gov/gett/home.htm

National Park Service site; provides an exhaustive virtual tour covering each day of the battle in great detail.

Map of the Battle-field of Gettysburg with Position of Troops, July 2nd 1863. Top1 Office, A.N.V., by L. Howell Brown, 1st Lieut. Engr. Troops . . . / from: Atlas to accompany the Official Records of the Union and Confederate Armies, 1861–1865

http://www.lib.berkeley.edu/EART/digital/gettysb-lg.gif

Very large scale map of battlefield, prepared by U.S. engineers after the battle.

Military History Online—Battle of Gettysburg

http://www.militaryhistoryonline.com/gettysburg

Contains essays, documents, and highly detailed descriptions of the battle.

M A N A S S A S / B U L L   R U N

The Battle of Bull Run (1st Manassas) (July 21, 1861)

http://www.civilwarhome.com/1manassa.htm

Includes primary sources and later historical accounts.

The Battle of 2nd Manassas (The Second Battle of Bull Run) August 28–30, 1862

http://www.civilwarhome.com/2manassa.htm

Includes primary sources and later historical accounts.

A Last Salute

http://www.espdesigns.com/salute/

Made by an educational technology design firm; documents ongoing archaeological excavations of human remains and armaments at the Manassas Battlefield.

Manassas National Battlefield Park

http://www.nps.gov/mana/home.htm

National Park Service site; includes a good overview of the First and Second Battles of Manassas, with much of the material designed especially for students.

M A R Y L A N D

See also Antietam

Monocacy: The Battle that Saved Washington

http://www.nps.gov/mono/mo_hist.htm

Brief overview of this little-studied battle, part of larger National Park Service site.

N E W   M A R K E T

The Battle of New Market, Virginia, May 15, 1864

http://www.vmi.edu/archives/Civil_War/cwnm.html

A brief background essay, the names and portraits (if available) of the entire corps that fought, and biographical sketches of the men who were killed during, or from wounds sustained in, the battle.

NORTH CAROLINA

Bentonville Battleground

http://www.ah.dcr.state.nc.us/sections/hs/bentonvi/bentonvi.htm

Part of a large web site on North Carolina historic places; contains an overview of the battle as well as outstanding maps.

PENINSULA CAMPAIGN

See Richmond

PETERSBURG

Petersburg National Battlefield

http://www.nps.gov/pete/mahan/PNBhome.html

National Park Service site; provides a thorough overview of the important events in and around Petersburg during the Civil War.

The Siege of Petersburg

http://members.aol.com/siege1864/

Contains highly detailed information about armies and leaders during Grant's long siege of Petersburg.

RICHMOND

Appomattox Courthouse National Historic Park

http://www.nps.gov/apco

Provides an overview of the events leading up to the surrender as well as an interesting explanation of how Confederate soldiers were paroled.

The 1862 Peninsula Campaign

http://www.peninsulacampaign.org/

Well-designed site with brief details of battle; especially good on technology and fortifications.

Richmond National Battlefield Park Homepage

http://www.nps.gov/rich/home.htm

National Park Service site; contains material on the Peninsula Campaign of 1862 as well as Grant's overland campaign of 1864.

Staunton River Battlefield State Park

http://www.stauntonriverbattlefield.org

Created by the Historic Staunton River Foundation; contains a description of the battle of Staunton River Bridge, June 25, 1864, fought in southeast Virginia and a map of troop movements in the region.

SHERMAN'S MARCH

"General William T. Sherman: Would the Georgia Campaigns of the First Commander of the Modern Era Comply with Current Law of War Standards?"

http://www.law.emory.edu/EILR/volumes/fall95/robisch.html

Scholarly article in *Emory International Law Review* 9, no. 2 (1995); mostly yes, says the author, Thomas G. Robisch, a military lawyer.

Grant Tells the Story

http://members.aol.com/_ht_a/historiography/grant4.html#Ch-59

Grant was Sherman's superior officer and helped plan the March through Georgia.

James Ford Rhodes, "Sherman's March"

http://www.bartleby.com/252/pages/page398.html

Excellent overview by a leading historian of the 1890s; *History of the Civil War, 1861–1865* (1917), pp. 398–429.

Sherman's March Through South Carolina

http://members.aol.com/x69xer/sherman2.html

This was a continuation of the March through Georgia and even more devastating.

Sherman's Memoirs

http://www.sonshi.com/sherman.html

Sherman's memoirs are almost as good as Grant's; they contain many useful documents. Chapters 20–24 cover the March through Georgia and South Carolina.

SHILOH

The Battle of Shiloh (Pittsburg Landing), April 6–7, 1862

http://www.civilwarhome.com/shiloh.htm

Short collection of primary documents and historical accounts of the first major battle of the war, in which Grant was whipped on the first day, but on the second day he recovered and snatched victory. For more links, see http://saints.css.edu/mkelsey/shil.html

Grant Tells the Story

http://members.aol.com/_ht_a/historiography/grant2.html#Ch-24

Grant's *Memoirs*, Chapter 24, contain a brilliant narration.

The Mississippi and Shiloh

http://cdl.library.cornell.edu/cgi-bin/moa/sgml/moa-idx?notisid=ABP2287-0036-148

Lincoln aides John Nicolay and John Hay explain the strategy from a Washington perspective in an 1888 magazine article, which became a chapter in their great biography of Lincoln.

SOUTH CAROLINA

See also Sherman's March

Civil War@Charleston

http://www.awod.com/gallery/probono/cwchas/cwlayout.html

A local reenactor has created an attractive site covering the naval and land battles fought around Charleston, including the very first battle at Fort Sumter, and Battery Wagner, location of the assault of July 18, 1863, that formed the basis of the movie *Glory* (1989).

SPOTSYLVANIA

See Fredericksburg

TENNESSEE

See also Chickamauga, Chattanooga, and Lookout Mountain

The Battle of Nashville (December 15–16, 1864)

http://www.civilwarhome.com/nashville.htm

Primary sources and historical accounts.

Britton Lane Battlefield Association: "The Battle That History Forgot"

http://www.brittonlane1862.madison.tn.us/

Made by a local preservation agency; contains a brief secondary account, reenactment photographs, and an interesting map of this "forgotten" battle in Tennessee.

VICKSBURG

See Western Theater

VIRGINIA

See also Appomattox, Fredericksburg, Manassas/Bull Run, New Market, Petersburg, Richmond, Wilderness

Civil War in the Shenandoah Valley, 1863–1865

http://www.rockingham.k12.va.us/EMS/Civil_War_in_the_Shenandoah/Civil_War_in_the_Shenandoah.htm

Includes brief narratives of the numerous battles in this valley.

Harpers Ferry National Historic Park

http://www.nps.gov/hafe/home.htm

National Park Service site; provides brief overviews of the military campaigns in and around Harpers Ferry, (West) Virginia.

Jackson's Valley Campaign, and the Seven Days' Battles

http://cdl.library.cornell.edu/cgi-bin/moa/sgml/moa-idx?notisid=ABP2287-0037-27

1888 study from the White House viewpoint, by Lincoln aides J. G. Nicolay and John Hay

Shenandoah Valley Campaign of Jackson, May–June 1862

http://www.civilwarhome.com/valleycampaignOR.htm

Primary sources and historical accounts of Stonewall Jackson's incredible exploits.

WESTERN THEATER

The Battle of Galveston (1 January 1863)

http://www.lsjunction.com/events/galvestn.htm

Part of a commercial web site on Texas history; provides a one-page description of the Confederate recapture of the port of Galveston.

The Battle of Mill Springs/Fishing Creek

http://www.geocities.com/Pentagon/Quarters/1864/Default.htm

Privately made site; features Orders of Battle, *Official Records*, photographs, diagrams of weapons, casualty lists, and unit rosters pertaining to the Battle of Mill Springs, Kentucky, in 1862.

The Battle of Perryville

http://www.battleofperryville.com/

Provides detailed accounts of Bragg's invasion of Kentucky, the battle itself, and the post-battle Confederate retreat into Tennessee.

The Battle of Wilson's Creek (Oak Hills), August 10, 1861

http://www.civilwarhome.com/wilsoncreekintro.htm

Includes primary sources and later historical accounts.

The Civil War in Arkansas

http://www.civilwarbuff.org

Made by the Arkansas Civil War Round Table; features a searchable (by location and date) database of Civil War events that took place in Arkansas.

Corinth: Crossroads of the Confederacy

http://www.corinth.org/

The local tourist agency provides a tour of the scenes of battles and skirmishes fought around Corinth, Mississippi.

The First Advance on Vicksburg, 1862

http://www.encompass.net/ctyson/civwar/farrago8.htm

Chapters 8 and 9 of Alfred Thayer Mahan's biography of David Farragut.

Grant Tells the Story

http://members.aol.com/_ht_a/historiography/grant3.html

Grant's *Memoirs* cover the campaign brilliantly, Chapters 30 to 38.

Handbook of Texas: Civil War

http://www.tsha.utexas.edu/handbook/online/articles/view/CC/qdc2.html

Part of the monumental online encyclopedia of the state with cross references to other scholarly articles in the handbook.

The Red River Campaign (10 Mar.–22 May 1864)

http://www.civilwarhome.com/redriverrecords.htm

Primary sources and historical accounts of the Yankee fiasco.

The Siege of Vicksburg (May 18–July 4, 1863)

http://www.civilwarhome.com/siegeofvicksburg.htm

Primary sources and historical accounts of the final days of Grant's triumphant campaign against the main Confederate stronghold in the West.

Vicksburg National Military Park

http://www.nps.gov/vick/home.htm

National Park Service site covers the entire Vicksburg campaign and contains a database of paroled Confederate soldiers.

The *War Times Journal*: Visiting the Battle of Picacho Pass Historic Site

http://www.wtj.com/articles/picacho/

Part of a larger commercial site; provides an interesting account of this little-studied New Mexico battle.

Wilson's Creek National Battlefield

http://www.nps.gov/wicr

National Park Service site; provides a lively account of this battle as well as a good analysis of the political and military events in Missouri throughout the war.

W I L D E R N E S S

The Battle of the Wilderness, May 5–7, 1864

http://www.civilwarhome.com/wildernessor.htm

Primary sources and historical accounts of how Lee mauled Grant, who nevertheless turned south and kept fighting.

The Battle of the Wilderness: A Virtual Tour

http://home.att.net/~hallowed-ground/wilderness_tour.html

Two Civil War enthusiasts tell the story of the incredibly bloody battle through the use of photographs and explanatory narrative.

POLITICAL AND MILITARY LEADERS

G E N E R A L   S I T E S

Biographical Directory of the United States Congress, 1774–Present

http://bioguide.congress.gov/biosearch/biosearch.asp

Short biographies of all members of the U.S. Congress; includes Confederates who served in Washington before or after the war.

Biographies of North Georgia

http://ngeorgia.com/people/

Well-done short biographies of Civil War political and military leaders. This is a rebel site that staunchly supports the War for Southern Independence.

HarpWeek: Presidential Elections from 1860 to 1884

http://elections.harpweek.com

Campaign broadsides and political cartoons digitized to the highest standards and accompanied by excellent explanatory material.

Selected Civil War Photographs

http://lcweb2.loc.gov/ammem/cwphome.html

Part of the Library of Congress's American Memory Project; houses photographs of dozens of Civil War leaders.

Shotgun's Home of the American Civil War: Biographies

http://www.civilwarhome.com/biograph.htm

Useful short biographies of one hundred military and civilian leaders on each side.

United States Civil War

http://www.us-civilwar.com/

Brief biographical sketches of dozens of Civil War notables.

The *War Times Journal* Civil War Series: Grant, Longstreet, Sherman, Hood, and Gordon

http://www.wtj.com/wars/civilwar/

Lengthy excerpts from public domain memoirs of these five important Civil War generals.

LEADERS—NORTH

CHAMBERLAIN, JOSHUA L.

Chamberlain Biography

http://www.curtislibrary.com/pejepscot/joshbiog.htm

Made by a Maine historical society; features a scholarly, concise essay on the life of the hero of Little Round Top. Several recent full-length biographies have appeared in print.

CUSTER, GEORGE ARMSTRONG

George Armstrong Custer, 1839–1876

http://georgearmstrongcuster.com/

Short biography and many links to one of the youngest generals of the war.

FARRAGUT, DAVID GLASGOW

Admiral David Glasgow Farragut (1801–1870)

http://www.encompass.net/ctyson/civwar/farmain.htm

Features Alfred Thayer Mahan's 1892 biography of this famous Union admiral.

GRANT, ULYSSES S.

An SR Books
**BEST
CIVIL
WAR
SITE**
Selection

The Ulysses S. Grant Association

http://www.lib.siu.edu/projects/usgrant

Sponsored by the editors of the multivolume edition of Grant's papers. Features memoirs by Grant himself and some colleagues, a chronology of Grant's life, and an essay by Bruce Catton.

Ulysses S. Grant Home Page

http://www.mscomm.com/~ulysses/

Fascinating tidbits, quotes, and topics about Grant the soldier.

Ulysses Grant *Memoirs*

http://members.aol.com/_ht_a/historiography/grant.html/

Richard Jensen's edition of the full text, with a hyperlinked table of contents.

Ulysses S. Grant Network

http://saints.css.edu/mkelsey/gppg.html

Maintained by the Ulysses S. Grant Network; designed to dispel myths.

HANCOCK, WINFIELD SCOTT

Winfield Scott Hancock

http://www.geocities.com/superbhancock/home.html

Very well-illustrated site regarding the Yankee hero at Gettysburg; many documents.

LINCOLN, ABRAHAM

Abraham Lincoln Online

http://www.netins.net/showcase/creative/lincoln.html

A volunteer effort by a group of Lincoln partisans; features Lincoln This Week as well as a useful timeline and some speeches by Lincoln.

Abraham Lincoln Papers at the Library of Congress

http://lcweb2.loc.gov/ammem/alhtml/malhome.html

Part of the Library of Congress's American Memory Project; consists of 20,000 letters written to Lincoln during the war, plus hundreds that he wrote. There are 61,000 images and 10,000 transcriptions. Some have been retyped for legibility. Users must have a good Lincoln biography to understand the material.

Abraham Lincoln Research Site

http://members.aol.com/RVSNorton/Lincoln2.html

Made by a retired history teacher; features a wealth of material on Lincoln's family life as well as a well-documented and fascinating account of the national mourning that followed Lincoln's assassination.

Ford's Theatre National Historical Site

http://www.nps.gov/foth/index2.htm

National Park Service site; contains an interesting hyperlinked narrative on Lincoln's assassination.

Lincoln: Man, Martyr, Myth

http://xroads.virginia.edu/~CAP/LINCOLN/lincoln.htm

Analytical essays by University of Virginia students focus on the language used by Lincoln, and especially about him after his martyrdom. Recommended for advanced users only.

Lincoln/Net: The Abraham Lincoln Digitization Project

http://lincoln.lib.niu.edu/

Major project based at Northern Illinois University, this site is focused on Lincoln before his presidency, with a biography, photographs, maps, and original documents. It includes extensive material on frontier life, especially religion, women, farming, trade, law, and the status of African Americans and Native Americans. It has a searchable database of campaign songs from 1860 and 1864; it also promises to be the largest source of research material on Abraham Lincoln.

Sheet Music about Lincoln, Emancipation, and the Civil War

http://memory.loc.gov/ammem/scsmhtml/scsmhome.html

Part of the Library of Congress's extensive American Memory Project; features a searchable collection of 200 song lyrics and scans of sheet music about Lincoln, emancipation, and the Civil War.

M C C L E L L A N ,   G E O R G E   B .

Major General George McClellan

http://www.swcivilwar.com/mcclellan.html

Short biography and some documents.

The McClellan Society's MG George B. McClellan Pages

http://www.georgebmcclellan.org/

Features exhaustive research by avid McClellan partisans; refutes "frequently asserted claims" against McClellan and reviews several books assessing McClellan's generalship.

M E A D E ,   G E O R G E   G O R D O N

An SR Books
BEST CIVIL WAR SITE
Selection

The Meade Archive

http://adams.patriot.net/~jcampi/welcome.htm

Made by a group of Meade fans; contains documents as well as interesting essays.

S H E R M A N ,   W I L L I A M   T E C U M S E H

Memoirs

http://www.sonshi.com/sherman.html

Sherman's memoirs are almost as good as Grant's; they contain many useful documents.

Sherman

http://www.spartacus.schoolnet.co.uk/USACWsherman.htm

Capsule biography and revealing documents.

THOMAS, GEORGE H.

The George H. Thomas Home Page

http://home.att.net/~dmercado/index.htm

Privately made site; features a chronology and essay about this Virginian who fought for the Union; contains an annotated bibliography.

LEADERS—SOUTH

BEAUREGARD, P. G. T.

General P. G. T. Beauregard

http://www.beau.lib.la.us/~belflowr/bgard/pgtbgard.htm

Created by the public library of Beauregard Parish, Louisiana; offers a short overview of Beauregard's life, with an emphasis on his Confederate military career and his postwar political activity.

BRAGG, BRAXTON

General Braxton Bragg

http://www.ils.unc.edu/nc/BraxtonBragg.html

Aimed at elementary school students; contains a short sketch of the life of Bragg.

CLEBURNE, PATRICK R.

Confederate States of America: General Patrick R. Cleburne

http://www.westga.edu/~cscott/general.html

Made by a professor; briefly sketches career of Cleburne, an Irish-born Confederate general in Tennessee. He made the controversial proposal to arm (and emancipate) slaves to fight with the Confederate army.

COOPER, SAMUEL

General Samuel Cooper

http://www.generalcooper.com/

Cooper served as the adjutant and inspector general of the Confederate army.

DAVIS, JEFFERSON

The Papers of Jefferson Davis

http://jeffersondavis.rice.edu/

Rice University offers selections from its definitive multivolume edition of Jefferson Davis's collected papers. Index online to vol 7–8–9–10, covering 1861–64. For some primary documents go to http://jeffersondavis.rice.edu/site.cfm#docs

EARLY, JUBAL A.

Autobiographical Sketch and Narrative of the War between the States.

http://docsouth.unc.edu/early/menu.html

Complete text of memoirs of important Confederate general.

FORREST, NATHAN BEDFORD

Forrest's Headquarters

http://members.aol.com/GnrlJSB/index.html

Made by an avid Forrest partisan; essays about this controversial Confederate, plus battlefield tours.

JACKSON, THOMAS J. "STONEWALL"

John Esten Cooke, The life of Stonewall Jackson. From official papers, contemporary narratives, and personal acquaintance. By a Virginian.

http://moa.umdl.umich.edu/cgi/sgml/moa-idx?notisid=ACP4502

Complete text of admiring 1863 book.

Jackson's Valley Campaign

http://cdl.library.cornell.edu/cgi-bin/moa/sgml/moa-idx?notisid=ABP2287-0037-27

1889 study by Lincoln aides J. G. Nicolay and John Hay

Shenandoah Valley Campaign of Jackson

http://www.civilwarhome.com/valleycampaignOR.htm

Primary sources and historical accounts.

Stonewall Jackson Resources at the Virginia Military Institute Archives

http://www.vmi.edu/archives/Jackson/Jackson.html

Extensive collection of primary documents about this famous general, who before the war had been a professor at the Virginia Military Institute.

JOHNSON, EDWARD "ALLEGHANY"

Edward Alleghany Johnson World Wide Web Page

http://www.fsu.edu/~ewoodwar

Made by a Florida State University researcher; contains extensive reprints of articles and primary sources about this colorful Rebel.

LEE, ROBERT E.

The Apotheosis of Robert E. Lee

http://xroads.virginia.edu/~CAP/LEE/lee.html

Made by University of Virginia students for a class project; focuses on historiographical debates about Lee.

The Robert E. Lee Papers at Washington and Lee University

http://miley.wlu.edu/LeePapers/

Beautiful digital reproductions of a few of Lee's official letters as Confederate general and as president of Washington College (now Washington and Lee University).

Stratford Hall Plantation: The Birthplace of Robert E. Lee

http://www.stratfordhall.org

Made to encourage visits to Lee's birthplace; paints a complimentary picture of Lee through the use of primary documents and essays.

LONGSTREET, JAMES

See also The War Times Journal: The Civil War Series, in "General Sites"

The Longstreet Chronicles

http://tennessee-scv.org/longstreet/

Created by a Longstreet fan intent on rehabilitating Longstreet's reputation; contains essays and an impressive collection of primary sources.

LORING, WILLIAM WING

The William Wing Loring World Wide Website: 50 Years a Soldier

http://home.earthlink.net/~atomic_rom/loring.htm

Features a long, hyperlinked biography of this general who fought in the Seminole Wars and Mexican-American War before leaving the U.S. Army to serve as a Confederate general. After the war he became an adviser to the Egyptian army.

MOSBY, JOHN SINGLETON

The Memoirs of Colonel John S. Mosby

http://docsouth.unc.edu/mosby/menu.html

Complete text of his autobiography, which was published in 1917.

WHEELER, JOSEPH

Pond Spring and the Joe Wheeler Home

http://www.wheelerplantation.org

Made to encourage visits to the Wheeler Plantation; consists of a brief, illustrated biography of this lieutenant general of cavalry for the Confederate Army of the Mississippi. In 1898 he served as a U.S. general in the war against Spain.

LIFE OF THE SOLDIER

CAMP LIFE

An SR Books **BEST CIVIL WAR SITE** Selection

Camp Life: Civil War Collections from Gettysburg National Military Park

http://www.cr.nps.gov/museum/exhibits/gettex/

Handsome National Park Service site features images of artifacts from the Gettysburg National Military Park museum as well as informative explanations.

CONSCRIPTION

The Enrollment and the Draft

http://cdl.library.cornell.edu/cgi-bin/moa/sgml/moa-idx?notisid=ABP2287-0037-201

Scholarly 1889 magazine article by Lincoln aides J. G. Nicolay and John Hay.

ETHNIC GROUPS

Ethnic Groups and Immigrants

http://www.cwc.lsu.edu/cwc/links/links10.htm#Ethnic

Excellent links assembled by Louisiana State University.

"The Fighting 69th": 69th New York State Volunteers, Company A, First Regiment, Irish Brigade, "Faugh a Ballagh"

http://www.69thnysv.org/

Regimental history.

Geschichtstheatergesellschaft 1848 e.v.

http://www.gtg1848.de/

A German site devoted to German '48ers (refugees from the failed Revolution of 1848), who played a major role in the war. Mostly in English.

An SR Books
BEST
CIVIL
WAR
SITE
Selection

Jews in the Civil War

http://www.jewish-history.com/civilwar.htm

Contains a fascinating collection of firsthand accounts of the war by Jewish soldiers as well as correspondence from North and South.

FLAGS

Battle Flags of the Confederacy

http://members.tripod.com/~txscv/csa.htm

Over a dozen images and short descriptions of flags.

F O O D

An SR Books **BEST CIVIL WAR SITE** Selection

Feeding Billy Yank: Union Rations between 1861 and 1865

http://www.qmfound.com/feeding_billy_yank.htm

This informative essay, part of the U.S. Army Quartermaster Museum web site, provides a lively account of how Union soldiers managed to remain comparatively well fed throughout the course of the war.

H O S P I T A L S   A N D   M E D I C I N E

Casualties

http://www.cwc.lsu.edu/cwc/links/links13.htm#casualties

Good links assembled by Louisiana State University.

Civil War Medicine

http://www.powerweb.net/bbock/war/

Privately made site; consists largely of illustrated essays by the designer discussing developments in medical technology and hospital design over the course of the war; includes complete bibliography suggesting avenues for further research.

Hospitals in Richmond during the Civil War

http://www.mdgorman.com/hospitals.htm

Details and newspaper clippings about every hospital in this key medical center.

Leaves from the diary of an army surgeon; or, Incidents of field, camp, and hospital life

http://moa.umdl.umich.edu/cgi/sgml/moa-idx?notisid=ACK4209

Full text of 1863 memoir by Thomas T. Ellis.

Medicine in the Civil War

http://www.cl.utoledo.edu/canaday/quackery/quack8.html

Part of a large web site on the history of medicine created by the University of Toledo Library; describes wounds inflicted by different types of ammunition and explains how they were treated; contains drawings taken from *Medical and Surgical History of the War of the Rebellion*.

United States Sanitary Commission

http://www.netwalk.com/~jpr/index.htm

An excellent source of material on medical care for Civil War soldiers.

The Western Sanitary Commission; a sketch of its origin, history, labors for the sick and wounded of the Western armies, and aid given to freedmen and Union refugees, with incidents of hospital life

http://www.hti.umich.edu/cgi/t/text/text-idx?sid=fe61668e25ea3803&idno=ABV 3185.0001.001&view=header&c=moa

Full text of 1864 report.

Whitman's *Drum Taps* and Washington's Civil War Hospitals

http://xroads.virginia.edu/~CAP/hospital/whitman.htm

Made by a University of Virginia student as a class project; a compelling documentary account of military hospitals in Washington during the Civil War.

LETTERS AND DIARIES

American Civil War Collection at the Electronic Text Center

http://etext.virginia.edu/civilwar/#Letters

Massive, searchable collection of Civil War letters, diaries, and memoirs, all transcribed in full and with beautifully digitized scans of many of the originals.

American Civil War Resources in the Special Collections Department, University Libraries, Virginia Tech

http://spec.lib.vt.edu/civwar/

An impressive collection of Civil War letters—some transcribed and scanned, some transcribed but not scanned, and some only described. Maintained by the Virginia Polytechnic Institute.

The Calvin Shedd Papers

http://www.library.miami.edu/archives/shedd/index.htm

Made by the University of Miami Archives; contains the transcribed letters of a Yankee soldier stationed in Florida.

Civil War Diaries

http://sparc5.augustana.edu/library/civil.html

Created by the library of Augustana College; contains two Civil War diaries, one of which, by Basil H. Messler of the Mississippi Marine Brigade, has been painstakingly transcribed and annotated.

Civil War Diary of Bingham Findley Junkin

http://www.iwaynet.net/~lsci/junkin/

Diary of Bingham F. Junkin, of the 100th Pennsylvania Volunteer Infantry ("Roundheads"). It covers Junkin's experiences in the battles of the Wilderness and Cold Harbor.

Civil War Letters of the Christie Family

http://www.mnhs.org/library/Christie/intropage.html

Letters to home from three brothers from Minnesota.

Dwight Henry Cory Letters and Diary

http://homepages.rootsweb.com/~lovelace/cory.htm

Features transcription of letters written by Cory, 6th Ohio Volunteer Cavalry, as he took part in many of the major battles of the Eastern theater.

Illinois Greyhounds

http://www.ketzle.com/diary/

Made by a descendent of Henry Ketzle, who served in the 37th Illinois Volunteer Infantry; contains Ketzle's postwar memoirs.

An SR Books
BEST
CIVIL
WAR
SITE
Selection

Letters from an Iowa Soldier in the Civil War

www.civilwarletters.com

Created by descendents of the letters' authors; features transcriptions of more than a dozen letters written by Newton Robert Scott of the 36th Iowa Infantry to friends and family at home, with links from names and places mentioned in the letters to explanatory information.

[Iowa] Letters, Journals, Diaries, Oral Accounts and Historical Information from the Civil War

http://iowa-counties.com/civilwar/letters.htm

Assorted letters, diaries, reminiscences.

Letters of the Civil War (from the Newspapers of Massachusetts)

http://www.geocities.com/Pentagon/7914/

Privately made site; compilation of letters written by Massachusetts soldiers to their hometown newspapers.

Mary Chesnut Diary

http://docsouth.unc.edu/chesnut/menu.html

Chesnut (1823–1886) kept a voluminous diary in Richmond, where she knew everyone of importance and commented with clever insight into their strengths and foibles. Considered one of the great diaries of all time.

The Memoirs, Diary, and Life of Private Jefferson Moses, Company G, 93rd Illinois Volunteers

http://www.ioweb.com/civilwar/

Made by a descendent; contains the diary of Private Jefferson Moses, Company G, 93rd Illinois Volunteers, which has been transcribed and broken down by date and which covers events in 1864 and 1865 in the Carolinas.

Overall Family Civil War Letters

http://www.geocities.com/Heartland/Acres/1574/

Created by descendents of the Overall family to share the letters of Isaac Overall, a member of the 36th Ohio Volunteer Infantry, and his family at home; contains both transcriptions and scanned images of the letters as well as a helpful summary page.

Samuel S. Dunton Civil War Letters

http://home.pacbell.net/dunton/SSDletters.html

Made by a descendent; contains twelve letters written by Dunton while he was stationed near Washington and in Louisiana.

The Steubing Letters: The Civil War Letters of W. J. and Nancy Steubing

http://www.geocities.com/Athens/Cyprus/6533/

Contains transcriptions of sixteen letters written between William J. Steubing, a German immigrant who served as a blacksmith in the 26th Texas Cavalry, CSA, and his wife.

MILITARY LAWS AND REGULATIONS

Civil War—War Crimes: Rape During the War

http://hometown.aol.com/cwrapes

Made by a private researcher in France; contains transcriptions from soldiers' compiled military service records showing thirty-two U.S. soldiers executed for raping Southern women.

Laws of War: General Orders No. 100

http://www.yale.edu/lawweb/avalon/lieber.htm

Official legal instructions for Union soldiers, as prepared by Francis Lieber.

Revised Regulations for the Army of the United States, 1861

http://members.tripod.com/howardlanham/unireg.htm

Official details on uniforms.

M U S I C   A N D   P O E T R Y

Civil War Music of the Western Border

http://www.mid-mo.net/dpara/civilwar/

Created by a team of Missouri musicians to advertise their recordings; contains full lyrics of Civil War songs as well as liner notes from their albums.

Poetry and Music of the War Between the States

http://users.erols.com/kfraser/

Privately made site; contains lyrics and names of lyricists for hundreds of songs about the Civil War, most of which were composed during the war itself; songs can be heard with the proper plug-in.

P E N S I O N S

Civil War Records in the Florida State Archives

http://dlis.dos.state.fl.us/barm/fsa/civilwar.htm

Digitized files for 7,300 Confederate pensions.

P R I S O N S

Alton in the Civil War: Alton Prison

http://www.altonweb.com/history/civilwar/confed/index.html

Contains a brief history of this prison in southern Illinois as well as a database of the approximately 1,300 men who died while held there.

Archeology at Andersonville

http://www.cr.nps.gov/seac/andearch.htm

National Park Service site; contains a brief history of the notorious prison for captured Union soldiers and a description of the ongoing excavations at the site.

Camp Ford, C.S.A.

http://www.campford.org/

Contains a short history of Camp Ford, Texas, the largest Confederate prisoner of war camp west of the Mississippi River, a list of units to which the men imprisoned there belonged, and the number in each unit who died or escaped.

Famous Trials: The Trial of Captain Henry Wirz, Commandant, Andersonville Prison, 1865

http://www.law.umkc.edu/faculty/projects/ftrials/wirz/wirz.htm

Created by a team of law students at the University of Missouri-Kansas City; contains a detailed analysis of the trial and execution of the Confederate commander of Andersonville Prison.

Salisbury Confederate Prison

http://www.ci.salisbury.nc.us/prison/csprison1.htm

Made by the town of Salisbury, North Carolina; features original drawings and other documents about the Confederate prison there and a description of a disastrous escape attempt.

WWW Guide to Civil War Prisons

http://tigger.uic.edu/~rjensen/prisons.htm

Links and documents, compiled by Richard Jensen

NAVAL OPERATIONS

Official Records of the Union and Confederate Navies in the War of the Rebellion

http://library5.library.cornell.edu/moa/browse.monographs/ofre.html

Official Records Navy ser. 1, vol. 1; the basic original documents of both navies.

Index of Civil War Naval Forces, Confederate and Union Ships

http://www.tarleton.edu/~kjones/navy.html

Extremely thorough and organized links to material on Civil War ships.

Admiral David Glasgow Farragut (1801–1870)

http://www.encompass.net/ctyson/civwar/farmain.htm

Features Alfred Thayer Mahan's biography of this famous Union admiral.

Battle Between the *Monitor* and the *Virginia*

http://www.ironclads.com/

Privately made site; features an illustrated description of this famous naval battle.

Civil War@Charleston

http://www.awod.com/gallery/probono/cwchas/cwlayout.html

Made by a Civil War reenactor; describes naval battles in and around Charleston Harbor.

Confederate Navy Collection Index at the Virginia State Library

http://image.vtls.com/collections/CN.html

Contains the digitized records of Confederate navy veterans.

C.S.S. *Alabama* Digital Collection

http://www.lib.ua.edu/libraries/hoole/digital/cssala/main.shtml

Made by the University of Alabama W. S. Hoole Special Collections Library; features extensive resources about this famous Confederate raider.

CSS *Neuse* State Historic Site

http://www.ah.dcr.state.nc.us/sections/hs/neuse/neuse.htm

Created by the North Carolina Department of Cultural Resources; covers the CSS *Neuse*, a Confederate ironclad built in eastern North Carolina but destroyed before it could be put to use against the enemy; considers the problems the Confederacy faced in building a strong naval fleet; contains a description and photographs of the ship's remains.

CSS *Virginia* Home Page

http://cssvirginia.org

Made by a descendent of an officer aboard the CSS *Virginia* (a.k.a. *Merrimack*) during its battle with the USS *Monitor*; contains primary documents.

The *Denbigh* Project

http://nautarch.tamu.edu/projects/denbigh/index.htm

Maintained by the Institute of Nautical Archaeology at Texas A&M University, which has embarked on a project to identify, document, and preserve the wreck of the *Denbigh*, one of the most successful blockade runners; contains a capsule history, a small collection of documents, and photographs of the wreck.

Friends of the *Hunley*

http://www.hunley.org

Professionally designed site; provides an informative history of the *Hunley*.

Index of Civil War Naval Forces: Confederate and Union Ships

http://www.tarleton.edu/~kjones/navy.html

Very useful collection of links assembled by a professor at Tarleton University in Texas.

Ironclads and Blockade Runners of the American Civil War

http://www.ameritech.net/users/maxdemon/ironclad.htm

Privately made site; features an extensive collection of facts and frequently asked questions about naval aspects of the Civil War; also contains a bibliography, excerpts of documents, lists of commanders, and photographs.

Legacy of the USS *Monitor*

http://home.att.net/~iron.clad/

Made by a researcher at the Monitor National Marine Sanctuary; covers the status of the ongoing recovery effort; features underwater photographs, the *Monitor*'s crew list, and an essay on the history of this most famous of the Union ironclads.

Maple Leaf Shipwreck

http://www.mapleleafshipwreck.com/

Online collection of essays contributed by marine engineers, curators, amateur historians, and archaeologists about the *Maple Leaf*, a Union army transport ship sunk in 1864 by a Confederate torpedo; also features a lengthy bibliography.

Monitor: History and Legacy

http://www.mariner.org/monitor/

Created by the Mariners' Museum in Newport News, Virginia, the site provides an informative history of the *Monitor* as well as an overview of Union naval strategy.

Shotgun's Home of the American Civil War: Naval War

http://www.civilwarhome.com/navalwar.htm

Contains a large collection of excerpts of out-of-print books and primary sources.

St. Louis' Ships of Iron

http://www.usgennet.org/~ahmostlu/ironclads.htm

Exploration of the history of the St. Louis shipyard of James B. Eads and Company, which constructed the famous gunboats designed by Samuel Pook; contains digital photographs and drawings of the ships built there as well as a number of crew rosters.

Steam Machines

http://www.archaeology.org/online/features/steam/index.html

Created by the Museum of the Rockies; consists of an essay by a professor of historical archaeology at Montana State University describing the USS *Monitor*, the CSS *H. L. Hunley*, and other famous Civil War naval vessels.

"The Union Navy's Blockade Reconsidered"

http://www.nwc.navy.mil/press/Review/1998/autumn/art5-a98.htm

A 1998 scholarly article by economics professor David G. Surdam.

U.S. Marine Detachment: Washington Navy Yard (1859–1865)

http://www.geocities.com/Heartland/Plains/4198/

Made by a historical reenacting group; dedicated to documenting the contributions made by the U.S. Marine Corps in the Civil War.

U.S.S. *Harvest Moon*

http://members.aol.com/WaltESmith/hmhome.htm

Sponsored by the *Harvest Moon* Historical Society in Wilmington, North Carolina; documents the history of the blockade ship USS *Harvest Moon*, now resting on the ocean floor off the South Carolina coast, where the ship was sunk by a Confederate torpedo.

Wakulla County, Florida: Some Civil War Action

http://www.polaris.net/~rblacks/st-marks.htm

Privately made site; contains reprints of two previously published articles by the site's designer.

Wars and Conflicts of the United States Navy

http://www.history.navy.mil/wars/index.html#anchor4162

Made by the U.S. Navy; all aspects of the navy in the Civil War; includes a brief discussion of the CSS *Alabama*, a detailed chronology, and transcriptions of a few documents.

The *War Times Journal*: Civil War Navies

http://www.wtj.com/archives/acwnavies/

Selections from the official Navy records regarding the *Monitor* and the *Merrimack*.

When Liverpool Was Dixie

http://www.csa-dixie.com/Liverpool_Dixie/

Explains how Commander James Bulloch, CSN, purchased and outfitted raiders. He was the uncle of Theodore Roosevelt, but remained in England after the war and died in exile.

Yazoo Naval Preservation Foundation

http://www.geocities.com/Pentagon/5106/index.html

Made by the Yazoo Naval Preservation Foundation; contains a brief history of naval action in Yazoo, Mississippi.

THE EXPERIENCE OF THE U.S. COLORED TROOPS

GENERAL SITES

An SR Books
BEST CIVIL WAR SITE
Selection

The African American Experience in Ohio, 1850–1920

http://dbs.ohiohistory.org/africanam

Made by the Ohio Historical Society; contains a searchable database of newspaper articles, pamphlets, and photographs written by and about Ohio's African Americans.

An SR Books
BEST CIVIL WAR SITE
Selection

The African American Odyssey: A Quest for Full Citizenship

http://lcweb2.loc.gov/ammem/aaohtml/exhibit/aointro.html

Small part of the Library of Congress's American Memory Project; narrative about the experience of African American Union soldiers; includes letters written by the sons of Frederick Douglass to their father.

African Americans at Petersburg

http://www.nps.gov/pete/mahan/eduhistafam.html

Section of the National Park Service site about Petersburg; describes the role of the USCT in the Union siege, especially the Confederate victory at the Battle of the Crater.

An SR Books
BEST CIVIL WAR SITE
Selection

The Battle of Olustee

http://extlab1.entnem.ufl.edu/olustee/

Made by a private researcher employed by the University of Florida; contains a detailed discussion of the role played by USCT regiments in this Florida battle.

Fort Pillow: Lincoln Retaliates

http://cdl.library.cornell.edu/cgi-bin/moa/moa-cgi?notisid=ABP2287-0037-200

Scholarly article, published in 1889, by Lincoln aides J. G. Nicolay and John Hay.

Fort Pillow Massacre (April 12, 1864)

http://www.civilwarhome.com/ftpillow.htm

Documents regarding episode where colored soldiers were massacred by General Forrest's troops.

Fort Scott National Historic Site

http://www.nps.gov/fosc/

National Park Service site; contains a page on African American units raised in the Fort Scott, Kansas, area.

Freedmen and Southern Society Project: The Black Military Experience

http://www.history.umd.edu/Freedmen/

Contains a powerful collection of transcribed primary source documents drawn from the multivolume book series, *Freedom: A Documentary History of Emancipation, 1861– 1867.*

"Freedom Fighters": United States Colored Troops in the Civil War

http://www.coax.net/people/lwf/data.htm

By Bennie J. McRae Jr.; features an extensive collection of documents in addition to interesting timelines.

National Park Service Civil War Soldiers and Sailors System: History of African Americans in the Civil War

http://www.itd.nps.gov/cwss/history/aa_history.htm

National Park Service site; consists of a searchable database of all the men who served in the USCT, brief histories of every USCT regiment, and biographical sketches of USCT Congressional Medal of Honor recipients.

The Negro in the American Rebellion.

http://www.hti.umich.edu/cgi/t/text/text-idx?c=moa;idno=ABY0202

Full text of 1867 scholarly book by leading African American scholar William Wells Brown.

Teaching with Historic Documents Lesson Plan: The Fight for Equal Rights—Black Soldiers in the Civil War

http://www.archives.gov/digital_classroom/lessons/blacks_in_civil_war/blacks_in_civil_war.html

National Archives site designed primarily for teachers and students; contains background material and digitized primary sources valuable for researchers at all levels.

United States Colored Troops at Camp Nelson, Kentucky

http://www.campnelson.org/colored

Made by the Camp Nelson Restoration and Preservation Foundation; describes the history of Camp Nelson, which during the Civil War served as an American Missionary Society school and a refugee center for black soldiers' families as well as a recruiting place for more than 10,000 men for the USCT.

The Valley of the Shadow: Two Communities in the American Civil War

http://valley.vcdh.virginia.edu/

An extensive multimedia archive created at the University of Virginia that takes two communities—Augusta County, Virginia, and Franklin County, Pennsylvania—through the experience of the Civil War. The War Years section contains rich material on the USCT.

REGIMENTAL HISTORIES

Like the sites listed in the Civil War Regiments index, these sites generally contain a combination of one or more of the following: rosters, *Official Records*, letters and diaries, and photographs.

Museum of the Kansas National Guard: Historic Units

http://skyways.lib.ks.us/kansas/museums/kng/kngunits.html

Developed by the Kansas National Guard; contains the histories of every Kansas-based military regiment, including the 1st Kansas (Colored) Volunteer Infantry and the 2nd Kansas (Colored) Volunteer Infantry, which are considered by some to be the first officially raised troops of African American soldiers in the Civil War.

5th Regimental Cavalry, United States Colored Troops

http://mywebpages.comcast.net/5thuscc/

7th Regiment Colored Infantry

http://members.aol.com/BlountAL/7th.html

8th United States Colored Troops

http://extlab1.entnem.ufl.edu/olustee/8th_USCI.HTML

29th Infantry, United States Colored Troops

http://www.illinoiscivilwar.org/cw29col.html

35th United States Colored Troops (First North Carolina Colored Volunteers)

http://extlab1.entnem.ufl.edu/olustee/35th_USCI.html

54th Massachusetts Company B

http://www.54thmass.org/

History of 73rd U.S.C.T. (1st Louisiana Native Guards)

http://www.siteone.com/tourist/blakeley/73rdUSCT.htm

The Louisiana Native Guards

http://www2.netdoor.com/~jgh/

Records of the 105th US Colored Troops

http://www.awod.com/gallery/probono/cwchas/usct105.html

111th Regiment Colored Infantry

http://members.aol.com/BlountAL/111th.html

U.S. Colored Troops formed in North Carolina

http://www.rootsweb.com/~ncusct/usct.htm

S LAVERY AND EMANCIPATION

Abolitionism

http://www.hti.umich.edu/cgi/t/text/text-idx?c=moa;idno=ABT7101

Speeches, lectures, and letters as well as an 1872 collection of writings by leading white abolitionist Wendell Phillips.

The African American Odyssey: A Quest for Full Citizenship

http://lcweb2.loc.gov/ammem/aaohtml/exhibit/aointro.html

Part of the Library of Congress's extensive American Memory Project; tells the story of slavery and emancipation through important documents and explanatory narrative.

African American Women: On-line Archival Collections

http://scriptorium.lib.duke.edu/collections/african-american-women.html

Transcribed letters from slave women to their owners and former owners.

Africans in America

http://www.pbs.org/wgbh/aia/

Made by the Public Broadcasting Service to serve as a companion to the television series of the same name; designed primarily for classroom teachers as an interactive textbook on the rise and fall of slavery in the United States.

American Slave Narratives: An Online Anthology

http://xroads.virginia.edu/~HYPER/wpa/wpahome.html

Created by a graduate student at the University of Virginia; contains transcriptions and some audio recordings of interviews with former slaves.

"Been Here So Long": Selections from the WPA American Slave Narratives

http://newdeal.feri.org/asn/

Collection of slave narratives assembled in the 1930s by the Works Progress Administration. Uses thematic organization of transcripts, with an eye toward classroom use.

The District of Columbia Emancipation Act

http://www.archives.gov/exhibit_hall/featured_documents/dc_
emancipation_act/

Small National Archives and Records Administration site; contains a scan of the original 1862 District of Columbia Emancipation Act, the only case of compensated emancipation in the United States, as well as a transcription and a brief explanatory essay.

Documenting the American South: North American Slave Narratives

http://docsouth.unc.edu/neh/neh.html

The University of North Carolina has built probably the most extensive online collection of nineteenth- and early twentieth-century slave narratives; they have been transcribed in full and are fully searchable.

The Dred Scott Case

http://library.wustl.edu/vlib/dredscott/

Transcribed and scanned court papers from Dred and Harriet Scott's first attempts to win their freedom through the court system.

Emancipation Proclamation

http://memory.loc.gov/ammem/alhtml/almintr.html

Part of the Library of Congress's American Memory Project; features a timeline that traces the evolution of federal emancipation policy over the course of the Civil War; also contains scans of early drafts of the Emancipation Proclamation as well as the official order issued in January 1863.

The Emancipation Proclamation

http://www.archives.gov/exhibit_hall/featured_documents/emancipation_proclamation/

National Archives online exhibit; contains explanatory narrative, a scan and transcription of the National Emancipation Act, an essay by John Hope Franklin, and audio files of Works Progress Administration slave interviews.

Excerpts from Slave Narratives

http://vi.uh.edu/pages/mintz/primary.htm

Developed by University of Houston history professor Steven Mintz; contains thematically organized transcriptions of forty-six previously published, public domain, firsthand accounts of slavery.

Free at Last: A History of the Abolition of Slavery in America

http://www.yale.edu/glc/archive/index.html

Created by the Gilder Lehrman Institute of American History; serves as an interactive textbook on the history of slavery and emancipation; features mostly secondary narrative written by prominent historians.

Freedmen and Southern Society Project

http://www.history.umd.edu/Freedmen/

Contains selections from the multivolume documentary book series by the same name, edited by scholars at the University of Maryland and other institutions; features a detailed timeline showing the development of emancipation policy over the course of the Civil War in addition to a rich collection of documents.

Jesuit Plantation Project: Maryland's Jesuit Plantations, 1650–1838

http://www.georgetown.edu/departments/amer_studies/jpp/coverjpp.html

Diaries and correspondence of the Jesuit priests who oversaw plantations in eastern Maryland and who attempted to reconcile their Christianity with slave owning.

John Brown's Holy War

http://www.pbs.org/wgbh/amex/brown/index.html

Companion to PBS television program on John Brown's efforts to start a slave rebellion.

Levi Jordan Plantation Project

http://www.webarchaeology.com

Uses the tools of archaeology and history to explore the lives of black and white residents of a Texas plantation before, during, and after the Civil War; includes descriptions of artifacts found at the plantation, which show evidence of direct African influence. A collaboration between university scholars, local historians, and descendents of plantation residents.

Sheet Music about Lincoln, Emancipation, and the Civil War

http://memory.loc.gov/ammem/scsmhtml/scsmhome.html

Section of the Library of Congress's American Memory Project; consists of a searchable collection—both scans of the original sheet music and transcriptions of the lyrics—of hundreds of Civil War-era songs, many of which are about the end of slavery.

Slavery in the United States

http://www.eh.net/encyclopedia/wahl.slavery.us.php

Scholarly article by economist Jenny B. Wahl, from the EH.Net Encyclopedia

Third Person, First Person: Slave Voices from the Special Collections Library

http://scriptorium.lib.duke.edu/slavery/

Online version of a Duke University Library exhibit; features scans of plantation records and slaveowner correspondence.

Toward Racial Equality: *Harper's Weekly* Reports on Black America, 1857–1874

http://blackhistory.harpweek.com

Scores of articles, illustrations, and cartoons pertaining to African American history accompanied by explanatory narrative and useful timelines.

Uncle Tom's Cabin and American Culture: A Multi-Media Archive

http://jefferson.village.virginia.edu/utc/

Extensive collection of transcribed documents and artifacts that place Harriet Beecher Stowe's famous antislavery novel in the context of the literary, political, and religious conventions of midnineteenth-century America.

The Valley of the Shadow: Two Communities in the American Civil War

http://jefferson.village.edu/vshadow2/

Created at the University of Virginia; allows visitors to recreate the world of slaves and slaveholders before, during, and after the Civil War through documents such as newspapers and letters, Freedmen's Bureau records, and the 1860 Augusta County, Virginia, slaveowner census.

Virginia Runaways Project

http://www.uvawise.edu/history/runaways/

A digital database of over 2,000 advertisements for runaway and captured slaves, servants, and military deserters from eighteenth-century Virginia newspapers.

WOMEN IN THE CIVIL WAR

American Civil War Civilians

http://reality.sgi.com/dianeg_corp/civil_war_civ/

Concentrates on female nurses—notably Dorothea Dix—as well as the Women's Loyal League; consists largely of essays by the site's designer.

The Civil War Comes to Hardin County

http://www.hardinhistory.com/history/war.htm

Created by the Hardin County Historical Society in Tennessee; includes many reports of hardship on the home front.

Civil War Richmond

http://www.mdgorman.com/

Privately made site; contains a discussion of women's work in Richmond's Civil War hospitals.

Civil War Women: On-line Archival Collections

http://scriptorium.lib.duke.edu/collections/civil-war-women.html

Created by Duke University; features the diaries and correspondence of Rose O'Neal Greenhow, the well-known Confederate spy; Sarah Thompson, an active pro-Union partisan in Tennessee; and Alice Williamson, a young pro-Confederate woman living under federal occupation in Gallatin, Tennessee.

Clara Barton: National Historic Site

http://www.nps.gov/clba/

National Park Service site; contains a chronology of the nurse's life; she later founded the American Red Cross.

Documenting the American South

http://metalab.unc.edu/docsouth/

Made by the University of North Carolina; contains dozens of memoirs and other fully transcribed and searchable documents chronicling the experiences of Southern women during the Civil War.

Hearts at Home: Southern Women in the Civil War

http://www.lib.virginia.edu/exhibits/hearts/

Created by the University of Virginia; features digitized letters, magazine illustrations, and rare books that capture the experience of Southern women during the Civil War.

Illinois Alive! Illinois in the Civil War: Private Albert D. J. Cashier (Jennie Hodgers)

http://www.alliancelibrarysystem.com/IllinoisAlive/files/iv/htm2/ivtxt002.cfm

Sponsored by the Illinois State Archives; tells the story of a woman who assumed a male identity, fought in the 95th Illinois, and maintained her disguise for decades after the war.

NARA Prologue: Women Soldiers of the Civil War

http://www.nara.gov/publications/prologue/women1.html

1993 scholarly article by DeAnne Blanton about women who disguised themselves as men to fight in the Civil War.

Shotgun's Home of the American Civil War: Civil War Biographies

http://www.civilwarhome.com/biograph.htm

Privately made site; includes short biographies of notable Civil War women, including Clara Barton, Belle Boyd, Varina Howell Davis, and Sojourner Truth

United States Sanitary Commission

http://www.netwalk.com/~jpr/index.htm

Made by a Civil War reenactor; consists of a thorough documentary account of this soldiers' aid organization staffed largely by women volunteers.

The Valley of the Shadow: Two Communities in the American Civil War

http://valley.vcdh.virginia.edu/

Major project from the University of Virginia; features letters and diaries, government documents, and transcriptions of newspaper articles from two communities—one in the North and one in the South—that capture the experience of women living at home in areas never far removed from the fighting.

Woman's Work in the Civil War: A Record of Heroism, Patriotism and Patience

http://www.hti.umich.edu/cgi/b/bib/bibperm?q1=ACP3511

Complete text, 810 pages, of detailed 1867 memorial volume by P. Brockett and Mrs. Mary C. Vaughan.

Women and the Freedmen's Aid Movement, 1863–1891

http://womhist.binghamton.edu/aid/intro.htm

Created by the State University of New York at Geneseo; considers how women, who played an active role in the antislavery movement, also led efforts to help freedmen build their new lives after the war; shows how they were frustrated by cautious officials and an apathetic public.

Women of the War: Their Heroism and Self-Sacrifice

http://www.hti.umich.edu/cgi/b/bib/bibperm?q1=abv3165

Complete text of important 1866 book by Frank Moore.

CIVIL WAR REGIMENTS

In general, regimental history sites are similar in their sponsorship and types of content. Most have been created by private individuals working on their own time, often with the sponsorship of a living history or reenactment organization. For the most part these sites contain at least two of the following types of material: rosters, excerpts from the *Official Records*, and excerpts from previously published histories of the unit. Some also contain photographs, letters, and diaries.

GENERAL SITES

National Park Service Civil War Soldiers and Sailors System

http://www.itd.nps.gov/cwss/regiments.htm

Contains brief histories and rosters of thousands of Union and Confederate regiments, searchable by side (Union or Confederate), state, unit number, and function (Infantry, Cavalry, Artillery, Sharpshooters, and Engineers).

ALABAMA

The Civil War Archive: Union Regiments—Alabama

http://www.civilwararchive.com/unional.htm

Gracie's—Moody's Alabama Brigade 1862–1865

http://www.tarleton.edu/~kjones/gracie.html

Law's Alabama Brigade 1862–1865

http://www.tarleton.edu/~kjones/lawsbrig.html

Morgan's Alabama Cavalry Brigade 1863–1865

http://www.tarleton.edu/%7Ekjones/morgan.html

1st Alabama Cavalry

http://www.geocities.com/coh41/1stRegAlCavCSA.html

4th Alabama "Roddey's" Cavalry, Confederate States Army

http://www.geocities.com/BourbonStreet/Delta/3843/4thalabama.htm

5th Alabama Battalion History

http://www.fred.net/stevent/5AL/5al.html

6th Alabama Infantry Regiment Home Page

http://www.archives.state.al.us/referenc/alamilor/6thinf.html

Mobile German Fusiliers, Co. H, 8th Alabama Infantry, CSA

http://www.37thtexas.org/html/gerfus1.html

History of the 16th Alabama

http://www.auburn.edu/~emmonmb/unit/history/

The 17th Alabama Regimental History

http://www.fred.net/stevent/17AL/17al.html

19th Alabama Infantry Regiment, C.S.A.

http://www.19thalabama.org

22nd Alabama Infantry Regiment

http://www.archives.state.al.us/referenc/alamilor/22ndinf.html

23rd Alabama Volunteer Infantry Regiment, CSA

http://www.canerossi.us/23ala/

25th Alabama Infantry Regiment

http://home.earthlink.net/~sdriskell/25th/25th.htm

O'Neal's 26th Alabama

http://www.rootsweb.com/~alcw26/26thala.htm

27th Alabama Infantry, Confederate States Army

http://www.datasync.com/~jtaylor/27th.htm

28th Alabama Infantry Regiment

http://members.aol.com/publishcon/index.html

32nd Infantry Regiment of Alabama

http://www.bensgenealogycorner.org/compdal.html
Roster only.

History of the 33rd Alabama Infantry, CSA

http://members.aol.com/wwhitby/33rd.html

Alabama 37th Regiment, CSA

http://gen.culpepper.com/military/civilwar/AL37/1862Apr-Aug.htm

41st Alabama Regimental Infantry

http://www.mindspring.com/%7Ecalrome/41st.htm

42nd Alabama Infantry

http://www.rootsweb.com/~al42inf/

43rd Alabama Infantry and Gracie's Alabama Brigade
http://www.geocities.com/Pentagon/Barracks/3313/index.html

44th Alabama Infantry
http://ephedrine2.tripod.com/CSA/main.html

46th Alabama Infantry Regiment
http://www.archives.state.al.us/referenc/alamilor/46thinf.html

The History of the 47th Alabama Volunteer Infantry Regiment in the American Civil War
http://www.geocities.com/Heartland/Ridge/9202/

62nd Alabama Volunteer Infantry
http://62ndalabama.org/

ARKANSAS

Arkansas Civil War Information
http://www.rootsweb.com/~arcivwar/

The Civil War Archive: Union Regiments—Arkansas
http://www.civilwararchive.com/unionar.htm

The Pulaski Lancers
http://www.couchgenweb.com/civilwar/lancers.html

3rd Arkansas Infantry Regiment
http://www.couchgenweb.com/civilwar/3rd-his.html

History of the 11th/17th Arkansas Mounted Infantry
http://www.geocities.com/Pentagon/1117/1117inf.html

CALIFORNIA

California in the Civil War
http://members.aol.com/bgandersen/civ_war/index.html

The California Historical Artillery Society

http://www.geocities.com/Athens/Crete/1870/

The Civil War Archive: Union Regiments—California

http://www.civilwararchive.com/unionca.htm

COLORADO

The Civil War Archive: Union Regiments—Colorado

http://www.civilwararchive.com/unionco.htm

CONNECTICUT

The Civil War Archive: Union Regiments—Connecticut

http://www.civilwararchive.com/unionct.htm

The 2nd Connecticut Volunteer Regiment

http://members.aol.com/fecook/cw/2ndct.htm

8th Regiment Connecticut Volunteers, Company A., Inc.

http://home.attbi.com/%7E8cv/8cv-frame.html

15th Connecticut Infantry

http://15ct.homestead.com/home.html

Roster of the 16th Connecticut Regiment, Volunteer Infantry

http://members.aol.com/Sholmes54/rost16ct.html

The 17th Connecticut Volunteer Infantry

http://home.att.net/~DogSgt/Seventeenth.html

The 18th Connecticut Volunteer Regiment

http://members.aol.com/fecook/cw/18thct.htm

The 26th Connecticut Volunteers

http://hometown.aol.com/conn26/myhomepage/index.html

DAKOTA TERRITORY

The Civil War Archive: Union Regiments—Dakota
http://www.civilwararchive.com/uniondt.htm

DELAWARE

The Civil War Archive: Union Regiments—Delaware
http://www.civilwararchive.com/unionde.htm

DISTRICT OF COLUMBIA

The Civil War Archive: Union Regiments—District of Columbia
http://www.civilwararchive.com/uniondc.htm

FLORIDA

Civil War Rosters: Florida Links
http://www.geocities.com/Area51/Lair/3680/cw/cw-fl.html

1st Battalion Florida Special Cavalry
http://www.geocities.com/yes_album/Special_Cavalry.html

1st Florida Regiment of Volunteer Infantry and Florida Brigade History
http://plaza.ufl.edu/moverton/html/1stFla.html

1st Florida Volunteer Infantry Unit History
http://extlab1.entnem.ufl.edu/olustee/1st_FL_History.html

Florida 2nd Infantry
http://www.psy.fsu.edu/%7Ethompson/cw/2-fl-inf/fl-2nd-inf.html

GEORGIA

The Georgia State Line
http://members.carol.net/~rickysahn/GSL/gslmain.htm

The Lawton-Gordon-Evans Georgia Brigade (CSA) (13th, 26th, 31st, 38th, 60th, & 61st Georgia Regiments, 12th Georgia Light Artillery Battalion)

http://users.erols.com/brant/GeorgiaBrigade/

1st Georgia Infantry (USA)

http://www.izzy.net/~michaelg/n-ga1.htm

1st Battalion Georgia Sharpshooters

http://members.tripod.com/k_thurman/1st_battalion_georgia_sharpshoot.htm

Co. "G," 3rd Regiment, Georgia Volunteer Infantry

http://www.forttejon.org/ga3/

The 5th Georgia Cavalry Regiment Home Page

http://www.pollette.com/5thcavalry/index.htm

8th Georgia Infantry Webpage

http://home.earthlink.net/~larsrbl/8thGeorgiaInfantry.html

Co. "A," 8th GA. Battalion Vols., Gist's Brigade, Army of Tennessee, Recruited from Bartow and Gordon Counties, Sept., 1861

http://www.hardlink.com/~rlk/roster.html

Historical Sketch of Company G, 8th Georgia, CSA

http://www.mindspring.com/~jtfleming/CoG_1.htm

9th Georgia Infantry CSA, 1861–65

http://members.aol.com/Gainf9reg/index2.html

11th Georgia Artillery Battalion—The Sumter Flying Artillery

http://www.sumterartillery.com/

12th Georgia Battalion Light Artillery

http://www.pollette.com/12thbat/staff.htm

22nd Georgia Infantry

http://www.mindspring.com/~jcherepy/22d_ga/22d_ga.html

27th Regiment Georgia Volunteer Infantry

http://www.cviog.uga.edu/Projects/gainfo/27th-rgt.htm

28th Georgia Volunteer Infantry

http://www.28thga.org/

32nd Georgia Infantry Regiment, 1862–1865

http://www.pollette.com/32d/home.htm

34th Georgia Regiment

http://members.aol.com/confed1864/34thGaindex.html

42nd Georgia Volunteer Infantry

http://www.42ndgeorgia.com/

52nd Regiment Georgia Volunteer Infantry

http://www.geocities.com/Pentagon/Bunker/6739/

65th Regiment Georgia Volunteer Infantry, Army of Tennessee, C.S.A.

http://www.izzy.net/~michaelg/65ga-vi.htm

ILLINOIS

The Civil War Archive: Union Regiments—Illinois

http://www.civilwararchive.com/unionil.htm

Database of Illinois Civil War Veterans in the Illinois State Archives

http://www.cyberdriveillinois.com/departments/archives/datcivil.html

Includes downloadable document on history of Illinois Civil War Regiments.

Illinois in the Civil War: Infantry, Cavalry, and Artillery Units

http://www.illinoiscivilwar.org/units_num.html

Illinois Greyhounds

http://www.ketzle.com/diary/

2nd Illinois Light Artillery, Battery G

http://www.grapevine.net/~battg2/BattGhom.html

4th Illinois Cavalry

http://www.4thillinoiscavalry.com/

**7th Illinois Mounted Infantry, Men of Company "H,"
1861 to 1865, Lincoln, Logan Co., Illinois**

http://members.tripod.com/~rjsnyder/Seventh.htm

9th Illinois Volunteer Infantry

http://www.4thillinoiscavalry.com/

30th Illinois Infantry, Company B

http://www.iltrails.org/randolph/military/cob3oil.htm

Roster only.

The History of the 35th Illinois Infantry

http://www.staff.uiuc.edu/~seadams/35thhis.html

36th Infantry Regiment

http://members.aol.com/fkt4387/36inf/36.htm

48th Illinois Infantry

http://members.evansville.net/cham/

48th Illinois Infantry

http://members.tripod.com/Black_eagle_129/index.html

59th Illinois Infantry

http://www.warmbrodtscivilwar.com/59index.html

63rd Illinois Infantry Regiment

http://www.rootsweb.com/%7Eilcivilw/reg_html/063_reg.htm

82nd Illinois Volunteer Infantry: A Regiment of Immigrants

http://www.geocities.com/Athens/Parthenon/7419/

89th Illinois Infantry

http://www.geocities.com/Athens/Parthenon/7419/

INDIANA

The Civil War Archive: Union Regiments—Indiana
http://www.civilwararchive.com/unionin.htm

Indiana in the Civil War: Indiana Regiments
http://www.indianainthecivilwar.com/rgmnt/regiment.htm

Union Regimental Histories
http://165.138.44.13/civilwar/INDREG.HTM

The Iron Brigade of the West [2nd, 6th, 7th Wisconsin; 19th Indiana; 24th Michigan; 4th U.S. Light Artillery]
http://carroll1.cc.edu/civilwar/ib.html

5th Battery—Indiana Light Artillery
http://www.7thkentucky.org/artillery.htm

The 7th Indiana Cavalry, 199th Regiment
http://www.indianacavalry.org/7th/home.htm

History of the 12th Indiana Cavalry
http://www.geocities.com/Heartland/Hills/4957/12thcav.html

31st Indiana Volunteer Infantry
http://www.psci.net/~hutch/

32nd Indiana Volunteer Infantry
http://www.serve.com/shea/germusa/infantry.htm

32nd Indiana Volunteer Infantry, "First German" Regiment
http://w3.one.net/%7Eedp/

32nd Volunteer Infantry: Indiana's German Sons
http://www-lib.iupui.edu/kade/peake/index.html

35th Indiana Infantry: "First Irish"
http://www-lib.iupui.edu/kade/peake/index.html

39th Indiana Regiment Infantry (Reorganized as 8th Indiana Regiment Cavalry)

http://www.rootsweb.com/%7Einhoward/data/military/39threghist.html

The 42nd Indiana Volunteer Infantry

http://www.geocities.com/indiana42nd/

47th Indiana Volunteer Infantry

http://mywebpages.comcast.net/klindsey/47thindiana.htm

49th Indiana Volunteer Infantry, "Company F"

http://www.kiva.net/~bjohnson/49th.html

70th Regiment, Indiana Volunteers

http://www.frontier.net/~pmross/

101st Indiana Infantry

http://home.att.net/%7Eb.d.henry/page9.html

INDIAN TERRITORY (OKLAHOMA)

Confederate Indian Units in the Civil War of the West

http://members.aol.com/ciiisiii/cherokeepage/indcsaunits.htm

IOWA

The Civil War Archive: Union Regiments—Iowa

http://www.civilwararchive.com/unionia.htm

Sioux City Cavalry

http://www.siouxvalley.net/%7Edrps484/

3rd Iowa Cavalry

http://www.iowa3rdcavalry.com/

Corporal Dennis Sasse's Iowa 4th Page

http://www.angelfire.com/ia/fourth/index.html

5th Iowa Volunteer Cavalry
http://www.scriptorum.org/c.html

5th Iowa Volunteer Infantry
http://www.scriptorum.org/i.html

14th Iowa Volunteer Infantry Regiment
http://www.iowa-counties.com/civilwar/14th_inf/index.htm

15th Iowa Infantry
http://www.iowa-counties.com/civilwar/15th_inf/

23rd Iowa Infantry Regiment
http://home.okstate.edu/homepages.nsf/toc/23rd.htm

24th Iowa Infantry
http://www.iowa-counties.com/civilwar/24th_inf/index.htm

27th Iowa Infantry
http://www.iowa-counties.com/civilwar/27th_inf/index.htm

32nd Regiment Iowa Volunteer Infantry, Company B
http://narn.jumpgate.net/~rbone/roster.htm
Roster only.

History of the 39th Iowa Infantry
http://www.angelfire.com/ia/captjoejoe/history.html

KANSAS

Museum of the Kansas National Guard: Historic Units
http://skyways.lib.ks.us/kansas/museums/kng/kngunits.html
Histories of all Kansas regiments.

1st Kansas Volunteer Infantry
http://www.firstkansas.org/index.html

12th Kansas Volunteer Infantry, Company K
http://www.geocities.com/MotorCity/1949/cok12ks.htm

KENTUCKY

The Civil War Archive: Union Regiments—Kentucky

http://www.civilwararchive.com/unionky.htm

The 1st Kentucky Brigade, CSA: The "Orphan Brigade"

http://www.rootsweb.com/~orphanhm/index.html

The 3rd Kentucky Cavalry

http://home.okstate.edu/homepages.nsf/toc/3rdCav.htm

The 5th Battery of Light Artillery

http://www.7thkentucky.org/ahistoric.htm

The 5th Kentucky Volunteer Infantry Regiment US (The Louisville Legion)

http://www.geocities.com/ky5thinfantry/

The 6th Kentucky Union Cavalry

http://www.users.mis.net/~chesnut/pages/sixth.htm

The 6th Kentucky Volunteer Infantry Regiment U.S.

http://www.geocities.com/jreinhart_us/

The 7th Kentucky Cavalry (Union)

http://members.tripod.com/~DutchR/7cav/index.html

The 7th Volunteer Infantry [U.S.]

http://www.7thkentucky.org/ioriginal.htm

The 8th Kentucky Infantry Regiment (CSA)

http://php.indiana.edu/~crabtre/8thky/8thky-main.htm

The 8th Kentucky Volunteer Cavalry Regiment (US)

http://www.geocities.com/~etelamaki_home/8thkent.html

9th Kentucky Infantry Regiment

http://home.okstate.edu/homepages.nsf/toc/9th.htm

9th Kentucky Volunteer Cavalry, Union
http://www.rootsweb.com/~kyhenry/9thky.htm

11th Kentucky ("Chenault's") Cavalry, CSA
http://www.geocities.com/BourbonStreet/Delta/3843/

11th Kentucky Infantry Regiment
http://home.okstate.edu/homepages.nsf/toc/11th.htm

14th Kentucky (Union) Cavalry
http://www.users.mis.net/~chesnut/pages/fourteen.htm

14th Kentucky Volunteer Infantry (USA), 1861–1865
http://freepages.military.rootsweb.com/~us14thkyinfantry/

16th Kentucky Volunteer Infantry [U.S.]
http://www.mt.net/~mtsysdev/civilwar/16thkyinf.htm

The 39th Kentucky Mounted Infantry Webpage [U.S.]
http://www.geocities.com/Heartland/Ridge/7616/

47th Kentucky Mounted Infantry
http://www.geocities.com/thomasspeed2/47kyinf.html

53rd Kentucky Mounted Infantry [U.S.]
http://www.geocities.com/Heartland/5170/53rdkent.htm

54th Regiment Kentucky Infantry, Union
http://www.rootsweb.com/~kyhenry/54.htm

Kentucky State Guard
http://members.aol.com/jweaver302/CW/kystgrd.htm

LOUISIANA

The Civil War Archive: Union Regiments—Louisiana
http://www.civilwararchive.com/unionla.htm

1st Battalion Louisville Zouaves National Website

http://www.angelfire.com/la/CoppensZouaves/

1st Louisiana Cavalry Regiment, Confederate States Army

http://members.tripod.com/%7Etcc230/lacavreg.htm

3rd Louisiana Cavalry, C.S.A.

http://www.cnnw.net/~rebcav/history/3lacavhis.htm

The Washington Artillery of New Orleans—5th Company and The 6th Massachusetts Light Artillery

http://www.geocities.com/Heartland/Woods/3501/

8th Louisiana Regiment, Army of Northern Virginia

http://www.geocities.com/BourbonStreet/Bayou/4566/tigers.html

9th Infantry Regiment Louisiana Volunteers

http://tcc230.tripod.com/9thlainf/Page_1x.html

10th La. Vol. Infantry: "Lee's Foreign Legion"

http://users.interlinks.net/rebel/10th/10th.htm

The 14th Louisiana Regimental History

http://www.fred.net/stevent/14LA/14la.html

Henry Gray's 28th Infantry Regiment

http://members.tripod.com/~pipeslines/

Thomas's 28th Infantry Regiment

http://www.geocities.com/Pentagon/Quarters/5361/

MAINE

Summary Unit Histories and Related Materials at the Maine State Archives

http://www.state.me.us/sos/arc/archives/military/civilwar/reghis.htm

1st Maine Heavy Artillery

http://www.cwoodcock.com/firstmaine/

History of the 3rd Maine Regiment

http://www.powerlink.net/mcgill/page2.html

The 7th Maine Regiment

http://hometown.aol.com/ME7THCOK/index.html

Civil War Service of the 9th Maine Infantry

http://members.aol.com/heavsusan/ninthmaine.html

The 11th Regiment Maine Infantry Volunteers

http://members.tripod.com/~Scott_Michaud/11th-Maine.html

13th Regiment, Maine Volunteer Infantry at Ship Island, Mississippi

http://www.ametro.net/~bouchard/civilwar/cosdf13me.html

MARYLAND

The Civil War Archive: Union Regiments—Maryland

http://www.civilwararchive.com/unionmd.htm

Battalion History of 1st Maryland Cavalry Battalion, CSA

http://www.cybcon.com/~warren/FirstMaryland/generate.cgi

History and Battles of the 1st Maryland Artillery, CSA

http://www.angelfire.com/md/freestaterebel/1stMD2.html

The 2nd Maryland Infantry, U.S., 1861–1865

http://home.att.net/%7Esecondmdus/2md.html

6th Maryland Regiment of Infantry

http://home.earthlink.net/%7Eearthalive/familystories/SixthMDdescendants.html

MASSACHUSETTS

The Civil War Archive: Union Regiments—Massachusetts

http://www.civilwararchive.com/unionma.htm

Massachusetts Volunteer Cavalry 1st Regiment

http://members.aol.com/Shortyhack/1stmass.html

1st Massachusetts Volunteer Infantry

http://members.rogers.com/catrinka/1massinf.html

"Gordon's Regulars": The 2nd Massachusetts Infantry in the Civil War

http://www.geocities.com/Pentagon/2126/

The Washington Artillery of New Orleans—5th Company and The 6th Massachusetts Light Artillery

http://www.geocities.com/Heartland/Woods/3501/

9th Massachusetts Battery

http://members.tripod.com/9thmassartillery/

10th Mass. Volunteer Infantry Homepage

http://members.aol.com/mass10th/index.html

Sleeper's Battery: The 10th Battery, Massachusetts Light Artillery, 1862–1865

http://www2.control.com/~emoore/tmba.html

11th Massachusetts Infantry

http://morssweb.com/hookrbde/11maindex.shtml

15th Massachusetts Volunteer Infantry in the Civil War

http://www.nextech.de/ma15mvi/

16th Massachusetts Volunteer Infantry: "Iron Sixteenth"

http://members.aol.com/inf16mavol/16thmass.html

18th Massachusetts Volunteer Infantry

http://www.18thmass.com/

An SR Books
BEST CIVIL WAR SITE
Selection

The Harvard Regiment: 20th Regiment of Massachusetts Volunteer Infantry, 1861–1865

http://www.harvardregiment.org

History of the Original 22nd

http://www.geocities.com/Pentagon/3622/history.html

25th Mass. Volunteer Infantry

http://hometown.aol.com/cw25mass/index.html

28th Massachusetts Volunteer Infantry

http://www.28thmass.org/

37th Massachusetts Volunteer Infantry

http://hometown.aol.com/mass37th/index.html

53rd Massachusetts Volunteer Infantry

http://www.intac.com/~blenderm/53rd_Mass_f/53rd_Mass.html

55th Massachusetts Volunteer Infantry

http://www.coax.net/people/lwf/55hist.htm

MICHIGAN

Michigan Cavalry Regiments

http://hometown.aol.com/dlharvey/cavalry.htm

Michigan Infantry Regiments

http://hometown.aol.com/dlharvey/infantry.htm

2nd Michigan Cavalry Homepage

http://members.aol.com/craffe1486/

2nd Michigan Volunteer Infantry: Company "A"

http://www.geocities.com/Pentagon/Quarters/8558/

3rd Battery, 1st Michigan Light Artillery, 1861–1865

http://www.cwartillery.org/3rdbattery/civwar.html

The Third Michigan Infantry Project

http://www.oldthirdmichigan.org/

4th Michigan Infantry Regiments

http://www.4thmichigan.com/

24th Michigan Infantry Regimental Website, 1862–1865

http://www.geocities.com/CapeCanaveral/Lab/1419/

The Iron Brigade of the West [2nd, 6th, 7th Wisconsin; 19th Indiana; 24th Michigan; 4th U.S. Light Artillery]

http://carroll1.cc.edu/civilwar/ib.html

MINNESOTA

The Civil War Archive: Union Regiments—Minnesota

http://www.civilwararchive.com/unionmn.htm

Brackett's Battalion Minnesota Cavalry

http://dlwgraphics.com/BBindex.htm

1st Minnesota Volunteer Infantry

http://www.firstminnesota.com/

1st Minnesota Volunteer Infantry

http://www1.minn.net/~cbarden/firstmn.html

MISSISSIPPI

The Civil War Archive: Union Regiments—Mississippi

http://www.civilwararchive.com/unionms.htm

Most are units of "African Descent."

Civil War Rosters: Mississippi Links

http://www.geocities.com/Area51/Lair/3680/cw/cw-ms.html

Mississippi Civil War Information

http://www.misscivilwar.org/

2nd Mississippi Infantry Homepage

http://www.2ndmississippi.org/

4th Mississippi Cavalry

http://www.gwest.org/4thms.htm

Company A, 5th Regiment Mississippi Cavalry

http://freepages.genealogy.rootsweb.com/%7Ebclayton/coa5reg.html

7th Mississippi Infantry

http://www.cbcag.edu/7miss/

History of the 8th Mississippi Infantry Regiment, Confederate States of America

http://www.datasync.com/~davidg59/8th_miss.html

14th Mississippi Infantry Regiment

http://www.izzy.net/~michaelg/14ms-1.htm

17th Mississippi Infantry

http://www.17thmississippi.com/

The 19th Mississippi Infantry

http://www.rootsweb.com/%7Ems19inf/

A Short History of the 20th Mississippi Infantry, with emphasis on Company E

http://www.cnnw.net/~rebcav/history/20thmiss.html

26th Mississippi Infantry, C.S.A.

http://www.26thmississippi.com/

31st Mississippi Infantry Regiment

http://freepages.genealogy.rootsweb.com/%7Ebclayton/31stinf.html

33rd Mississippi Infantry Regiment

http://www.hal-pc.org/~rhall/33rd.html

A Brief History of Bradford's Battery Confederate Guards Artillery of Pontotoc County, Miss.

http://www.misscivilwar.org/artillery/bradfords/bradfbtty.html

Harvey's Scouts

http://www.rootsweb.com/~msmadiso/harveyscouts/index.htm

MISSOURI

The Civil War Archive: Union Regiments—Missouri

http://www.civilwararchive.com/unionmo.htm

1st Missouri Confederate Brigade

http://home.carolina.rr.com/cloverwrights/2ndMo.htm

2nd Missouri Cavalry (C.S.A.)

http://members.tripod.com/2ndmocavcsa/

14th Missouri State Militia Cavalry

http://art50.home.mindspring.com/14thMO.htm

21st Missouri Volunteer Infantry Regiment

http://www.geocities.com/mo21infantry/index.html

The 23rd Missouri Volunteer Infantry

http://members.aol.com:/rgooch6760/23rdMoVol.html

24th Missouri Volunteer Infantry

http://www.geocities.com/yankdoodle_99/

26th Missouri Volunteer Infantry

http://www.angelfire.com/mo2/26thmo/

Missouri State Guard

http://members.aol.com/ozrkreb/hist3.htm

NEBRASKA

The Civil War Archive: Union Regiments—Nebraska
http://www.civilwararchive.com/unionne.htm

NEVADA

The Civil War Archive: Union Regiments—Nevada
http://www.civilwararchive.com/unionnv.htm

NEW HAMPSHIRE

The Civil War Archive: Union Regiments—New Hampshire
http://www.civilwararchive.com/unionnh.htm

3rd New Hampshire Regiment
http://www.usgennet.org/usa/nh/topic/civilwar/nh3rdreg.htm

4th New Hampshire Regiment
http://www.usgennet.org/usa/nh/topic/civilwar/nh4threg.htm

5th Regiment New Hampshire Volunteers
http://members.aol.com/ozrkreb/hist3.htm

NEW JERSEY

The Civil War Archive: Union Regiments—New Jersey
http://www.civilwararchive.com/unionnj.htm

New Jersey. Adjutant-General's Office. Record of Officers and Men of New Jersey in the Civil War, 1861–1865.
http://www.njstatelib.org/cyberdesk/DIGIDOX/Digidox20.htm
Searchable database of 1876 compendium of all soldiers.

3rd New Jersey Cavalry
http://www.geocities.com/rdenm76900/

Homepage of the 3rd Regiment, New Jersey, Volunteer Infantry
http://www.geocities.com/Athens/Delphi/1316/thirdjersey.html

8th New Jersey Volunteer Infantry

http://www.8thnj.com

14th Regiment New Jersey Volunteers, Company K: "The Monocacy Regiment"

http://www.rci.rutgers.edu/~eweber/14thnjvols.htm

History of the 39th New Jersey Volunteer Infantry

http://www.geocities.com/Heartland/Lane/5626/39th/39th.htm

NEW MEXICO

The Civil War Archive: Union Regiments—New Mexico

http://www.civilwararchive.com/unionnm.htm

NEW YORK

The Civil War Archive: Union Regiments—New York

http://www.civilwararchive.com/unionny.htm

New York 2nd Regiment Veteran Cavalry

http://www.geocities.com/Heartland/2101/2dvetcav.html

5th New York Volunteer Infantry: Duryée's Zouaves

http://www.zouave.org/

NY 8th Home Page

http://www.geocities.com/Pentagon/Quarters/1380/

9th New York Volunteers Inf. (Hawkins' Zouaves)

http://members.aol.com/NY9Zouaves/index.html

10th New York Volunteer Cavalry

http://www.ggw.org/~nycav/

12th New York Cavalry

http://web.cortland.edu/woosterk/12cav.html

New York 16th Regiment Infantry Home Page

http://www.geocities.com/Heartland/2101/16index.html

20th New York Volunteer Cavalry

http://ourworld.compuserve.com/homepages/marko6/

The 34th NY Volunteer Infantry

http://www.rootsweb.com/~nyherkim/civros34.html

36th New York State Volunteers

http://www.conversantcomm.com/36thNY/Welcome.htm

37th New York Infantry

http://www.shreve.net/~japrime/37thnyvi/index.htm

44th New York Infantry Regiments

http://home.earthlink.net/~cwashburn/44th_ny.html

52nd New York State Volunteers

http://www.geocities.com/pvt52ny/index.html

62nd New York Volunteer Infantry

http://www.io.com/~jhaller/acw/62-ny.html

64th Regiment New York State Volunteer Infantry, Also Known as "Cattaraugus Regiment"

http://www.vanvlack.net/64thRegiment.htm

"The Fighting 69th": 69th New York State Volunteers, Company A, First Regiment, Irish Brigade, "Faugh a Ballagh"

http://www.69thnysv.org/

69th New York State Militia

http://www.hourigan.com/69thny/index.htm

76th New York State Volunteer Regiment

http://www.bpmlegal.com/76NY/index.html

89th New York Volunteer Infantry Regiment
http://www.rootsweb.com/~nybroome/br89his.htm

97th New York Volunteer Infantry
http://www.rootsweb.com/~nyherkim/regiments/civros97.html

102nd New York Infantry of Volunteers
http://www.geocities.com/newyork102nd/

109th Voluntary Infantry Unit
http://www.rootsweb.com/~nybroome/brmi109.htm

112th New York Infantry: The Chautauqua Regiment
http://home.earthlink.net/~cwashburn/112th_ny.html

115th NY Volunteer Infantry
http://www.rootsweb.com/~nyherkim/regiments/general115.html

History and Times of the 124th New York Volunteers: The Orange Blossoms
http://www.ussaga.com/orange.html

128th NY Volunteer Infantry
http://home.rochester.rr.com/ny128th/

The 134th New York Volunteer Infantry
http://www.axworthy.com/134th/

The 149th New York State Volunteer Infantry Home Page
http://www.149th-NYSV.org/

Hardtack Regiment: 154th New York Volunteer Infantry
http://hometown.aol.com/nyvi154th/hardtackregiment.html

The 162nd New York Volunteer Infantry: 3rd Regiment, Metropolitan Guard
http://members.aol.com/DAP4477575/index.html

The 165th Regiment, N.Y. Volunteer Infantry, 2nd Battalion Duryee Zouaves

http://www.geocities.com/Heartland/Plains/8675/ny165_nd.htm

178th NY Volunteer Infantry

http://www.io.com/~jhaller/acw/178-ny.html

188th New York Volunteers

http://home.swbell.net/jcanders/index.html

NORTH CAROLINA

The Civil War Archive: Union Regiments—North Carolina

http://www.civilwararchive.com/unionnc.htm

McRae's Battalion, North Carolina Cavalry

http://members.aol.com/jweaver301/nc/mcrae.htm

North Carolina Civil War Home Page

http://members.aol.com/jweaver303/nc/nccwhp.htm

The Pender/Scales Brigade North Carolina Infantry (13th, 16th, 22nd, 34th, 38th North Carolina Infantry Regiments)

http://www.angelfire.com/wv/wasec5/

1st North Carolina Regiment of Cavalry: Stuart's Tarheels

http://firstnccav.home.mindspring.com/

3rd North Carolina Mounted Infantry, US

http://www.nctroops.com/3usmnt.htm

7th Regiment, North Carolina Troops

http://www.homestead.com/cranfords/index.html

13th Infantry Battalion

http://www.angelfire.com/nc/twsj/page2.html

25th North Carolina Infantry

http://home.att.net/~jddlhd/index.html

26th North Carolina State Troops

http://members.aol.com/jweaver301/nc/26nchis.htm

37th North Carolina Troops

http://www.geocities.com/nc37th/

42nd Regiment

http://home.earthlink.net/~eabosti/html/42nd_regiment.html

The 49th North Carolina Troops

http://home.earthlink.net/~cmc49nct/49nct.htm

57th Regiment

http://home.earthlink.net/~eabosti/html/57th_regiment.html

58th North Carolina Infantry

http://members.aol.com/jweaver301/nc/58ncinf.htm

OHIO

Ohio in the Civil War

http://www.ohiocivilwar.com

History of Battery L, 1st Ohio Light Artillery

http://www.geocities.com/Heartland/5060/civilwar.htm

2nd Ohio Volunteer Infantry, April, 1861 to October, 1864

http://members.aol.com/afs2ovi/2nd/2ndpage.htm

3rd Ohio Volunteer Cavalry

http://freepages.genealogy.rootsweb.com/~thirdovc/

Ohio Volunteer Infantry 4th Regiment: Three Months and Three Year Service

http://members.aol.com/Shortyhack/Ohio4.html

7th Ohio Volunteer Infantry

http://members.tripod.com/Larry_Hardman/

15th Ohio Volunteer Infantry

http://www.webspawner.com/users/15thovvi/

16th Ohio Volunteer Infantry, 1861–1864

http://www.mkwe.com/home.htm

22nd Ohio Volunteer Infantry

http://www.bright.net/~lrrp/22nd.html

The 24th Ohio Volunteer Infantry Regiment

http://www.geocities.com/CapitolHill/Senate/1861/

25th Ohio Volunteer Infantry

http://www.geocities.com/Pentagon/Barracks/3727/

36th Ohio Volunteer Infantry

http://www.angelfire.com/oh/36OVI/

The 41st OVI Unit History

http://members.tripod.com/~dmcclory/history/

45th Ohio Volunteer Infantry

http://www.homestead.com/ohio45/index.html

48th Ohio Veteran Volunteer Infantry

http://www.48ovvi.org/

49th Ohio Volunteer Infantry

http://www.geocities.com/Pentagon/Bunker/7349/page2.html

Ohio Volunteer Infantry 51st Regiment

http://members.aol.com/Shortyhack/ohio51.html

60th Ohio Volunteer Infantry

http://freepages.genealogy.rootsweb.com/%7Evolker/60thOhio.html

63rd Ohio Volunteer Infantry

http://www.geocities.com/Heartland/Plains/4688/ovi.html

64th Ohio Volunteer Infantry
http://www.geocities.com/sixtyfourth_ovi/

65th Ohio Volunteer Infantry
http://my.ohio.voyager.net/%7Elstevens/65oh.html

Ohio Volunteer Infantry 66th Regiment
http://hometown.aol.com/Shortyhack/66ohio.html

72nd Regiment Ohio Volunteers
http://www.udata.com/users/hsbaker/ohio72.htm

73rd Ohio Volunteer Infantry
http://home.adelphia.net/~73rdovi/

76th Ohio Volunteer Infantry
http://my.ohio.voyager.net/%7Elstevens/civwar/

89th Ohio
http://www.89thohio.com/

93rd Regiment Ohio Volunteer Infantry
http://www2.daytonaccess.net/wschmidt/93rd%20O.V.I/93rdOVI.htm

The 126th Ohio Volunteer Infantry: Letters, Accounts, Oral Histories
http://www.iwaynet.net/~lsci/

Ohio Volunteer Infantry 142nd Regiment (100 Day Service)
http://members.aol.com/Shortyhack/142ohio.html

155th Regiment, Ohio Volunteers
http://home.mindspring.com/%7Emtmitchell/index.html

175th Regiment Ohio Volunteers
http://www.udata.com/users/hsbaker/175th.html

PENNSYLVANIA

The Civil War Archive: Union Regiments—Pennsylvania
http://www.civilwararchive.com/unionpa.htm

Pennsylvanian Militia of 1862
http://maley.net/1862militia/

1st Pennsylvania Cavalry Regiment (44th Pennsylvania Volunteers)
http://www.geocities.com/Heartland/Hills/7117/1stPACAV.html

2nd Pennsylvania Heavy Artillery Volunteers (112th Pa Regiment)
http://home.sc.rr.com/pa2ndheavy/

The 6th Pennsylvania Cavalry, "Rush's Lancers"
http://www.rushslancers.com/

7th Pennsylvania Cavalry
http://clix.to/7thpacavalry

11th Pennsylvania Cavalry Regiment (108th Volunteers)
http://64.225.103.104/11-PA-Cav/

12th Pennsylvania Cavalry
http://12thpacavalry.8k.com/

The 15th Pennsylvania Volunteer Cavalry (The Anderson Cavalry)
http://www.swcivilwar.com/cw_15th.html

43rd Pennsylvania Volunteers
http://www.geocities.com/Pentagon/Quarters/8343/

53rd Pennsylvania Militia of 1863
http://www.geocities.com/Heartland/Valley/9931/militia.htm

61st Pennsylvania Volunteers
http://members.aol.com/dick744/

74th Pennsylvania Volunteer Infantry Regiment
http://www.olypen.com/tinkers/74th%20Pennsylvania/Webpage/default.htm

77th Pennsylvania Volunteers: On the March
http://jefferson.village.virginia.edu/vshadow2/HIUS403/77pa/main.html

93rd Pennsylvania Infantry
http://www.angelfire.com/pa/Stump44/index.html

History of the 97th Pennsylvania Volunteer Infantry
http://the97thpvi.tripod.com/Sutlers.htm

100th Regiment, Pennsylvania Veteran Volunteer Infantry
http://www.100thpenn.com/100TH_PVI_MAIN.htm

"Collis' Zouaves": 114th Pennsylvania Volunteer Infantry, Co. E
http://colliszouaves.tripod.com/

138th Pennsylvania Volunteer Infantry
http://www.faitnet.com/138th/

148th Regiment Pennsylvania Volunteers
http://www.pa-roots.com/148th/148thindex.html

200th Regiment Pennsylvania Volunteers in the Civil War, 1861–1865
http://www.geocities.com/Heartland/Pines/9366/

A Brief History of the 210th Pennsylvania Infantry Regiment
http://www.geocities.com/WallStreet/3958/penn210.html

RHODE ISLAND

The Civil War Archive: Union Regiments—Rhode Island
http://www.civilwararchive.com/unionri.htm

Brown's Battery B, 1st Regiment Rhode Island Light Artillery

http://www.geocities.com/BourbonStreet/3604/

SOUTH CAROLINA

John T. Kanapaux's Battery, Lafayette's Light Artillery, South Carolina Volunteers

http://freepages.genealogy.rootsweb.com/~york/Kanapaux/index.html

1st South Carolina Cavalry

http://members.tripod.com/~Bowesl/1stsc.html

13th Regiment of South Carolina Volunteers of the Confederate States of America

http://hometown.aol.com/adj61/page3.htm

The 14th South Carolina Regiment: Gregg's/McGowan's Brigade Army of Northern Virginia

http://www.geocities.com/rickysahn/SC14/sc14main.htm

The 16th South Carolina C.S.A.

http://www.geocities.com/BourbonStreet/Square/3873/franklina.html

18th Infantry, Co. G, Mountain Guards, York County, South Carolina Volunteers

http://freepages.genealogy.rootsweb.com/~york/18thSCV/G.htm

History of the 20th South Carolina Volunteer Infantry

http://www.geocities.com/Heartland/Hills/9908/20hist.html

Company B of the 22nd Regiment of South Carolina Volunteers

http://hometown.aol.com/adj61/page5.htm

TENNESSEE

Tennessee Civil War Home Page: Confederate Unit Information

http://members.aol.com/jweaver303/tn/tncsunit.htm

Tennessee Civil War Home Page: United States Army Units

http://members.aol.com/jweaver303/tn/tnusunit.htm

Allison's Cavalry

http://tennessee-scv.org/Camp1513/allison.htm

Archer's Brigade: "Victory or Death" [Tennessee]

http://www.fred.net/stevent/home.html

Huwald's Battery: Tennessee Mountain Howitzers

http://tennessee-scv.org/Camp1513/huwald.htm

2nd Tennessee Infantry Regiment U.S.A.

http://home.cinci.rr.com/secondtennessee/

7th Tennessee Cavalry—Company D

http://pages.prodigy.net/rebel7tn/

Company C, 8th Tennessee Infantry Regiment, CSA

http://home.att.net/~dmelear/hist_sgb1.htm

9th Tennessee Cavalry

http://tennessee-scv.org/Camp1513/9th.htm

20th (Russell's) Tennessee Cavalry

http://home.olemiss.edu/~cmprice/cav.html

44th Tennessee Infantry

http://www.geocities.com/BourbonStreet/4455/

TEXAS

2nd Texas Confederate Infantry Regiment

http://www.cba.uh.edu/~parks/tex/irg0020.html

Terry's Texas Rangers Website (8th Texas Volunteer Cavalry)

http://www.terrystexasrangers.org/

Official Historic Website of the 10th Texas Infantry

http://members.aol.com/SMckay1234/

Parson's Brigade 12th Texas Cavalry Regiment

http://www.rootsweb.com/%7Etxellis/parson.htm

A Sketch of the History of Debray's (26th) Regiment of Texas Cavalry by Col. X. B. Debray (1884)

http://www.geocities.com/Athens/Cyprus/6533/26TX/History.html

VERMONT

A Short Chronology of the War

http://www.vermontcivilwar.org/units.shtml

Dozens of short histories of Vermont units.

The Civil War Archive: Union Regiments—Vermont

http://www.civilwararchive.com/unionvt.htm

History of the 2nd Regiment Vermont Volunteer Infantry

http://home.earthlink.net/%7Ecoe2vt/history.html

VIRGINIA

Russell County, Virginia, 1860–1865

http://rhobard.com/russell/

Lists soldiers, units, pensions, 1869 census; some photographs.

The Valley of the Shadow: Two Communities in the American Civil War, The War Years

http://jefferson.village.virginia.edu/cwhome.html

Map showing battles fought by regiments from one Virginia county, with each battle linked to information about that unit's experience there. Also features newspapers, letters and diaries, *Official Records*.

Virginia Civil War Home Page: Military Units

http://members.aol.com/jweaver300/grayson/vaunit.htm

Short histories of dozens of units.

3rd Virginia Volunteer Infantry

http://www.geocities.com/pentagon/8245/

18th Virginia Cavalry

http://www.angelfire.com/pa2/Stump45/

24th and 42nd Virginia Infantry

http://www.geocities.com/Heartland/Ranch/2320/index.html

33rd Regiment Virginia Volunteer Infantry, Company A, Potomac Guard

http://members.aol.com/Vir33rdreg/index.html

42nd Virginia Infantry Regiment, 1861–1865, Company I, Campbell Guards

http://users.erols.com/va42nd/61-65.html

48th Virginia Infantry

http://www.rootsweb.com/~vascott/48th/index48.htm

WEST VIRGINIA

The Civil War Archive: Union Regiments—West Virginia

http://www.civilwararchive.com/unionwv.htm

West Virginia in the Civil War

http://www.wvcivilwar.com/

Bibliographies and short histories for dozens of regiments.

West Virginia Military Research

http://www.rootsweb.net/~wvgenweb/military/index.html

1st West Virginia Cavalry

http://www.lindapages.com/1wvc/1wvc.htm

3rd West Virginia Infantry 6th West Virginia Cavalry

http://www.rootsweb.net/~wvgenweb/military/6wvcavrh.html

4th West Virginia Volunteer Infantry

http://www.geocities.com/Heartland/Hollow/8127/page2.html

11th West Virginia Infantry Volunteers

http://www.geocities.com/cok11wv/

12th West Virginia Infantry

http://www.lindapages.com/12wvi/12thcover.htm

WISCONSIN

Wisconsin Civil War Regimental Histories

http://museum.dva.state.wi.us/Res_regiments.asp

2nd Wisconsin Volunteer Infantry Association Inc.

http://www.secondwi.com/

The Iron Brigade of the West [2nd, 6th, 7th Wisconsin; 19th Indiana; 24th Michigan; 4th U.S. Light Artillery]

http://carroll1.cc.edu/civilwar/ib.html

4th Wisconsin Volunteers

http://www.hughesfamilies.com/fourth/fourth.cfm

15th Wisconsin Volunteer Infantry: The Scandinavian Regiment

http://www.15thwisconsin.net/

The 26th Wisconsin Infantry Volunteers

http://www.russscott.com/~rscott/26thwis/

28th Regiment Wisconsin Volunteer Infantry, 1862–1865

http://www.28thwisconsin.com/

GENERAL HISTORY, HISTORIC DOCUMENTS, LINKS, AND ONLINE BOOKSTORE SITES

GENERAL HISTORY

Ehistory

http://www.ehistory.com

Standard fare of articles by historians and writers of varying qualifications, plus a full-text searchable *Official Records* and a nice collection of letters.

The History Channel

http://www.historychannel.com

Civil War content consists of reprints from *The Reader's Companion to American History*, with articles by Stephen Sears, James McPherson, and other notable scholars.

The History Net

http://www.historynet.com/

Other than full-text articles from the current issue of *America's Civil War* and *Civil War Times*, most of the American Civil War content is geared toward K–12 students.

HISTORIC DOCUMENTS

American Memory: Historical Collections for the National Digital Library

http://memory.loc.gov/ammem/amhome.html

With over 7 million digitized items from more than 100 collections, this is America's largest digital archive. Four of its collections have been designated Best of the Web in other sections of this book.

Congressional Globe

http://memory.loc.gov/ammem/amlaw/lwcg.html

Massive official compilation of complete texts of all congressional speeches, 1833–1873. Researchers can read famous speeches delivered during debates over the Compromise of 1850, the Kansas-Nebraska Act, the secession crisis, the Civil War, and Reconstruction.

Documenting the American South: The Southern Homefront, 1861–1865

http://docsouth.dsi.internet2.edu/imls/index.html

Over 400 digitized printed works and manuscripts accompanied by images of currency, manuscript letters, maps, broadsides, title pages, illustrations, and photographs. Taken together, they show Southern people attempting to build a national state and culture during the Civil War.

DOUGLASS: Archive of American Public Address

http://douglassarchives.org

Northwestern University collection of famous speeches. Includes addresses by Frederick Douglass and Abraham Lincoln.

The Historical *New York Times* Project

http://www.nyt.ulib.org/

Images of every page of the daily newspaper. Navigation takes the user directly to the edition of interest. Articles about key Civil War events have been clipped and scanned at a resolution high enough to allow for easy reading.

Making of America

http://moa.umdl.umich.edu/

Over 8,500 books and 50,000 journal articles from nineteenth-century America. Full-text searchable, although articles themselves are in image files and have not been transcribed. Researchers can read slave narratives, sentimental domestic literature, news accounts of battles and political debates, and dozens of early histories and memoirs of the Civil War.

Secession Era Editorials Project

http://history.furman.edu/~benson/docs/

Hundreds of transcribed editorials from 1850s newspapers, showing how the press fanned the flames of discord.

LINK SITES

The American Civil War

http://www.homepages.dsu.edu/jankej/civilwar/civilwar.htm

The sites are broken down by topic. Many links are to courses, clubs, and stores as well as to traditional web sites.

The American Civil War Homepage

http://sunsite.utk.edu/civil-war/warweb.html

Mammoth collection of links, some to sites of little use to serious scholars.

Richard Jensen's Civil War Guides

http://tigger.uic.edu/~rjensen/civilwar.htm

Of all the link sites on the Civil War, this is the most geared toward the interests and needs of serious scholars. Many links are to memoirs and other primary documents buried deep in large digital collections such as Making of America and Documenting the American South. Some links are to sites requiring institutional subscription.

United States Civil War Center Index of Civil War Information

http://www.cwc.lsu.edu/cwc/civlink.htm

Probably the most comprehensive of the link sites, it occasionally sacrifices quality for quantity.

ONLINE BOOKSTORES

Abraham Lincoln Book Shop

http://www.alincolnbookshop.com/

Attractive site with excellent collection of books and multimedia. Graphics-heavy homepage takes time to download, and navigation is fairly difficult.

History Book Club

www.historybookclub.com

You can't beat the introductory offer, and the selection of Civil War books is certainly strong.

Military Book Club

http://www.militarybookclub.com

Strong selection of Civil War books along with historical fiction, general reference works, and histories of armed conflicts since ancient times.

Morningside Bookshop

http://www.morningsidebooks.com

Devoted entirely to books on the Civil War, with offerings from its own press as well as from other publishers.

The *War Times Journal* Store

http://www.wtj.com/store/

Sells a strong list of books through an affiliate relationship with Amazon.com.

More Great Books on the Civil War Era!

Look for more great books in *The American Crisis Series: Books on the Civil War Era* and other titles from SR Books on this fascinating period in U.S. history.

Atlanta Will Fall: Sherman, Joe Johnston, and the Yankee Heavy Battalions
by Stephen Davis
Paperback 0-8420-2788-2 $17.95
in *The American Crisis Series: Books on the Civil War Era*

Beneath a Northern Sky: A Short History of the Gettysburg Campaign
by Steven E. Woodworth
Paperback 0-8420-2933-8 $14.95
in *The American Crisis Series: Books on the Civil War Era*

Crisis in the Southwest: The United States, Mexico, and the Struggle over Texas
by Richard Bruce Winders
Paperback 0-8420-2801-3 $17.95
in *The American Crisis Series: Books on the Civil War Era*

Gotham at War: New York City, 1860–1865
by Edward K. Spann
Paperback 0-8420-5057-4 $17.95
in *The American Crisis Series: Books on the Civil War Era*

The Human Tradition in the Civil War and Reconstruction
edited by Steven E. Woodworth
Paperback 0-8420-2727-0 $19.95
in *The Human Tradition in America series*

Lessons of War: The Civil War in Children's Magazines
edited by James Marten
Paperback 0-8420-2656-8 $18.95

The Men of Secession and Civil War, 1859–1861
by James L. Abrahamson
Paperback 0-8420-2819-6 $17.95
in *The American Crisis Series: Books on the Civil War Era*

The Mosby Myth: A Confederate Hero in Life and Legend
by Paul Ashdown and Edward Caudill
Paperback 0-8420-2929-X $17.95
in *The American Crisis Series: Books on the Civil War Era*

On the Brink of Civil War: The Compromise of 1850 and How It Changed the Course of American History
by John C. Waugh
Paperback 0-8420-2945-1 $17.95
in *The American Crisis Series: Books on the Civil War Era*

(continued)

One Damn Blunder from Beginning to End: The Red River Campaign of 1864
by Gary Dillard Joiner
Paperback 0-8420-2937-0 $17.95
in *The American Crisis Series: Books on the Civil War Era*

Retreat to Victory? Confederate Strategy Reconsidered
by Robert G. Tanner
Paperback 0-8420-2882-X $17.95
in *The American Crisis Series: Books on the Civil War Era*

A Short History of the Civil War at Sea
by Spencer C. Tucker
Paperback 0-8420-2868-4 $17.95
in *The American Crisis Series: Books on the Civil War Era*

A Single Grand Victory: The First Campaign and Battle of Manassas
by Ethan S. Rafuse
Paperback 0-8420-2876-5 $17.95
in *The American Crisis Series: Books on the Civil War Era*

Virginians at War: The Civil War Experiences of Seven Young Confederates
by John G. Selby
Paperback 0-8420-5055-8 $17.95
in *The American Crisis Series: Books on the Civil War Era*

War and Ruin: William T. Sherman and the Savannah Campaign
by Anne J. Bailey
Paperback 0-8420-2851-X $17.95
in *The American Crisis Series: Books on the Civil War Era*

Also available:
World War II on the Web: A Guide to the Very Best Sites
by J. Douglas Smith and Richard Jensen
Paperback 0-8420-5021-3 $23.95 with free CD-ROM

SR Books are available at bookstores across the country, from online retailers, and directly from Scholarly Resources.

SR Books (an imprint of Scholarly Resources)
104 Greenhill Avenue * Wilmington, DE 19805-1897
800-772-8937 • 302-654-7713 • FAX 302-654-3871
Order online: www.scholarly.com

Prices subject to change without notice.

ABOUT THE CD

The CD version of *Civil War on the Web*, CW.pdf, can be viewed only with Adobe Acrobat Reader, which is provided on this CD.

OPENING CW.PDF IF ACROBAT READER IS INSTALLED ON YOUR COMPUTER

Macintosh: CW.pdf will open immediately upon placing the CD in your drive.

Windows: There are several ways to open a file on a CD:

1. From the desktop: double click on the hard-drive icon (My Computer), double click on the CD-drive icon, double click on the file named CW.pdf. Acrobat Reader will launch and the file will open.

2. From the Menu Bar: Go to Start—Find and type in the file name CW.pdf. Hit Enter when the file is located on the CD drive.

3. From Acrobat Reader: Launch Acrobat Reader. Click on File in the menu bar and select Open. Then locate the file CW.pdf on the CD in the drive and hit Enter.

OPENING VR2.PDF IF ACROBAT READER IS NOT INSTALLED ON YOUR COMPUTER

Macintosh: double click on the Acrobat Reader Installer icon on the CD and follow the setup instructions.

Windows: There are several ways to install a program from a CD:

1. From the desktop: double click on the hard-drive icon (My Computer), double click on the CD-drive icon, double click on the file named "ar505enu.exe"—this is the Acrobat Installer. The program will launch, and then simply follow the setup instructions.

2. From the Menu Bar: Go to Start—Run—Browse and highlight the CD drive in the drop-down window. The file named "ar505enu.exe" will appear. Double click on the file and proceed as in (1) above.

Acrobat Reader is provided free of charge by Adobe (http://www.adobe.com) and can also be downloaded from their web site at: http://www.adobe.com/products/acrobat/readstep2.html.

README.PDF

Provided in text, rtf, and pdf formats, this document lists system requirements for using Acrobat Reader, describes the interactive features of CW.pdf, and provides important information for users new to Acrobat Reader. The text and rtf versions can be viewed in WordPad or NotePad (Windows), in SimpleText (Mac), or in your word-processing software. The pdf version can be viewed only in Acrobat Reader.

ABOUT THE CD

The CD version of *Civil War on the Web*, CW.pdf, can be viewed only with Adobe Acrobat Reader, which is provided on this CD.

OPENING CW.PDF IF ACROBAT READER IS INSTALLED ON YOUR COMPUTER

Macintosh: CW.pdf will open immediately upon placing the CD in your drive.

Windows: There are several ways to open a file on a CD:

1. From the desktop: double click on the hard-drive icon (My Computer), double click on the CD-drive icon, double click on the file named CW.pdf. Acrobat Reader will launch and the file will open.

2. From the Menu Bar: Go to Start—Find and type in the file name CW.pdf. Hit Enter when the file is located on the CD drive.

3. From Acrobat Reader: Launch Acrobat Reader. Click on File in the menu bar and select Open. Then locate the file CW.pdf on the CD in the drive and hit Enter.

OPENING VR2.PDF IF ACROBAT READER IS NOT INSTALLED ON YOUR COMPUTER

Macintosh: double click on the Acrobat Reader Installer icon on the CD and follow the setup instructions.

Windows: There are several ways to install a program from a CD:

1. From the desktop: double click on the hard-drive icon (My Computer), double click on the CD-drive icon, double click on the file named "ar505enu.exe"—this is the Acrobat Installer. The program will launch, and then simply follow the setup instructions.

2. From the Menu Bar: Go to Start—Run—Browse and highlight the CD drive in the drop-down window. The file named "ar505enu.exe" will appear. Double click on the file and proceed as in (1) above.

Acrobat Reader is provided free of charge by Adobe (http://www.adobe.com) and can also be downloaded from their web site at: http://www.adobe.com/products/acrobat/readstep2.html.

README.PDF

Provided in text, rtf, and pdf formats, this document lists system requirements for using Acrobat Reader, describes the interactive features of CW.pdf, and provides important information for users new to Acrobat Reader. The text and rtf versions can be viewed in WordPad or NotePad (Windows), in SimpleText (Mac), or in your word-processing software. The pdf version can be viewed only in Acrobat Reader.
